0
9

D1309617

Money Talk

A Financial Guide For Women

Written by

Patricia Q. Brennan, M.A., CFP®, CRPC®, AFC, CHC, CFCS
Rutgers Cooperative Extension

Barbara M. O'Neill, Ph.D., CFP®, CRPC®, AFC, CHC, CFCS
Rutgers Cooperative Extension

Natural Resource, Agriculture, and Engineering Service (NRAES)
Cooperative Extension
PO Box 4557 • Ithaca, New York 14852-4557

NRAES–160
Revised 2009

April 2009

ISBN 978-0-935817-94-2

Natural Resource, Agriculture, and Engineering Service (NRAES)
Cooperative Extension
PO Box 4557
Ithaca, New York 14852-4557
Phone: (607) 255-7654 • Fax: (607) 254-8770
E-mail: NRAES@CORNELL.EDU • Web site: WWW.NRAES.ORG

TABLE OF CONTENTS

SESSION I

Financial Basics

SESSION II

Are You Covered? Insurance Basics

SESSION III

Investing Basics

Acknowledgments

The authors thank the following peer reviewers for offering comments to improve the quality and accuracy of the text:

Karen P. Bennett
Extension Professor and Specialist/Forest Resources
University of New Hampshire Cooperative Extension

Mary L. Carsky, Ph.D.
Professor of Marketing
University of Hartford/Barney School of Business

Cynthia Needles Fletcher, Ph.D.
Professor and Extension Specialist
Human Development and Family Studies
Iowa State University

Gail M. Gordon
Business Development and Family Economics Specialist
University of Wyoming Cooperative Extension Service
Agricultural and Applied Economics

Patricia K. Gorman
Family Resource Management Field Specialist
Iowa State University Extension

Louis Gorr
Extension Agent, Family and Consumer Sciences/
Management, Housing, and Consumer Education
Virginia Cooperative Extension
Virginia Polytechnic Institute and State University

Lynne C. Grant
Extension Educator, Family and Consumer Sciences
University of Connecticut Cooperative Extension System

Joanne Bordelon Hamilton, AFC
Extension Educator
University of Maryland

Celia Ray Hayhoe, Ph.D., CFP®
Family Financial Management Extension Specialist
Apparel, Housing, and Resource Management
Virginia Polytechnic Institute and State University

Beverly Healy
Extension Educator
University of Idaho Cooperative Extension System

Suzann Enzian Knight
Extension Professor and Specialist
University of New Hampshire Cooperative Extension
Family Studies Department

Robin L. Kuleck
Family Living Educator, Resource Management
Penn State Cooperative Extension

Geri Mason
Family and Consumer Science Educator
University of Maryland/Wicomico County Extension

Barbara S. Poole, Ph.D.
Associate Professor, Finance
Roger Williams University

Patricia Swanson, Ph.D.,CFP®
Extension State Specialist and Adjunct Assistant Professor
Human Development and Family Studies
Iowa State University

Elizabeth S. Trent
Associate Professor, Emerita
University of Vermont

Josephine Turner, CFP®
Professor, Family, Youth, and Community Sciences
University of Florida

The authors also thank Linda Intili at Rutgers Cooperative Extension of Morris County, for typing the original manuscript, and Money Talk class participants, who provided helpful feedback and encouragement. The authors offer special thanks to Marty Sailus and Cathleen Walker at NRAES for supporting the project; to Joy Drohan for her exceptional and meticulous copy editing; to Andrea Gray for creating a sensible and attractive design; and to Jeff Miller of The Art Department, Ithaca, New York, for the cover design. (Cover art is from Getty Images, Inc., www.gettyimages.com.)

About the Authors

Patricia Q. Brennan, a Certified Financial Planner (CFP®), was a Family and Consumer Sciences Educator with Rutgers Cooperative Extension of Morris County from 1981 to 2008. She held the tenured faculty rank of associate professor at the School of Environmental and Biological Sciences, Rutgers University. Professor Brennan is a chartered retirement planning counselor (CRPC), an accredited financial counselor (AFC), and a certified housing counselor (CHC). She taught more than 80 personal finance classes annually and wrote and recorded a weekly five-minute morning radio program on station WMTR. She wrote for Morris County newspapers, appeared regularly on the Cablevision cable TV show "Money Counts," and made guest appearances on CNBC and News 12 New Jersey. Professor Brennan made more than 30 national professional conference presentations and contributed numerous articles for professional journals and proceedings. She earned a B.S. in Home Economics from Immaculata University and an M.A. in Education from Montclair State University.

Barbara M. O'Neill, Ph.D., holds the rank of Professor II in the Department of Agricultural, Food, and Resource Economics at the School of Environmental and Biological Sciences, Rutgers University, where she has been a faculty member since 1978. She currently serves as Rutgers Cooperative Extension's Specialist in Financial Resource Management. She is a certified financial planner (CFP®), a chartered retirement planning counselor (CRPC), an accredited financial counselor (AFC), a certified housing counselor (CHC), a Certified Financial Educator (CFEd), and certified in family and consumer sciences (CFCS). Dr. O'Neill has written more than 1,500 consumer newspaper articles and more than 100 articles for professional journals and conference proceedings. She served as national president of the Association For Financial Counseling and Planning Education in 2003. She is the author of five books—three financial case-study books published by Rutgers University, and *Saving On A Shoestring* and *Investing On A Shoestring,* trade books published by Dearborn Financial Publishing.

Dear Money Talk Reader,

Money Talk: A Financial Guide For Women was developed because women have unique financial needs. Statistics tell us that it is only a matter of time before most (85–90%) women will be on their own financially. Some will never marry, some will see their marriages end in divorce, and some will outlive their husbands.

Women have unique financial needs for the following reasons.

- We live longer, on average, than men, so our money has to last longer.
- We earn less, on average, than men do.
- We may have gaps in our employment history, due to family care giving, that will affect future retirement benefits.
- Some women rely on a spouse for income and are at risk for becoming a "displaced homemaker" if the relationship ends (e.g., in death and divorce).
- Some women lack financial experience because "the man is supposed to handle the money."

This guidebook will provide you with information that you need to take charge of your financial future. Each of the five class sessions includes a number of investment lessons. They will also introduce you to important financial terms such as "net worth" and "expense ratio."

Each class session also features a number of exercises. They were included so that you could "personalize" the information. In other words, instead of just reading about how to calculate your net worth, you have a form to calculate your own (Session I). In Session III, there are forms to compare different types of investments and calculate your investment risk tolerance.

Simply reading *Money Talk: A Financial Guide For Women* will not change your financial situation. You need to take action (e.g., starting an individual retirement account [IRA]) to achieve your financial goals. That's why the exercises are included. You'll find a list of Minimum "Need to Knows" at the end of each session. These are the most important facts covered in each lesson.

Your local Cooperative Extension office is a resource that can help you improve your financial well-being through classes, speaking engagements, publications, financial consultations, Web sites, newspaper articles, and other outreach methods. Feel free to get in touch if we can be of assistance.

Patricia Q. Brennan, CFP®
Senior Extension Trainer Emeritus

Dr. Barbara M. O'Neill, CFP®
Extension Specialist in Financial
Resource Management

April 2009

No matter how much women prefer
to lean, to be protected and supported,
nor how much men prefer to have them do so,
they must make the voyage of life alone,
and for safety in an emergency
they must know something
of the laws of navigation.

Elizabeth Cady Stanton, 1892

Financial Basics

Mary has a little jar
And in it she drops change
Twenty years from now, she hopes
It'll be in the ten-thousand dollar range

What will be covered in Session I

Financial Planning Lessons

1. Understanding Your Relationship to Money
2. Money Values and Goals
3. Testing Your Financial Fitness
4. Managing Household Cash Flow
5. Calculating Your Net Worth
6. Tips for Smarter Borrowing
7. Financial Record Keeping

Terms to Learn (bolded in the text)

Cash flow	Fixed expenses	Net worth
Compound interest	Flexible expenses	Periodic expenses
Debt-to-income ratio	Liquidity	Spending plan
Emergency fund	Money "baggage"	Values

Exercises

1. Money Coat of Arms
2. Emotional Uses of Money
3. Ten Things I Love to Do
4. Evaluate Your Financial Goals
5. Financial Fitness Quiz
6. Checklist of Expenses
7. Household Expenses: Week by Week
8. Anticipated Occasional Expenses in Next 12 Months
9. Spending Plan Worksheet
10. Finding Money to Save Worksheet
11. Net Worth Statement
12. Credit Card Comparison Worksheet
13. Credit File Request Form
14. Credit Card Safety Record
15. How Organized Are You?
16. A Record of Important Family Papers

Understanding Your Relationship to Money

People's feelings about money are often a stronger influence on their spending and saving decisions than the amount of money they earn. People often use money in connection with a number of emotions and motivations, including security, power, control, status, and success, and to build self-esteem. Understanding these emotions is a key to successful financial management.

We are also influenced by "money messages" in society (e.g., advertising). People receive money messages from a variety of places. Sources of money messages include parents, religion, media, friends, and financial institutions.

> *"Money baggage."* Harmful thoughts and beliefs about money that can hold people back from achieving personal and/or financial success.

Examples of negative money baggage include:

- "My net worth determines my self worth,"
- "It's just too complicated,"
- "Live for today—the future doesn't matter," and
- "The man should make all financial decisions."

Understanding your money baggage is the first step in making changes to improve your finances. To better understand your money baggage, reflect on what you've heard about money from society, your parents, your friends, and/or your spouse. Also, what do you say about money? What does money mean to you?

A number of books have been written about money personalities, which is another way of looking at factors that influence financial decisions. *Money Harmony*, by Olivia Mellan, for example, classifies money personalities as hoarder, spender, money monk, avoider, and amasser.

Another way to probe your money decisions, values, and financial goals is to ask yourself some tough questions:

- What is the meaning and purpose of your life?
- What would you do if you found out you had less than 10 years to live?
- How do you want to be remembered?

Many people take stock of their lives at some point, often in midlife or after a "wake-up call" such as cancer or a heart attack. Very often the things we like to do best cost little or nothing. A life assessment process includes weighing needs and wants and pausing to enjoy simple pleasures. As the old saying goes, the best things in life are often free.

Use the *Money Coat of Arms* (Exercise I-1) on page 4 to better understand your relationship with money. In the five sections of the coat of arms, describe the following items:

- one thing you do well with money
- one thing you don't do well with money
- your money motto (e.g., "happiness is positive cash flow")
- a way that you enjoy spending money
- a way that you have a hard time spending money

Use the *Emotional Uses of Money* worksheet (Exercise I-2) on page 5 to better understand the underlying emotions associated with your spending decisions.

Making Positive Financial Changes

Why do some women achieve their financial goals while others, who earn the same income or more, fail to make progress? Probably dozens of answers to this question exist, including a person's age, income, employment, marital status, and access to employer savings plans (e.g., 401(k)s and credit unions). Another explanation for financial goal achievement is personal qualities, such as:

- a positive attitude,
- a desire to achieve a specific goal,
- focus and self-control,
- financial knowledge, and
- specific actions taken (e.g., investing $3,000 annually in an IRA) to reach a financial goal (e.g., accumulate $100,000 for retirement). In other words, "where there's a will, there's a way."

Achieving financial goals is not just a matter of money. It's about an internal desire to improve one's finances and "walk the walk" with specific practices (e.g., enrolling in a 401(k) plan) that move you forward. According to a popular theory, behavioral change occurs in defined stages, based on a person's readiness to change.

At the precontemplation stage of change, people may not even be aware that a problem (e.g., high debt load) exists or that adjustments should be made in their lives. At the contemplation stage, they gain knowledge about alternative behaviors and begin to understand ways to change (e.g., reduce spending). At the preparation stage, people commit to make a change and gain required skills (e.g., read a book on personal finance). At the action stage, they "take the plunge" and actually change their behavior. In the maintenance stage, people work to sustain their change and reap the rewards of their efforts (e.g., increased bank balance).

In the precontemplation and contemplation stages, a key process is consciousness-raising, or raised awareness. An example of this process is that news stories about the benefits of saving small dollar amounts on a regular basis might cause a person to think, "I should save some money." Commitment takes place during the preparation stage of change. An example of commitment is, "I will save $25 per paycheck." At the action stage of change, countering is an important process. This means substituting a healthy response (e.g., saving $3 per day) for an unhealthy one (e.g., spending $3 per day on lottery tickets).

Another action stage change process is environmental control. This means restructuring your environment to reduce the probability of a problem-causing event. An example is signing up for a mutual fund automatic savings plan (e.g., $50 per month) so that part of your income can be invested in fund shares before it is spent. Another is having your paycheck directly deposited at a bank.

Personal change is difficult, and it doesn't happen just because we want it to. Most successful changes require persistence, positive thoughts, and a strong support system. Believe in yourself and your ability to make changes that will improve your finances. Even small amounts of savings add up over time.

Remember this phrase: "If it is to be, it's up to me." You, alone, control your financial destiny. When facing financial challenges, having a positive attitude is important. You can give up and say "I'll never save enough money," or you can resolve to take action to improve your life. People who think positively generally experience greater success than "naysayers" because they believe that there's a connection between what they do today and what will happen in the future.

Today is the first day of the rest of your financial life. Make the most of it.

Money Coat of Arms

Fill in each section of the Money Coat of Arms with the information that is requested.

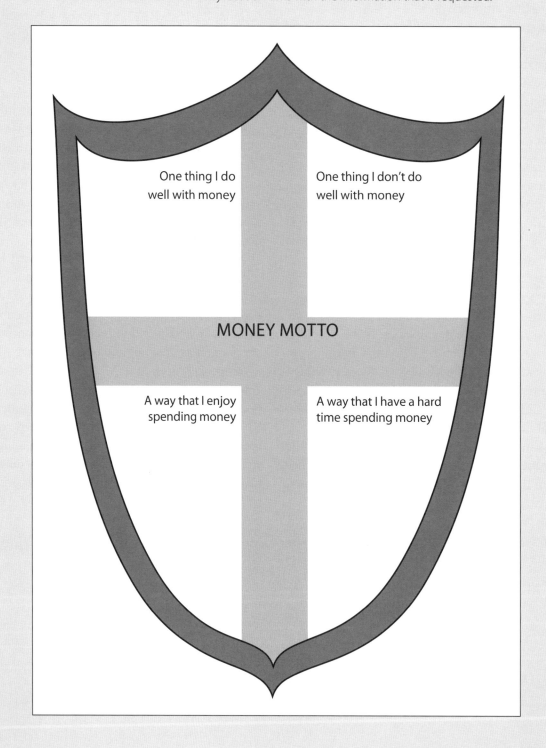

One thing I do well with money

One thing I don't do well with money

MONEY MOTTO

A way that I enjoy spending money

A way that I have a hard time spending money

EXERCISE I-2

Emotional Uses of Money

Money is powerful. It can bring out the best and worst in people. So, understanding money's influence can help a family gain control over their finances. Insight into emotional uses of money can help a family handle sensitive issues when they arise. Some emotional uses are positive—security, comfort, freedom, sharing, etc. Some can also work against a family—fear, greed, overspending, control, etc.

Answer the following true-false questions about your use of money. Be honest!

1.	T	F	I buy things I don't want or need because they are on sale.
2.	T	F	I feel anxious and defensive when asked about my finances.
3.	T	F	I can never have enough money saved to feel secure.
4.	T	F	I buy things I don't need or want because they are "in."
5.	T	F	I overspend regularly on "extras."
6.	T	F	I often insist on paying more than my share at a restaurant or on a group gift.
7.	T	F	I spend money freely, even foolishly, on others, but seldom on myself.
8.	T	F	I feel "dumb" if I pay more for something than a neighbor did.
9.	T	F	I don't trust others in my family to spend money wisely.
10.	T	F	If I earn the money, I think I should have the right to decide how it is spent.
11.	T	F	If someone in my family acts selfish in spending our money on him/herself, I feel I have the right to do the same.

Analysis: If you answered *true* to any of questions 1–3, you may feel insecure concerning money. Money provides a form of security, but not the only one. What reasons other than money or material possessions might be causing insecurity? Think about it.

Did you answer *true* to either 4 or 5? Then you may use money for *status*. Money sometimes reflects the values of our friends rather than our own. What are your values?

True answers to questions 6, 7, or 8 might mean that you use money in ways that reflect your low *self-esteem*. Spending on others does not win the affections of family members, friends, or coworkers. Your spending is your business. It has nothing to do with the spending of your neighbors. You cannot buy *self-esteem*. If yours is low, seek help through reading, therapy, or changes in habits or actions, but not through money.

If you answered *true* to questions 9 and/or 10, you may use money to *control* others in the family. In two-earner families, his/her money divisions can cause resentment. Not involving family members often results in lack of cooperation. A dictator may secure obedience, but not love. Which do you want from your family?

A true answer to question 11 may indicate that money is used for *retaliation*, to get back at someone. This often causes fairness to become such an issue that it blocks love and affection. If you need to disagree, do so without using money as your weapon.

Adapted from: Dollar, P. (1991). *Family Communications about Money.* University of Georgia Cooperative Extension, Athens, GA.

Money Values and Goals

People generally spend money in ways that are consistent with their values. Values are also the building blocks of financial goals. They are the foundations on which people base their dreams and plans. A family that values education, for example, will probably make college savings a high priority. Another family that values religion might tithe a certain portion of its income.

> **Values.** Beliefs about what is important in a person's life.

Examples of values that affect personal finances are family togetherness, image and personal appearance, community service/helping others, independence, religion/faith, security, happiness, job success, close friendships, and education/knowledge.

What are your values as they relate to your use of time and money? Complete *Ten Things I Love to Do* (Exercise I-3) on page 7 to gain insight into your time and money use decisions. This exercise will help you decide whether you can refocus some of your activities to save money while still enjoying yourself.

Do you have a financial goal, or is it a dream? A dream is vague, such as "I want to send my child to a good college," or "I want to be comfortable in retirement." These are dreams. A goal is specific, achievable, written, and includes dates for beginning and ending. For example, "In 4 years, we will save the $20,000 we need for the down payment on a townhouse," or "By the time my child is 18, I will have $40,000 in savings to pay part of his or her college tuition."

Setting financial goals is like planning your next vacation. To develop both a financial plan and a travel itinerary, you must know your starting point and destination and the time frame and cost of the "journey."

What is your financial itinerary? Have you made specific plans to reach your financial goals?

Financial goals should be "SMART" goals. SMART is an acronym for specific, measurable, attainable, realistic, and time-related. In other words, financial goals should have a definite outcome and deadline and be within reach, based upon personal income and assets.

How do you set a financial goal? Write the goal down, answering the questions who, what, when, where, and why. Since this is *your* goal, begin your goal statement with "I/We." State exactly what you want to accomplish (e.g., "I will save $5,000 by the end of next year"). Include specific dates and dollar amounts in your goal statement. Then state exactly what you will do to achieve the goal and how you will do it (e.g., save 10% of pay annually in a 401(k) plan or save $2,000 annually in an IRA). Repeat this process until you've developed goal statements for each of your financial goals.

Keep rewriting your goals until they are specific and achievable. Tell select people about your goals so that they can hold you accountable and support your goals. Track your progress and, if necessary, make changes to your goals as personal circumstances or economic conditions change. Use the *Evaluate Your Financial Goals* worksheet (Exercise I-4) on page 8 to describe your financial goals along with a date and cost and the amount of savings required to achieve them.

Some financial goals, such as "make a list of debts" and "calculate net worth" require only time. Many financial goals, however, such as "put $3,000 per year into an IRA" or "buy a $15,000 'new used' car in 5 years" require saving money. The more specific a financial goal, the easier it is to determine how much savings is required. You simply work backward to break a large goal into smaller pieces. For example, that $15,000 car in 5 years will require $3,000 in annual savings or about $58.00 weekly ($3,000 divided by 52).

Goals provide a framework for investment decisions and help narrow down your choices. For example, if you have a short-term goal, such as freshman-year college tuition in a year or a new car purchase in 3 years, you'll want to keep this money in cash assets (e.g., a money market mutual fund) so that there's no loss of principal. Equity investments such as stock (a security that represents a unit of ownership in a corporation) or growth mutual funds (a portfolio of stocks that is collectively owned by many investors and managed by a professional investment company) would be a poor choice due to the historical volatility of the stock market in short time frames.

On the other hand, if you have a long-term goal, such as college expenses for a newborn or retirement in 20 years, cash assets are a poor choice due to the risk of loss of purchasing power. Stocks or growth mutual funds would be better places to save for these long-term goals. We know from research by Ibbotson Associates (a Chicago investment research firm) that stocks are less volatile in longer time frames (a principle called time diversification) and provide the best historical return (gain or loss you receive from investing) of any asset class.

Several studies have shown a link between the act of planning and subsequent financial behavior. A survey sponsored by NationsBank and the Consumer Federation of America found that, no matter what their income, people with a plan save more money, save or invest in smarter ways, and feel better about their financial progress than those without a plan.

According to a recent Retirement Confidence Survey (RCS), workers who have done a retirement savings calculation have saved considerably more than those who have not. Thus, doing a retirement savings calculation appears to be related to changing saving behavior. Almost two-thirds (59%) of workers who calculated a retirement savings goal reported that they saved or invested more.

Bottom line: determine your financial goals before you spend or invest your money and know what you're investing for. A key to investment success is financial goal setting. Remember that *people don't plan to fail, they fail to plan* and set financial goals.

EXERCISE I-3

Ten Things I Love to Do

To help determine the things you value, list 10 things you love to do. After making your list, put a check mark by those activities that are free or inexpensive to do. Can you save money by spending more time doing free or less expensive things you love?

1. _____
2. _____
3. _____
4. _____
5. _____
6. _____
7. _____
8. _____
9. _____
10. _____

Evaluate Your Financial Goals

Use the worksheet below to list your financial goals and calculate the time and dollar amount required to achieve them. Be sure to categorize your goals according to the time frames suggested below. Review and update this worksheet periodically.

1 Goals	2 Approximate $ amount needed	3 Month and year needed	4 Number of months to save	5 Date to start saving	6 Monthly $ amount to save (col. 2 ÷ col. 4)
Short-term (less than 3 years)					
Intermediate-term (3–10 years)					
Long-term (more than 10 years)					

Date prepared _____/_____/_____

Starting an Emergency Fund

A financial goal that everyone should have is to establish some type of **emergency fund**. This is savings set aside specifically to meet emergencies or unanticipated bills or to cover monthly living expenses if your paycheck stops (e.g., unemployment). Too often people use credit cards or borrow from family members in an emergency because they don't have a savings account to fall back on when unexpected things happen. This just digs them further into debt when interest is charged on unpaid balances. Decide up front what constitutes an emergency so that money from the fund is not used for recurring expenses, such as birthdays.

Make establishing an emergency fund a priority. Fund it with approximately 3–6 months or more of living expenses or whatever gives you peace of mind. Whenever you withdraw from the emergency fund, pay yourself back based on a predetermined schedule as you would any other bill. Discipline yourself to use this money only for real emergencies (e.g., car repairs, broken appliances, sickness, etc.).

Keep your emergency fund in a liquid savings product such as a money market mutual fund or short-term certificate of deposit (CD). A **liquid** investment can be converted quickly to cash without loss of value. To get started, save even $5 or $10 per paycheck or whatever you can afford. Another way to start an emergency fund is to save $1 per day, plus pocket change. At the end of each month, you should have about $50 saved, or $600 after 1 year.

Testing Your Financial Fitness

Do you get an annual physical each year from your doctor and periodic screening tests such as mammograms and Pap tests? You should. Frequent monitoring of your physical health and early detection of health problems, such as cancer or heart disease, is very important. Likewise, a "financial checkup" is also advisable to:

- monitor progress from year to year (e.g., increased savings)
- identify problems (e.g., a high debt-to-income ratio)
- identify solutions to problems (e.g., reducing household expenses)
- set and monitor financial goals (e.g., a child's college education)
- identify needed action (e.g., purchasing additional life insurance)

Use the Financial Fitness Quiz (Exercise I-5) on pages 11–12 to assess your financial health. At the end of the quiz is a description of how to interpret your score. Questions that you mark with a 1 (never) or 2 (seldom) indicate areas for improvement.

Want to get your finances in order? Below are a dozen financial management strategies to consider to improve your financial fitness. Many of these will be discussed in depth later in this session.

Do a savings analysis. Determine how much money is needed to fund future financial goals. For example, if you need $10,000 for a new car in 4 years, you'll need to save $2,500 per year or $96.15 ($2,500 divided by 26) per biweekly paycheck. Break down large goals into smaller doable pieces.

"Pay yourself first." Implement automated savings methods such as direct deposit of your paycheck, payroll deductions for a credit union or 401(k) plan, and automatic investment plans offered by mutual funds or company direct stock purchase programs. For automatic investment plans, your bank checking or savings account is debited monthly for the amount of share purchases.

Debt analysis. Determine the percentage of household take-home pay spent on consumer debt such as credit cards, car loans, and student loans. If your consumer debt ratio exceeds 15–20% of take-home pay, this is an indication that you are becoming over-extended (e.g., $350 of monthly consumer debt with a $2,200 monthly net income = a 16% debt ratio [{350 ÷ 2,200} x 100]).

Accelerate debt repayment. One way to accelerate debt repayment is to obtain a PowerPay© analysis (see www.powerpay.org). PowerPay© will help you save money by allocating the monthly payment from debts that are repaid to remaining creditors.

Develop a spending plan. A spending plan (a.k.a., budget) is a written plan for spending and saving money. Basically, you total all income sources and all monthly expenses, including 1/12 of the annual cost of occasional expenses such as quarterly property taxes, then adjust the figures and your spending habits until income = expenses + savings.

Organize your financial records. Make a list of important financial data, such as names and addresses of financial advisors and insurance agents, locations of important papers, and bank and investment account information.

Calculate your net worth. Net worth is household assets minus debts. Try to calculate your net worth annually to measure your financial progress.

Determine your marginal tax bracket (the rate you pay on the last (highest) dollar of personal or household (if married) earnings)—Then use this information to make investing decisions (e.g., tax-exempt municipal bonds versus taxable corporate bonds). Marginal tax bracket information can be found on page 109 and on the Web site http://njaes.rutgers. edu/money/taxinfo/.

Check your credit file. Request a report annually from the three major credit bureaus. If you find erroneous information, request a correction in writing.

Periodically review insurance coverage and cover "large loss" risks. Examples of "big ticket" risks that can devastate a household's finances are liability, major damage to a home, and the loss of a breadwinner's income due to death or disability.

Maximize tax-deferred investing opportunities. Examples of ways to reduce income tax are employer-sponsored tax-deferred retirement plans (e.g., 401(k)s and 403(b)s), IRAs, simplified employee pension plans (SEPs), and the long-term capital gains tax rate on investments held for more than 12 months.

Maintain and develop your earning ability. Often people increase their earning ability by taking college courses or other programs that improve job skills. Another recommended strategy is increasing your financial literacy through personal finance classes, publications, and Web sites.

EXERCISE I-5

Financial Fitness Quiz

Want to improve your personal finances? Start by taking this quiz to get an idea of how well you've managed your money so far. Choose the score that best describes your current financial management practices:

5 = always
4 = usually
3 = sometimes
2 = seldom
1 = never

When you're done, add up your scores for each of the 20 questions below. The summary at the end of the quiz tells how you're doing.

Financial Management

____ 1. I have a bank checking account (or credit union share draft account) with which to pay bills

(write "5" for "yes" and "1" for "no" for this question).

____ 2. I have enough money each month to pay my rent/mortgage and other household expenses.

____ 3. I have enough money to pay for an emergency, such as a large car repair.

____ 4. I have written financial goals with a date and dollar cost (e.g., $10,000 for a car in four years).

____ 5. I have a written plan (budget) for spending and/or saving my money.

____ 6. I keep organized financial records and can find important documents easily.

____ 7. I know my federal marginal tax bracket (e.g., 15%, 25%).

____ 8. I calculate my net worth (assets minus debts) annually.

Financial Fitness Quiz

(continued)

Saving/Investing

___ 9. I save regularly for long-term financial goals, such as education for my children, a house, or retirement.

___ 10. I have money to cover at least 3 months of expenses set aside in a readily accessible account (e.g., money market mutual fund).

___ 11. I increase my savings when I receive a salary increase.

___ 12. I have a personal investment account for retirement (other than an employee pension).

___ 13. I have money spread across more than one type of investment (e.g., stocks, bonds, mutual funds, CDs).

___ 14. The after-tax yield of my savings and investments is greater than the rate of inflation.

Insurance & Estate Planning

___ 15. I have insurance to cover "big" unexpected expenses, such as a hospital bill or disability.

___ 16. I have a current will (write "5" for "yes" and "1" for "no" for this question).

Credit

___ 17. Less than half of 1 week's pay goes to my credit card revolving balances, student loans, and car payments.

___ 18. I pay credit card bills in full to avoid interest charges.

Shopping

___ 19. I comparison shop for major purchases by checking at least three sources.

___ 20. I avoid impulse purchases and don't use shopping as a form of recreation.

Scoring for the Financial Fitness Quiz is as follows:

0–20 points   You need lots of help, but don't despair. It's never too late to take action to improve your finances.

21–40 points   You are headed for financial difficulty. Now is the time to take action to reverse the trend.

41–60 points   You are doing a fair job of managing your finances and have taken some steps in the right direction.

61–80 points   You are doing a good job and are above average in managing your finances.

81–100 points   You are in excellent financial shape. Keep up the good work!

Note: Items that you scored with a 1, 2, or 3 indicate actions that you should consider taking in the future to improve your finances.

Managing Household Cash Flow

To get a handle on your household's cash flow, you need a spending plan.

In other words, you need to do a realistic side-by-side comparison of what you earn (income) and where the money goes (savings and household expenses). A spending plan provides direction for future financial decisions and indicates whether there is sufficient income with which to pay expenses.

> **Cash flow.** The relationship between household income and expenses.
> **Spending plan.** A plan for spending and saving money.

If this sounds like "budgeting," you're right. "Spending plan" is a fancy way of saying "budget." Still, there are subtle differences between the two. First, "spending plan" is a more positive term because it includes the word "spending." Most people like to spend money. The word "plan" also emphasizes control of your money, rather than letting your money control you. The word "budget," on the other hand, is often perceived negatively (e.g., deprivation) and discourages people from taking financial control of their lives.

Spending plans provide a number of advantages.

- They help determine where money is currently being spent.
- They force you to make spending choices and prioritize needs and wants.
- They help you live within your income.
- They can include savings for "big ticket" financial goals such as a new car or retirement.
- They can reduce worrying, out-of-control feelings, and family fights about money.

Although not nearly as "sexy" a topic as some "hot" new investment, spending plans are the foundation of financial planning. Why? Unless money is left over after covering household expenses, little can be done in other areas of personal finance, such as investments or retirement planning.

To prepare a spending plan, it is first necessary to know what you earn and spend. To do this, track your household income and expenses for a full month. Start with gross income so that taxes are viewed as an "expense." Try to choose a "typical" month rather than the December holiday season, in which people tend to spend more than usual. Household earnings include net (after-tax) income from a job, benefit payments (e.g., Social Security, pension, unemployment, disability), child support or alimony, public assistance, self-employment income, and other income sources (e.g., rental income). Add all income from family members who contribute to household expenses together to obtain a total of monthly household net income.

Now total your monthly expenses for an entire typical month. Using your spending records as a guide, make a list of **fixed expenses** such as housing, car loan payments, and insurance premiums that don't vary over time. Next, make a list of **flexible expenses** such as food, transportation, and gifts that vary from month to month. Finally, make a list of **periodic expenses** (e.g., holiday expenses, quarterly property taxes) that come around only once or a few times a year and divide the annual cost by 12 to arrive at a monthly cost. For example, $4,000 of annual property taxes would cost $333 monthly.

Be sure to set aside money to meet financial goals (e.g., $100 deposited monthly into a mutual fund) as a monthly "expense." If you lack an emergency fund of 3 months' expenses, include a "line item" in your spending plan to gradually build up your reserves. If you have access to "automated" savings plans, such as a 401(k), sign up today. Even small amounts of savings (e.g., $15 per paycheck) will grow substantially over time.

Four worksheets are included in this unit to help you manage your money. Use the *Checklist of Expenses* (Exercise I-6) on page 16 as you track your spending so that you don't forget any expense categories. Use the *Household Expenses: Week by Week* (Exercise I-7) worksheet on page 17 to record your actual expenses. Use the *Anticipated Occasional Expenses in Next 12 Months* (Exercise I-8) worksheet on page 18 to determine the annual and monthly cost of nonmonthly expenses (e.g., vacation, quarterly insurance premiums, and property taxes). Use the *Spending Plan Worksheet* (Exercise I-9) on pages 19–20 to total income and expenses and adjust the numbers so that income equals expenses, including savings.

Earn more than you spend and you have positive cash flow. Spend more than you earn and you have negative cash flow. You have three ways to manage cash flow and make it a positive number: earn more, spend less, or do a little of both.

Ways to Increase Household Income

- Adjust tax withholding (e.g., a $1,000 refund is equal to an additional $83 per month).
- Add a second job or work overtime.
- Start a home-based business or freelance your talents and skills.
- Increase/collect child support and alimony. (Note: This may require court intervention.)
- Access public benefits (e.g., low-cost health screenings and pet rabies clinics).
- Sell assets (e.g., sell a car, have a garage sale).
- Upgrade job skills through additional education or training.
- Charge adult children room and board.
- Use tax benefits not previously used (e.g., earned income tax credit).
- Collect money previously loaned to others.
- Establish a barter network (e.g., child care cooperative).
- House share or take in a compatible boarder or roommate.

Painless Ways to Reduce Expenses

Literally hundreds of books are available about ways to live on less. Many are organized by spending category. Below are some ideas to consider.

Housing

- Consider refinancing an existing mortgage if savings exceed the up-front cost (e.g., points).
- Ask your mortgage lender to cancel private mortgage insurance when home equity reaches 20% of home value (e.g., $20,000 of equity on a $100,000 home).
- Purchase appliances with a high energy efficiency ratio.

Food

- Combine coupons with store sales and/or product rebates for additional savings.
- Buy in bulk when items are on sale or in season (e.g., produce and canned goods).
- Buy store or generic brands if they have the cheapest price.

Utilities

- Use e-mail in lieu of phone calls to reduce telephone charges.
- Sign up for a long-distance telephone savings plan and/or generous "anytime" minutes cell phone plan, or use inexpensive prepaid phone cards.
- Eliminate add-on features to phone service (e.g., caller ID).
- Compare the cost of cable television and satellite service.
- Close off unused rooms in the winter to conserve heat.
- Insulate your hot water heater and reduce the temperature to 120°F.

Transportation

- Keep a car as long as possible to reduce depreciation and financing costs.
- Consider buying a late model used car instead of a new one.

- Purchase airline tickets during fare wars and check whether staying over a Saturday night will lower your fare.

Clothing

- Shop department store clearance sales, consignment stores, factory outlets, and thrift shops for clothing discounts.
- Buy washable clothing to avoid dry cleaning costs.
- Build a wardrobe around just a few dominant colors or neutrals to enhance "mixing and matching" possibilities.

Financial Management

- Switch to credit cards with a low annual percentage rate (APR) if you carry a balance from one month to the next.
- Increase collision and comprehensive deductibles and drop these coverages completely on older cars. (Note: This assumes adequate emergency reserves to pay for damage.)
- Inquire about insurance discounts (e.g., for buying all property insurance from the same company).
- Reorder checks and deposit slips from a mail order firm instead of a bank.

Other

- Eliminate expenses for services you rarely use, possibly including health club dues, call waiting, and premium cable channels.
- Trim gambling expenses (e.g., lottery tickets, casino trips, and bingo) and expensive habits (e.g., smoking and morning coffee stops).
- Always inquire about discounts, especially when traveling and paying cash for items.

Spending plans should balance the "bottom line." It may take several attempts to get income and expense numbers to balance. This is perfectly normal. (Hint: Do your spending plan in *pencil*). As you make expense adjustments, try to make small cuts in several categories rather than large cuts in only one or two areas. Psychologically, this is more appealing because there is less feeling of deprivation. Use the *Finding*

Money to Save Worksheet (Exercise I-10) on page 21 to identify strategies.

Many U.S. households lack a spending plan (budget). This is unfortunate. A spending plan is a tool for improved financial planning, not a financial "straightjacket." If you don't currently have a spending plan in place, start today.

Methods of Keeping Spending Plan Records

Two keys to developing a successful spending plan are using realistic figures for each expense category (e.g., food) and developing an easily manageable record-keeping system. Looking for an easy way to manage your finances? Below are descriptions of six commonly used spending plan record-keeping methods.

Computer programs. Many people use personal finance software or spreadsheet programs (e.g., Quicken and Microsoft Money) to keep income and expense records. Some of these programs print a summary of differences between planned and actual spending and provide a cumulative annual summary so you can see exactly where your money went for an entire year and the percentage of income spent in each expense category (e.g., mortgage, 35%). Of course, as with any computer program, the output is only as good as the numbers that are used. Otherwise, it's "garbage in, garbage out." Initially, it may take some time to set up records in a computer that will later save time and effort.

Envelope system. Many people also use envelopes as a spending plan tool. Every payday, they divide their money among envelopes for various expense categories. When an envelope is empty, spending in that category ends unless "transfers" are made (e.g., $50 from food envelope to utilities envelope). An advantage of the envelope system is easy access to money. Disadvantages are the possibility of loss or theft due to keeping money at home and lack of interest on savings.

Account system. Instead of placing money physically into envelopes, each paycheck is deposited into a bank or credit union account and divided "on paper"

Checklist of Expenses

Child/elder care

- [ ] Babysitter
- [ ] Day care
- [ ] Other

Clothing

- [ ] Cleaning & laundry
- [ ] Purchases
- [ ] School and work uniforms
- [ ] Other

Contributions

- [ ] Donations to charities
- [ ] Dues, union, etc.
- [ ] Educational institutions
- [ ] Religious institutions
- [ ] Other

Education

- [ ] Books, papers, & magazines
- [ ] Calculators
- [ ] Computer & software
- [ ] Seminars
- [ ] Tuition
- [ ] Other

Food

- [ ] Bakery & delivered goods
- [ ] Groceries & meats
- [ ] Lunches
- [ ] Milk
- [ ] Other

Gifts

- [ ] Anniversaries
- [ ] Birthdays
- [ ] Holidays
- [ ] Other

Medical expenses

- [ ] Dentist
- [ ] Doctor
- [ ] Prescriptions & over-the-counter medicine/vitamins
- [ ] Other

Housing

- [ ] Appliances/appliance repair
- [ ] Cable TV
- [ ] Electricity
- [ ] Furnishings
- [ ] Garbage removal
- [ ] Gas or oil
- [ ] Insurance
- [ ] Internet provider
- [ ] Property taxes
- [ ] Rent/mortgage payments
- [ ] Sewage disposal
- [ ] Telephone/cell phone
- [ ] Utilities
- [ ] Water
- [ ] Other

Home entertainment

- [ ] Food
- [ ] Supplies
- [ ] Other

Personal care

- [ ] Allowances
- [ ] Barber & beauty shop
- [ ] Manicures
- [ ] Toiletries
- [ ] Other

Recreation

- [ ] Beverages
- [ ] Clubs & sports
- [ ] Dining out
- [ ] Entertainment
- [ ] Movies & plays
- [ ] Parties
- [ ] Video/DVD rentals
- [ ] Other

Retirement savings

- [ ] Contributions to any other pension plan
- [ ] Contributions to IRAs
- [ ] Employer retirement plan

Savings

- [ ] Bank and savings & loan (S&L) accounts (saving accounts, CDs, money market accounts)
- [ ] Mutual funds
- [ ] Stocks & bonds
- [ ] Other

Taxes

- [ ] Income: federal, state, local
- [ ] Real estate

Transportation (private)

- [ ] Fuel
- [ ] Insurance
- [ ] License fees
- [ ] Maintenance & repairs
- [ ] Purchases
- [ ] Other

Transportation (public)

- [ ] Bus
- [ ] Plane
- [ ] Train
- [ ] Other

Insurance

- [ ] Auto
- [ ] Disability
- [ ] Health
- [ ] Life
- [ ] Property
- [ ] Other

Vacations

Miscellaneous

- [ ] Carpooling
- [ ] Gifts
- [ ] Personal expenses
- [ ] Pet expenses
- [ ] Postage
- [ ] Tobacco products and alcoholic beverages
- [ ] Other

EXERCISE I-7

Household Expenses: Week by Week

Household expense	Week of _____	Week of _____	Week of _____	Week of _____	Week of _____
Allowance for children					
Beverages/snacks					
Child/elder care					
Clothing					
Contributions					
Education					
Entertainment					
Food at home					
Food eaten out					
Gifts					
Home furnishings					
Home maintenance					
Insurance					
Loan payments					
Personal care					
Rent/mortgage					
Savings					
Taxes					
Transportation					
Utilities					
Other: (list)					
_____					
_____					
Total					

Adapted from: Hogarth, J. (1991). *Take Control of Your Finances.* Cornell Cooperative Extension, Ithaca, NY.

Anticipated Occasional Expenses in Next 12 Months

Fill in the amounts of anticipated expenditures below as best you can. An example is provided. Some examples of occasional expenses are holidays and birthdays, school supplies, car license plates, insurance premiums, and property taxes paid directly to a local tax assessor.

Item	Jan	Feb	Mar	Apr	May	June	July	Aug	Sept	Oct	Nov	Dec	Add Monthly Figures*	Divide by 12 for Average Monthly Amount**
Auto Insurance			$415						$415				$830	$69
Totals														

Example: * $415 + $415 = $830
        ** $830 ÷ 12 = $69

This example shows that $69 per month should be set aside to pay the auto insurance premium.

Adapted from: *Anticipated Occasional Expenditures in Next 12 Months*. Rutgers Cooperative Extension, New Jersey Agricultural Experiment Station. Rutgers, The State University of New Jersey, New Brunswick, NJ.

Spending Plan Worksheet

Instructions: 1. Calculate monthly net income under heading 1.
2. Estimate monthly expenses (sum of fixed (2a), controllable (2b), and monthly portion of periodic expenses (2c)).
3. Compare income and expenses (3) and make adjustments.

1. Monthly net income

Gross* monthly wages $ _____

Gross monthly wages of others

    in home $ _____

Public assistance/food stamps $ _____

Unemployment/disability $ _____

Child support/alimony $ _____

Social Security/retirement $ _____

Other $ _____

Other $ _____

Total monthly income $ _____

2a. Fixed expenses

Housing

    Rent or mortgage $ _____

    Insurance/taxes $ _____

Utilities

    Telephone $ _____

    Heating (equal payment plan) $ _____

    Electricity (equal payment plan) $ _____

    Trash/garbage $ _____

    Water $ _____

    Sewer $ _____

    Cable $ _____

    Internet service provider $ _____

    Other: _____ $ _____

Credit card payments

_____ $ _____

_____ $ _____

_____ $ _____

Auto

    Loan payment $ _____

    Insurance** $ _____

    License $ _____

Child support/alimony $ _____

Life insurance** $ _____

Savings (regular amounts) $ _____

Payroll deductions

    Federal + state income tax $ _____

    Savings plans $ _____

    Social Security $ _____

    Insurance premiums $ _____

    Other $ _____

Other

_____ $ _____

_____ $ _____

_____ $ _____

Total monthly estimated fixed expenses $ _____

2b. Controllable expenses

Food

Groceries	$ _____
Food eaten out	$ _____

Household expenses

Repairs and supplies	$ _____
Furnishings and appliances	$ _____
Exterior upkeep	$ _____

Transportation

Gas and repairs	$ _____
Other transportation	$ _____

Personal care	$ _____
Medical care	$ _____
Education/reading	$ _____
Travel/entertainment	$ _____
Child/elder care	$ _____
Charity/gifts/special expenses	$ _____
Clothing	$ _____
Savings	$ _____
Other	$ _____
Total monthly estimated controllable expenses	$ _____

2c. Periodic expenses

Refer to Exercise I-8, page 18.

Periodic expenses come up infrequently (e.g., 1–4 times per year) and include taxes, insurance premiums, auto servicing, tires, licensing, birthdays and holidays, educational costs, vacations, etc. Fill in the estimated costs next to the months they are due. Do not include taxes withheld from your paycheck, but do include estimated tax payments you make to the Internal Revenue Service (IRS).

Adapted from: Matejic, D. (1999). *Programming My Dollars: Where Does My Money Go?* FS063, Rutgers Cooperative Extension. http://www.njaes.rutgers.edu/pubs/publication.asp?pid=FS063

Add your total periodic expenses for the year and divide by 12 to determine the total monthly portion.

January	$ _____
February	$ _____
March	$ _____
April	$ _____
May	$ _____
June	$ _____
July	$ _____
August	$ _____
September	$ _____
October	$ _____
November	$ _____
December	$ _____
Total periodic expenses	$ _____

$$\frac{\text{Total periodic expenses}}{12} = \frac{\text{Monthly portion}}{\text{periodic expenses}}$$

3. Compare income and expenses

Total monthly income	$ _____

Estimated expenses

Fixed	$ _____
Controllable	$ _____
Periodic (monthly portion)	$ _____
Total expenses	– $ _____
Balance	$ _____

Now that you have a spending plan, you should make every effort to stick to the designated amounts in each category. It is not enough just to have a plan on paper.

* Before tax withholding and other deductions.
** Monthly portion of premiums if *not* paid by employer *or* automatically deducted from your paycheck *or* listed with your periodic expenses on page 18.

(e.g., via a ledger with headings for different expense categories). Each time money is added or spent in a category, the balance changes. Surpluses or deficits in an expense category (e.g., food) can carry over from month to month. The amount in the overall bank account, however, should always remain "in the black."

Spreadsheet system. Two columns are listed on a sheet of paper: "target amount" and "actual amount." "Target amount" is anticipated income and expenses while "actual amount" lists what really happened. This method provides a comparison of planned and actual figures so that adjustments can be made, if needed.

"Running balance" system. This method tracks one account in which funds are held for bill paying. Using a calendar with paydays marked and a list of monthly and occasional (e.g., quarterly property tax) expenses, a projection is made of income and expenses for a 3- to 6-month period. "Extra" paychecks (e.g., a month with five weekly paydays) and occasional expenses (e.g., quarterly property taxes) are inserted as they occur. The ending balance is carried forward into subsequent projections.

Reserve accounts. Many people establish special accounts as a "parking place" for earmarked money.

An example is a reserve for occasional expenses. The annual cost for each expense is divided by 12 and saved monthly. Other common reserve accounts are money set aside monthly for home maintenance and emergencies (e.g., unemployment).

On page 22 are examples of three different ways to track expenses versus income.

Managing an Unpredictable Income

For many people, managing money is a fairly predictable process. They earn the same income each month and pay roughly the same expenses. Of course, there are occasional surprises (e.g., a flat tire), but more often than not, income and household expenses remain pretty much the same. This makes it easy to plan bank deposits so that sufficient money is available to pay bills.

For other people, however, income is irregular and can vary considerably from month to month. For example, real estate agents generally earn the most during the summer. Winter months, on the other hand, often bring a reduced income. Unpredictable and/or irregular income is also a fact of life for many other occupations, including landscapers and self-employed consultants.

Account Method

Example:	Food account
Balance 3/31:	$250
April 1:	(100)
April 8:	(100)
April 13: (paycheck)	+ 250
April 15:	(100)
$200	ETC.

Spreadsheet Method

	Target amount	Actual amount
Income		
Salary #1	$900	$1,000
Salary #2	1,200	1,200
	2,100	2,200
Expenses		
Savings	250	250
Mortgage	755	755
Utilities	235	295
Loan/credit	245	260
Insurance	130	130
Food	300	265
Other	100	280
	$2,015	$2,235

Running Balance Method

Previous month's balance (12/31)		$265
Jan. 1 bills	(250)	15
Jan. 3 paycheck	+ 400	415
Jan. 10 paycheck	+ 400	815
Midmonth bills	(215)	600
Jan. 17 paycheck	+ 400	1,000
Jan. 24 paycheck	+ 400	1,400
Jan. 31 paycheck	+ 400	1,800
Jan. 31 bills	(1,250)	550
"Fudge factor" (reserve)	(150)	$400
		Carryover

So how do you manage an irregular income? Plan, plan, plan. The key to developing a spending plan (budget) with an irregular income is stashing away money from high-earning months to draw from when income is lower. There is no other "magic" way.

The first step in managing an unpredictable income is tracking monthly expenses for an entire month. Once you know what it takes to run your household each month, the next step is to determine which months are "feasts" (income greater than expenses) and which are "famines" (income less than expenses). For example, if monthly expenses (including savings) total $2,000 and household monthly income ranges from $1,000 to $5,000, some of the surplus of high-earning months should be saved and doled out gradually over lean months to supplement income. Designate a bank savings account or money market fund to hold surplus income until it is needed.

The biggest problem experienced by irregular earners is not having the organization and/or discipline to set money aside. They spend freely during "the good times" and then have nothing to fall back on when income is reduced. To plan ahead, estimate anticipated income for each month, based on past earnings records. Be conservative with your estimates. Then subtract monthly expenses from income (e.g., $1,500 income minus $2,000 expenses equals a $500 deficit). Calculate the total deficit for all months in which expenses exceed income (e.g., 5 months with deficits: $500 + $1,000 + $1,500 + $2,000 + $500 equals $5,500).

Next, divide the total for the deficit months (in this example, $5,500) by the number of months in which income exceeds expenses. In this example, there are seven "good" (income greater than expenses) months, and $5,500 divided by 7 equals $786. This is the average amount that must be set aside during each "good" month. The actual amount saved per month can vary (some "good" months are better than others), however, as long as the total deficit ($5,500 in this example) is eventually set aside as a cushion.

Managing an unpredictable income need not be a nightmare. It does take some planning and attention to detail, however. The key to success is simulating a regular paycheck by accumulating funds to draw upon when income is reduced.

Calculating Your Net Worth

Imagine that you have gotten lost along a busy high way and have come to a rest stop looking for directions. Many rest stops have large wall maps with a large "X" indicating the location of the rest stop in relation to an entire state or region. When planning your finances, a net worth statement is like that "X" on a traveler's road map. It marks your finances at a particular point in time.

> **Net worth** = assets – liabilities (debts)

A net worth statement tells your current position financially and provides a starting point for your journey to future financial goals. Before you can plan where you are going in the future, you need to see where you stand today. A net worth statement provides a snapshot of your finances on a particular day and indicates how much you are worth in dollars and cents. As new snapshots are taken, your net worth will change. An extreme example is former Microsoft chairman Bill Gates' net worth, which can change significantly day to day, depending on the performance of his Microsoft stock.

Preparing a net worth statement is a relatively simple process and shouldn't take more than an hour or two. With financial records and a calculator in hand and using the *Net Worth Statement* worksheet (Exercise I-11) on page 24 as a guide, first list all of your **assets** (i.e., things of value that you own) at their **fair market value** (the value for which you could reasonably expect to sell the items). Next, make a similar list of all your debts (i.e., money owed to others). Net worth is calculated by subtracting the sum of debts from the sum of assets. For example, if a person has $250,000 of assets and $100,000 of debt, he or she would have a $150,000 net worth. If debts exceed assets, as is sometimes the case for college students and others, net worth is a negative number.

Assets can be divided into several categories. First, there are *cash assets,* including the actual cash that you have in your wallet as well as checking and savings accounts, money market funds, the cash value of life insurance policies, and other liquid assets. A second category of assets is *real estate assets,* including one's personal residence, land, and other property (e.g., vacation home).

A third category of assets is *investments.* This includes the market value of CDs, stocks, bonds, mutual funds, and annuities, as well as retirement accounts such as IRAs, 401(k) and 403(b) plans, and pensions. The final category of assets is *personal property,* including automobiles, recreational vehicles, appliances and home furnishings, collections (e.g., coins), jewelry and furs, and other possessions.

The debt side of the ledger is divided into four categories. The first, *current debts,* are outstanding bills that will be repaid within a year. This includes medical and utility bills, small credit card balances, and other short-term debts. The second debt category is *mortgages* on a home or land. The third category of debt is *loans,* such as car loans, student loans, and loans against a cash value (e.g., whole life or universal life) life insurance policy. The fourth category is *other debts* such as credit card balances that will take more than a year to repay.

Once you've completed your first net worth statement, resolve to do another at least once a year to monitor your progress. A good time to calculate net worth is during tax season because financial records are readily available. Aim to increase your net worth by at least 5% annually. Net worth statements are especially valuable when viewed comparatively from one year to the next. A net worth statement represents the results of all prior financial activities.

Net Worth Statement

An important step in gaining financial control is to take an accounting of your total financial worth. Every year, your net worth should be tabulated to enable you to review your progress and compare it with your financial goals. In addition, a net worth statement is a valuable aid in planning your estate and establishing a record for loan or insurance purposes.

Assets—what you own*

Cash on hand _____

Checking account _____

Savings account _____

Money markets _____

Other _____

Cash value life insurance _____

Real estate/property:

Home _____

Land _____

Other _____

Investments (market value):

Certificates of deposit _____

Stocks _____

IRAs _____

Bonds _____

Mutual funds _____

Annuities _____

401(k) or 403(b) plans _____

Pension plan _____

Other _____

Loans receivable: _____

Personal property (present value):

Auto _____

Recreational vehicle/boat _____

Home furnishings _____

Appliances and furniture _____

Collections _____

Jewelry and furs _____

Other _____

Total assets _____

Liabilities—what you owe

Current debts:

Household _____

Medical _____

Credit cards _____

Department store cards _____

Back taxes _____

Legal _____

Other _____

Mortgages:

Home _____

Land _____

Other _____

Loans:

Bank/finance company _____

Bank/finance company _____

Automobiles _____

Recreational vehicle/boat _____

Education _____

Life insurance _____

Personal (from family or friends) _____

Other:

Credit cards (long-term payoff) _____

Total debts _____

* Use the following codes for couples: (M) me, (P) partner, (J) joint, e.g., mutual funds $2, 000 (J), stock $5000 (P).

Tips for Smarter Borrowing

Credit is the use of someone else's money for a price, which is called interest. Other fees (e.g., late and over-the-limit fees) may also be charged. The use of credit creates debt, which is the outstanding balance owed to lenders. Debt repayment is a major expense for many families. Some people spend a day's pay (or more) per week repaying car loans, credit cards, and other debts. Not only is this expensive, but money that goes toward payments is unavailable for investing. Below are 24 tips for smarter borrowing.

1. Borrow as little as possible by making the largest down payment you can afford (e.g., on a car). When car payments end, continue making the previous monthly payment to yourself as a way to build savings for items such as your next car.

2. Shop for the best credit deal, just as you would for other purchases. Compare at least three credit issuers (e.g., banks) for the lowest APR and fees. Use the *Credit Card Comparison Worksheet* (Exercise I-12) on page 28 to compare three credit card offers.

3. Separate borrowing decisions from purchasing decisions. In other words, don't just accept the financing arrangement offered by a merchant (e.g., car dealer or furniture store). Shop around for better terms (e.g., through an employer credit union).

4. Always pay more than the minimum monthly payment. Otherwise, it could take years, even decades, to repay a loan. Even small amounts added to minimum payments produce awesome savings. For example, according to the book *Slash Your Debt,* send $25 a month more than the minimum on a 17% credit card with a $5,000 outstanding balance and you'll save $7,192 in interest and 352 payments (almost 30 years).

5. Say no to credit life or disability insurance if you already have adequate individual or group policies. If you don't currently have life or disability insurance and need it, shop around for the best buy in coverage.

6. Avoid being "upside down" on a car loan. This means that you owe more than a car is worth. Shorten the length of your car loan or make a larger down payment.

7. Pay credit card bills promptly to reduce the average daily balance on which interest is charged. Avoid cards using the two-cycle average daily balance calculation method. This method generally increases finance charges because it includes two billing cycle balances.

8. Limit credit card cash advances. The interest rate is high because most creditors charge interest from the date money is borrowed (i.e., there is usually no grace period), along with transaction fees (e.g., $2.50).

9. Transfer balances on high-rate credit cards to those with low 6-month "teaser rates." Try to pay off the balance before the low rate expires or seek another low-rate card. (Note: Doing this too frequently could lower your credit score.)

10. Request a copy of your credit file. Every U.S. resident is entitled to receive a free copy of their credit file each year from each of the major credit bureaus: Experian, Equifax, and TransUnion. Use the *Credit File Request Form* (Exercise I-13) on page 29 to make your request. If there are errors in your credit file, contact the credit bureau promptly and request a correction.

11. Request a copy of your credit score. Credit scores are three-digit numbers that range from the 300s (worst) through the 800s (best). Lend-

ers use them to assess a person's creditworthiness and to determine the interest rates charged for a loan or credit card. Credit scores are available online for a fee from www.myfico.com and from each of the three major credit bureaus (www.experian.com, www.transunion.com, and www.equifax.com), and for free from www.eloan.com.

12. Complete the *Credit Card Safety Record* (Exercise I-14) on page 30, which includes spaces to list the issuers of your credit cards, the card user(s), the account number, and the telephone number and mailing address of the issuer. Keep this form with your financial records in case a credit card is lost or stolen.

13. Calculate your **debt-to-income ratio** by dividing the total monthly payment for household consumer debts into net (after-tax) household income. For example, a family with a $250 car payment and $100 of monthly credit card payments and a $2,500 monthly net income would have a debt-to-income ratio of .14 ($350 divided by $2,500) or 14%. Financial experts generally recommend a debt-to-income ratio of no more than 15–20%. Above that, it is easy to become overextended and experience difficulty making payments. It is also recommended that consumer debt (e.g., credit cards, car loans, and student loans), plus housing costs (e.g., rent or mortgage payment), not exceed 40–50% of take-home pay.

14. Consider alternatives to credit cards to reduce interest costs. One example is using a home equity loan to consolidate high-interest credit card bills if you have the discipline not to run up credit card balances again. Interest on up to $100,000 of home equity debt is usually tax-deductible. Other lower cost sources of money are credit unions and loans against a 401(k) (note: certain limits apply) or cash value life insurance policy. Repay the loan promptly to protect your future financial security.

15. Avoid borrowing money from finance companies. Apply at a bank or credit union first. Finance companies generally charge high interest rates and can be considered a negative reference in credit reports, thus lowering your credit score. This is because potential lenders may see this as an indication that you couldn't get a loan elsewhere due to prior problems.

16. Consider closing less attractive credit card accounts so that you don't appear "credit heavy" to potential lenders. Don't close your oldest accounts, however, because this could lower your credit score. Good candidates for closure are high-interest department store accounts and credit cards that charge high annual membership fees.

17. Carry a list of credit card billing cycle dates with you when you shop. This will help you select the card that provides the longest "float" time between the date of purchase and the date that payment is due.

18. Select a credit card that best matches your debt repayment style. If you generally make minimum or partial payments, look for a credit card with a low interest rate. If you pay your bill in full, seek a grace period and no (or a low) annual fee. A grace period is the number of days you have before a credit card company starts charging interest on new purchases.

19. Design your own debt repayment schedule by paying more than the minimum amount required. For example, repay a home equity loan over 3–5 years, not a bank's 15–20-year schedule. Another is a "do-it-yourself" biweekly mortgage. Simply divide your mortgage payment (principal and interest) by 12 and add that amount to each monthly payment. This has the same effect as a biweekly mortgage (i.e., 13 payments per year).

20. Negotiate a discount from lenders, especially if you have a good credit history. Many credit card

issuers will reduce annual fees and/or interest rates upon request. Before calling, role play your request with a friend to sharpen your negotiating skills. If you have other credit cards or pre-approved offers, hint that you will close your account or switch to another card issuer unless your request is honored.

21. Read credit card disclosure charts and surrounding footnotes carefully. By law, all credit card offers must include a so-called "Schumer Box" (named for the sponsor of the bill) that includes the APR, various fees, and the minimum finance charge.

22. Complain if you get hit with an unjustified penalty (e.g., late fee). Many creditors will reverse these charges upon request, at least for the first time. Also be aware that many creditors have decreased the amount of time between when a bill is mailed and when payment is due. As a result, there is a greater chance of a late fee being charged. In addition, some creditors have moved payment-posting deadlines to earlier times of the day, such as 10 a.m. This effectively means that the company must receive the payment by the day before for it to be posted on the due date. Check your bill inserts for details.

23. Beware of credit traps. These are products and features that can greatly increase the cost of borrowing. Examples of credit traps include:

- late fees, which can be charged when payment is only a day late.
- over-the-limit fees charged for as long as a borrower's balance exceeds the credit limit.
- cash advances that charge interest immediately when a credit card is used to obtain cash.
- skip-a-month offers that allow borrowers to skip a payment but continue to accrue interest.
- rent-to-own agreements that allow consumers to rent items by the week for a stated time (often 78 weeks), resulting in a cost that is two to four times the amount it would cost to purchase an item outright.
- 125% equity loans that allow borrowers to receive loans greater than the value of their home, minus its outstanding mortgage. If you had to sell quickly, you'd be unlikely to get back all of what you owed. In addition, a portion of the loan would not be tax-deductible.

24. Visit www.powerpay.org for a PowerPay© analysis. This online program helps users accelerate debt repayment by printing out a repayment calendar that adds monthly payments from paid-off debts (e.g., Sears credit card) to remaining debts (e.g., MasterCard), resulting in hundreds, even thousands, of dollars of interest savings.

Credit Card Comparison Worksheet

Name of issuer	APR	Grace period	Annual fee	Other fees	Balance calculation method	Other features
ABC Credit	19.8%	25 days	$20	$20: late fee $20: over limit fee $2: cash advance fee	Average daily balance (including new purchases)	10% discount on phone calls if charged to credit card.
XYZ Credit	16.0%	None	None	$15: late fee $15: over limit fee $1: transaction fee	Two-cycle average daily balance (including new purchases)	Use of card provides discounts on auto purchases.

Annual Credit Report Request Form

You have the right to get a free copy of your credit file disclosure, commonly called a credit report, once every 12 months, from each of the nationwide consumer credit reporting companies - Equifax, Experian and TransUnion.

For instant access to your free credit report, visit www.annualcreditreport.com.

For more information on obtaining your free credit report, visit www.annualcreditreport.com or call 877-322-8228.

Use this form if you prefer to write to request your credit report from any, or all, of the nationwide consumer credit reporting companies. The following information is required to process your request. **Omission of any information may delay your request.**

Once complete, fold (do not staple or tape), place into a #10 envelope, affix required postage and mail to:
Annual Credit Report Request Service P.O. Box 105281 Atlanta, GA 30348-5281.

Please use a Black or Blue Pen and write your responses in PRINTED CAPITAL LETTERS without touching the sides of the boxes like the examples listed below:

A B C D E F G H I J K L M N O P Q R S T U V W X Y Z   0 1 2 3 4 5 6 7 8 9

Social Security Number:

☐☐☐ - ☐☐ - ☐☐☐☐

Date of Birth:

☐☐ / ☐☐ / ☐☐☐☐
Month   Day   Year

- - - - - Fold Here - - - - -   - - - - Fold Here - - - -

First Name   **M.I.**

Last Name   **JR, SR, III, etc.**

Current Mailing Address:

House Number   **Street Name**

Apartment Number / Private Mailbox   **For Puerto Rico Only: Print Urbanization Name**

City   **State**   **ZipCode**

Previous Mailing Address (complete only if at current mailing address for less than two years):

House Number   **Street Name**

- - - - - Fold Here - - - - -   - - - - Fold Here - - - -

Apartment Number / Private Mailbox   **For Puerto Rico Only: Print Urbanization Name**

City   **State**   **ZipCode**

Shade Circle Like This → ●

Not Like This → ⊗ ⊘

I want a credit report from (shade each that you would like to receive):
○ Equifax
○ Experian
○ TransUnion

○ Shade here if, for security reasons, you want your credit report to include no more than the last four digits of your Social Security Number.

31238

If additional information is needed to process your request, the consumer credit reporting company will contact you by mail.

Your request will be processed within 15 days of receipt and then mailed to you.

Copyright 2004, Central Source LLC

Credit Card Safety Record

Make a list of all of your credit card issuers, account numbers, and creditor contact information.

Name of card	Card user(s)	Account number	Creditor contact information

Financial Record Keeping

When was the last time you couldn't find an important document or receipt? Do you remember how frustrating it was looking for something you know you had carefully put away somewhere? That's why it's so important to keep good financial records. They can:

- prove that a bill has been paid.
- save time and stress by not having to search for certain papers.
- show legal proof of events (e.g., birth, death, marriage, divorce).
- prove ownership of property.
- document tax deductions.
- dispute errors in bank, investment, credit card, or other financial statements.
- document claims for benefits such as life insurance and Social Security.
- expedite the timely payment of bills, thereby avoiding late charges.
- simplify estate planning and the administration of your financial affairs.

Many financial records, such as canceled checks, tax records, and bank and credit card statements, can be stored at home, preferably in an insulated steel box or fire-resistant file cabinet. Some important documents are best kept in a bank safe deposit box. These include papers that you don't need to refer to very often and/or those that are difficult to replace.

Home storage can be divided into two categories: active and inactive. Both kinds of files should be stored in fireproof boxes that can be purchased at office supply stores. The active file includes papers that you may need immediately; the inactive file is more for historical value and may be used only occasionally. Items to keep in an active home file include:

- appliance manuals and warranties
- bank and investment account statements (for as long as you own an asset, plus at least 3 years)
- burial/funeral instructions
- canceled checks
- credit card information and loan payment records
- education (e.g., transcripts of college courses) and employment (e.g., resume) records
- health benefit information and family health records (e.g., immunizations)
- insurance policies
- inventory of the contents of safe deposit box
- keys to safe deposit box
- receipts for recently paid bills
- receipts for items under warranty
- Social Security information (e.g., benefit estimates)
- tax returns for the past 3 years
- original wills and trusts (Note: Another secure location for these papers is your attorney's office safe.)

Items to Keep in a Safe Deposit Box

- adoption papers
- birth certificates
- citizenship papers
- death certificates
- divorce records

- household inventory (list and photographs or videotape of possessions)
- important contracts
- marriage certificates

- military discharge papers
- real estate deeds and mortgages
- stock and bond certificates
- titles to automobiles
- wills and trusts (copy)

Items to keep in an inactive home file include:

- selected active file papers more than 3 years old
- copies of legal documents stored in one's safe deposit box (e.g., birth and death certificates)
- correspondence related to important legal matters (e.g., adoption or a lawsuit)
- insurance accident reports and claim forms
- property improvement records (e.g., receipts or paid vouchers)
- tax returns that are 4 or more years old

One way to take charge of your finances is to get your important papers organized. Use the *How Organized Are You?* worksheet (Exercise I-15) to analyze your current organizational skills and record-keeping practices. Use the six-page *A Record of Important Family Papers* worksheet (Exercise I-16) on pages 33–41 to record important household financial data. Another record-keeping suggestion is to have an emergency moveable file in case you need to leave your home in a hurry (e.g., hurricane).

EXERCISE I-15

How Organized Are You?

For each statement, place a check mark in the column that most accurately describes your own behavior or situation.

	Yes	No	Sometimes
1. I have a home filing system that works well for me.	☐	☐	☐
2. My spouse/partner, children, and/or another relative or friend know the whereabouts of my life insurance policy.	☐	☐	☐
3. I know the contents of all my storage boxes without having to look inside.	☐	☐	☐
4. I know where my income tax papers of 3 years ago are located, and in the event of my death, a relative or friend also would be able to locate them.	☐	☐	☐
5. I have a system for handling incoming mail.	☐	☐	☐
6. I have two copies of a household inventory—one is stored at home and one is in my safe deposit box.	☐	☐	☐
7. I make a written "to-do" list with identified priorities for the day or week.	☐	☐	☐
8. I expect interruptions to occur during the course of a normal day and keep my daily schedule flexible enough to allow for such occurrences.	☐	☐	☐
9. At the end of most days, I feel I've accomplished the most important tasks I had planned to do.	☐	☐	☐

Adapted from: Marilyn Sugden and Kathy Prochaska-Cue, Extension Family Economics and Management Specialists, as part of the *Can't Find It? Put Your House in Order!* lesson. Nebraska Cooperative Extension, 1983.

A Record of Important Family Papers

Name: _____

Copy 1 of this record stored at: _____

Safe deposit box number: _____ at _____

Social Security number: _____ - _____ - _____

Date recorded or revised: _____

Copy 2 stored at: _____

Bank key kept at: _____

Where Social Security cards are kept: _____

Names of advisers

Adviser	Name	Address	Phone number/e-mail address
Accountant			
Attorney			
Banker			
Broker			
Doctor			
Executor			
Insurance agent			
Financial planner			

A Record of Important Family Papers
(continued)

Insurance policies

Type	Company & address	Policy number	Effective date	Policy amount	Premium	Payment due	Beneficiary	Location of policy
Life								
Health & accident								
Hospitalization								
Major medical								
Disability								

A Record of Important Family Papers

(continued)

Insurance policies

Type	Company & address	Policy number	Effective date	Policy amount	Premium	Payment due	Beneficiary	Location of policy
Medicare								
Long-term care								
Vehicles								
Homeowner's/renter's								
Umbrella liability								

A Record of Important Family Papers
(continued)

Bank accounts, savings, and credit union accounts

Type	Name & address	Name on account	Account number	Location of records
Individual checking				
Joint checking				
Savings				
Other				

A Record of Important Family Papers
(continued)

U.S. savings bonds, certificates of deposit, Treasury bills, bonds, and notes

Serial number	Owner & co-owner	Purchase price	Date of purchase	Maturity date	Value at maturity	Beneficiary	Location of records

A Record of Important Family Papers
(continued)

Stocks, bonds, and mutual fund shares

Kind	Company	Number	Name on certificate	Date purchased	Number of shares	Cost per share	Income due	Location of certificate

A Record of Important Family Papers

(continued)

Vehicles

Make	Model & year	Engine number	Purchase price	Registration	Location of title

Real estate

Type	Location	Purchase price	Mortgage amount	Mortgage holder	Location of records

A Record of Important Family Papers
(continued)

Debts

Description	Name & address of person/company owed	Account #	Amount of debt	Interest rate	Number & amount of payments	Final payment due	Location of records

Payments due me/us

Description	Name & address of person owing	Amount of payment	Interest rate	Number & amount of payments	Final payment due	Location of records

A Record of Important Family Papers
(continued)

Other important papers

Type of paper	Location	Type of paper	Location	Type of paper	Location
Adoption papers		Deed to house & lot		Military service records	
Automobile title		Divorce papers		Organization membership	
Baptismal records		Education records		Passports	
Birth certificates		Employment records		Pension records/ retirement plans	
Business records		Guarantees and warranties		Patents & copyrights	
Canceled checks		Health records		Real estate abstract	
Charge account list		Household inventory		Rental property records	
Citizenship papers		Important keys		Social Security card & record	
Death certificates		Last instructions		Tax records	
Deed to burial plot		License to practice		Will for:_____	
Deed to farm & lots		Marriage certificates		Will for:_____	

Your Minimum "Need to Knows" about Financial Planning Basics

- People's feelings about money greatly influence spending and saving decisions.

- Personal qualities, such as focus, discipline, and a positive attitude, are related to financial success.

- Frequent monitoring of financial health is as important as an annual physical with a doctor.

- Even relatively small dollar amounts will grow to significant sums with **compound interest** (earning interest on interest).

- People generally spend money in ways that are consistent with their values.

- Financial goals should be specific, with an estimated time deadline and dollar cost.

- Investment decisions should be based on financial goals so that appropriate assets are chosen.

- Three to six months' expenses or more should be set aside in reserve as an emergency fund.

- Credit terms should be compared and negotiated just like any other consumer purchase.

- A spending plan is a plan for spending and saving money. Income should equal household expenses plus savings for financial goals.

- If earnings are irregular, base your budget on average expenses. Shift income from high-earning months to low-earning months to manage successfully.

- A net worth statement provides a snapshot of your finances (assets minus debts) and should be calculated annually to measure financial progress.

- Credit files and credit scores should be checked periodically and errors, if any, should be corrected promptly.

- Credit traps are products and features that can greatly increase the cost of borrowing; they should be avoided.

- Important papers that are difficult to replace should be kept in a safe deposit box.

- "If it is to be (i.e., financial success), it is up to me."

Action Steps

SESSION I: **Financial Basics**

Check off each of the following action steps as they are completed.

☐ Complete the *Money Coat of Arms* exercise (page 4) and use it to identify your values.

☐ List short-, intermediate-, and long-term financial goals with a date and cost for each.

☐ Start or increase emergency savings to equal 3 months of expenses.

☐ Take the *Financial Fitness Quiz* (pages 11–12) to identify financial strengths and weaknesses.

☐ Track household income and expenses for a month to identify spending patterns.

☐ Identify specific ways to increase income and/or reduce expenses.

☐ Use the *Spending Plan Worksheet* (pages 19–20) and expense tracking data to prepare a spending plan.

☐ Calculate your net worth (assets minus debts) annually to analyze financial progress.

☐ Contact existing creditors and request concessions, such as a lower interest rate.

☐ Request a copy of your credit file and correct any errors. Check your credit score.

☐ Complete the *Credit Card Safety Record* (page 30) to summarize credit card account data.

☐ Calculate your debt-to-income ratio (monthly consumer debt payments/net pay).

☐ Set up a simple, user-friendly financial record-keeping system.

References

A Money Management Workbook (1999). Washington, D.C.: American Association of Retired Persons (Women's Financial Information Program).

Dahl, B. (1996). *A Working Woman's Guide to Financial Security*. Urbana, Ill.: University of Illinois Cooperative Extension.

FACTA, The Fair and Accurate Credit Transactions Act: Consumers Win Some, Lose Some (2006, June). Available online at: www.privacyrifgts.org/fs/fs6a-facta.html.

Garman, E.T., and Forgue, R.E. (2008). *Personal Finance*. Boston, Mass.: Houghton Mifflin Company.

Hendricks, E. (2005). *Credit Scores and Credit Reports*. Cabin John, MD: Privacy Times, Inc.

High School Financial Planning Program (2007). Denver, Colo.: National Endowment for Financial Education.

The InCharge Guide to Debtor Education (2004). Orlando, FL: InCharge Education Foundation, Inc.

Johnson, A. (2000). *The Financial Check-Up*. Providence, Utah: Watkins Printing.

Keown, A.J. (2001). *Personal Finance: Turning Money into Wealth*. Upper Saddle River, N.J.: Prentice-Hall.

Mellon, O. (2002). *Money Harmony: Resolving Money Conflicts in Your Life and Relationships*. New York: Walker and Company.

O'Neill, B. et al. (2002). *Investing For Your Future*. NRAES–156. Ithaca, N.Y.: Natural Resource, Agriculture, and Engineering Service.

Prochaska, J.O., Norcross, J.C., and DiClemente, C.O. (1994). *Changing for Good*. New York: Avon Books.

Vitt, L.A. & Murrell, K.L. (2007). *You and Your Money*. Upper Saddle River, NJ: FT Press.

Warren, E. & Tyagi, A.W. (2005). *All Your Worth*. New York: Free Press.

Are You Covered? Insurance Basics

Mary has a lot of risks
With her car, her home, and health
That's why she buys insurance
So she can protect her wealth

What will be covered in Session II

Insurance Lessons

1. Managing Life's Risks
2. Insurance Basics
3. Life Insurance
4. Health Insurance
5. Disability Insurance
6. Long-Term Care Insurance
7. Auto Insurance
8. Homeowner's Insurance
9. Umbrella Liability Insurance

Terms to Learn (bolded in the text)

Any-occupation disability insurance	Liability insurance
Cash value	Managed care health plan
Coinsurance	Noncancelable
Copayment	Own-occupation disability insurance
Declarations page	Permanent life insurance
Deductible	Policy limit
Elimination period	Risk acceptance
Exclusions	Risk avoidance
Guaranteed renewable	Risk reduction
Indemnity plan health insurance	Risk transfer
Large-loss principle	Term life insurance

Exercises

1. Life Insurance Needs
2. Checklist for Financial Fitness
3. Insurance Evaluation and Goals

Managing Life's Risks

Life is full of risks.

Many of life's risks have financial consequences. Some examples of potential financial losses include:

- damage to your car in an auto accident.
- a fire that destroys your residence and personal possessions.
- loss of income due to disability (accident or illness).
- loss of a household earner's income due to death.
- loss of a homemaker's services (e.g., child care) due to death.
- large medical bills for a major disease (e.g., cancer) or injury (e.g., car accident).
- a court judgment holding you liable for damages to others.

> **Risk.** According to Webster's Dictionary, "exposure to loss, harm, or danger."

People manage the risk of financial loss in five different ways. Below is a description of each method and examples of each.

Do nothing and hope for the best. Deciding, consciously or by default, to take no action to deal with life's risks is a risk management strategy used by some people. For example, they forgo health insurance or property insurance that covers the loss or theft of personal possessions. Often, the cost of insurance is an obstacle to managing risks. Thus, people who can least afford to pay for a loss are often without coverage.

Risk avoidance. Eliminating the possibility of a loss by avoiding activities that expose you to a risk. For example, not driving in the snow avoids the chance of a weather-related traffic accident. Ditto for other potentially hazardous activities such as skiing, bungee jumping, cigarette smoking, and sun-tanning.

Risk reduction. Instead of avoiding an activity altogether, you take measures to reduce a loss, should one occur. Examples include wearing seat belts when driving, using smoke detectors and burglar alarms, taking a defensive driving course, and buying a car with airbags and/or an antitheft system.

Risk acceptance. Intentionally accepting small financial losses that you can afford to pay out-of-pocket, if needed. Generally, this is done to keep the cost of insurance policies affordable. Three common examples are the deductible (e.g., $500) for comprehensive and collision auto coverage, dropping collision coverage on an older car, and the copayment (e.g., 20%) for medical expenses and doctor's bills.

Risk transfer. Transferring the risk of loss to a third party (insurance company) in exchange for a specified payment (premium). Insurance coverage is especially recommended for potentially large losses such as disability and liability. Insurance companies pool premiums from many people to cover losses.

Insurance Basics

Insurance is the most common method that people use to protect themselves against potential financial losses.

> **Insurance.** According to Webster's Dictionary, a guarantee against risk of loss or harm in consideration of a payment proportioned to the risk involved (premium).

An important principle behind the purchase of insurance is the **large-loss principle**. This means that the size (amount) of a potential loss—rather than its probability—is the determining factor in purchasing insurance.

In other words, you want to spend the bulk of your insurance premium dollars to protect against risks that can wipe out your assets and/or claim future income for years to come (e.g., a court judgment). Small expenses, such as a dented fender or broken eyeglasses, should be covered through insurance deductibles or emergency fund savings.

On the other hand, certain types of insurance are clearly unnecessary. This includes insurance that duplicates coverage you already have, insurance that covers small losses, and very narrowly defined coverage (e.g., dread disease insurance). Below is a list of commonly sold, but generally unnecessary, types of insurance.

Credit (life and/or disability) insurance. This covers loan payments if a borrower becomes disabled or dies. According to the Consumer Federation of America, credit insurance is grossly overpriced. Credit insurance is generally calculated as a flat rate per $100 of loan balance. Sometimes it is added to a loan contract without a borrower's knowledge and/or consent, a practice known as "packing." Much better alternatives are to build up emergency reserves to cover small debts (e.g., $1,000 loan) and purchase or increase general life and disability coverage to cover large debts (e.g., $80,000 mortgage).

Term life insurance for children. The purpose of insurance is to protect dependents against the loss of a household earner's income. Children are generally dependents and have a low probability of dying. Therefore, insuring them is rarely necessary. Some people argue that policy proceeds could be used for a child's funeral or family grief counseling. However, it is likely that college funds, no longer needed, could be tapped for this, if necessary. As for the argument that children could get sick and be turned down for coverage later as an adult, they could probably still get insurance through an employer group plan.

Cancer insurance. Cancer makes headlines, but heart disease is actually America's most frequent killer. The bottom line is that no one knows what diseases they may or may not contract. Therefore, comprehensive major medical coverage is needed rather than "dread disease policies" that provide protection only against a specific illness.

"Double indemnity" insurance rider. This policy feature doubles the face amount of a life insurance policy if a person dies from accidental causes. In reality,

---

Major "Large-Loss" Risks that Can Greatly Affect a Family's Finances

- Loss of income due to disability (illness or accident).
- Loss of a household earner's income (death).
- Destruction of one's home due to fire, flooding, etc.
- Liability losses resulting from a court judgment.
- Large hospital and doctor expenses (e.g., expenses for cancer treatment).

---

most people do not die in accidents. If additional life insurance is needed, it should be purchased as part of a basic policy that provides coverage regardless of the cause of death.

Hospital indemnity policies. These policies provide a specific benefit for each day spent in a hospital. Generally, they pay much less than the amount that a patient is actually charged. Again, a much better alternative is a comprehensive major medical health insurance policy that covers expenses incurred both in a hospital and as an outpatient.

Flight insurance. This is life insurance sold in vending machines at airports. Like double indemnity, it is an unwise choice because it shouldn't matter if you die in a plane crash or by natural causes. Instead, life insurance should be purchased based on the needs of a spouse and/or children. In addition, some credit cards (e.g., "gold" bankcards) provide $100,000 of flight insurance coverage for free if you charge your plane ticket.

Collision-damage waivers (car rentals). This is coverage for the risk of damage to a rental car. It is expensive and can add as much as 50% to the cost of a car rental. Rental car use is probably covered under a personal auto policy, so check with your auto insurance agent. If not, a better alternative is to add a "rental car rider" to your policy.

Life insurance for people without dependents. If you are single and childless or have a working spouse that can get by without your income, there may be no economic reason to buy life insurance.

In addition to buying unnecessary coverage, the following four errors are often made:

- not following the "large-loss principle"—in other words, covering small losses (e.g., having a low deductible on auto collision) rather than large ones (e.g., having a high auto liability limit of at least $300,000 per occurrence).
- not becoming knowledgeable about employer-provided insurance benefits, especially if both spouses in a couple work and benefits need to

be coordinated. Ditto for public benefits for income-eligible families without health insurance.
- failing to carry disability insurance to cover the risk of loss of income due to accident or illness and umbrella liability insurance to cover large (e.g., $1 million and up) court judgements.
- not checking the credit rating of an insurance carrier, both at the time of policy purchase and periodically after that. You should select a company with at least an "A" rating.

One of the largest insurance company rating firms, A.M. Best, provides free reports to registered users through their Web site at www.ambest.com. Other insurance company rating firms, which may have reports in public libraries as well as information available by phone and online, are Duff & Phelps, Moody's, Standard & Poor's, and Weiss Research. Other sources of information about insurance company credit ratings are your insurance agent and company sales brochures. If an insurance company has a high rating, the rating will be featured prominently in marketing materials.

To summarize what you've learned so far about insurance, insurance companies aggregate risks and use laws of probability and large numbers to provide consumers with protection against financial losses caused by illness, death, accidents, natural disasters, and other destructive or damaging events. When you purchase insurance, you pool your risks and premium dollars with those of other people. You pay (or your employer pays for you) a premium to an insurance company that, in return, pays you (or someone else) for the damaging effects of a loss, should one occur.

Evaluating your insurance needs is an important part of financial planning. This includes determining how much coverage you need and what type of policy you should buy. When selecting insurance, you should:

- insure for major losses and cover small losses only if the premium is very inexpensive or paid by a third party.
- choose a company with a strong financial rating.

- select enough coverage to adequately insure your income (e.g., disability insurance) and assets (e.g., liability and property insurance).
- select the highest deductible you can afford.
- pay annually or semiannually rather than quarterly or monthly (to reduce premium costs).
- avoid duplicating coverage.
- ask about available discounts (e.g., price break for having all property coverage with one insurance company).
- follow "The Rule of Three" and compare prices from at least three competing insurers.
- take the time to read a policy and understand it, preferably *before* signing a contract.

The basic types of insurance that most people need are as follows:

- health/medical
- disability
- life
- property (for homeowners or renters)
- auto

In addition, for many people, the following types of policies should also be purchased, or at least explored:

- umbrella liability
- long-term care

No matter what the type of policy, you'll find the following sections in an insurance contract.

Declarations page. This is descriptive material about a particular person's insurance policy (e.g., name of the insured, beneficiary (if any), type and amount of coverage, policy deductibles and/or coinsurance, period (term) of coverage, premium amount and due date(s), policy number, name of insurance agent).

Insuring agreements. These are broad descriptions of coverage with definitions of important terms often in boldface.

Exclusions. This is a description of risks that are not covered by a policy. Common examples of policy exclusions are nuclear war, earthquakes, and floods (unless you have a special policy), a personal car used as a taxi, and business liability losses (e.g., a client comes to your home-based business and falls on the sidewalk) on a personal insurance policy.

Endorsements and riders. These are additional clauses to an insurance contract that add coverage in exchange for a higher premium. Common examples are theft coverage for property left in a vehicle, business use of a car, and a "scheduled property rider" to cover the total value of property such as jewelry and coins.

Insurance policies also contain the following features that specify coverage limits.

Benefit coordination clauses. This feature is designed to prevent people from collecting from two insurance policies for the same expense, especially in the case of two-worker families with employer-provided health coverage. Generally, a worker can claim from a spouse's policy only the amount not covered by his or her employer's policy. In other words, the total claim cannot exceed 100% of the cost.

Deductible. This is a dollar figure, usually a flat dollar amount (e.g., $200 or $500), that an insured person must pay out-of-pocket before an insurance policy reimburses him or her for the remainder of a loss. For example, with a $500 deductible and a $2,000 covered loss, the insured would pay $500 and the insurance company would pay the remaining $1,500.

Elimination period. With some types of policies (e.g., disability and long-term care), there is a certain number of days (e.g., 30, 60, or 90), starting from the date of an insurable event (e.g., injuries from an accident), before benefits are paid.

Copayment. Copayments are commonly used with prescription drug coverage and office visits to health maintenance organization (HMO) plan doctors. They are the amount (e.g., $5 per office visit or $10 per prescription) that an insured person must pay out-of-pocket. The remainder of the cost is covered by the medical plan.

Coinsurance. This is the amount (usually stated as a percentage) of a claim that an insured person is expected to pay out-of-pocket. For example, some health insurance policies pay 80% of approved charges and the insured is responsible for the balance. Generally, there is a limit (e.g., $2,000) on the amount you must copay per year. This limit is called a **stop-loss limit.**

Policy limit (a.k.a., lifetime maximum). This is the highest dollar amount that an insurance policy will pay. For example, an auto insurance policy with a $300,000 liability limit will not pay benefits greater than $300,000. Some health insurance policies pay benefits only up to $250,000 for an entire family. A much better policy limit is a maximum of $1,000,000, or no policy upper limit, for each family member.

Life Insurance

One of the costliest risks that families face is the death of a breadwinner (worker). This is especially true if a spouse and/or children depend upon that person for all or part of their support. Losing that income can be a tremendous financial blow. Another person who may also need life insurance protection is a full-time homemaker. Otherwise, his or her survivors may not have enough money to hire people to provide necessary services (e.g., child care).

To protect family members against financial disaster resulting from death, consider the purchase of life insurance. Life insurance makes sense if you have dependents who would suffer financially in the event of your death. No simple formula exists to determine the amount of life insurance you need. Instead, many factors must be considered, including:

- current assets and liabilities.
- earning power of surviving family members.
- other sources of income to the family.
- projected expenses and family support.

Carry too little insurance and you may not provide sufficient resources for your family after your death. Carry too much and you may not enjoy a reasonable level of living while you're alive. Many insurance companies have worksheets to calculate life insurance needs. They total up a family's economic needs and subtract available resources. You can also use the *Life Insurance Needs* worksheet (Exercise II-1) on page 52 to calculate your life insurance needs.

The worksheet assumes that you'll need 75% of your current income if a breadwinner is not alive. This is because living costs will be reduced. It also includes a calculation of lump sum cash needs such as mortgage liquidation (optional), debt repayment, and funeral expenses, as well as calculations for the income needs of children (e.g., college expenses) and the surviving spouse. After the total amount of money needed is calculated, existing income sources (e.g., government Social Security benefits), insurance, and assets are subtracted to determine the additional amount of insurance required.

Once you have calculated the amount of coverage that you need, choose an insurance product that is right for you. Two basic types of coverage exist, which, in one form or another, are the basis for virtually all forms of life insurance. The two basic types are term insurance and permanent (cash value) insurance.

Term life insurance is, as the name suggests, insurance that provides protection only for a specific period of time or term. It has no cash value or investment component. Term insurance is one of the best ways to solve an insurance need of short or limited duration (e.g., a worker with young children). It generally also has the lowest up-front premium cost.

Level term policies offer a level amount of protection for a given period of time (e.g., 10 years). Each time the policy is renewed, the premium increases to reflect the additional risk of loss as an insured person ages. The longer the time of the guaranteed premium (e.g., 15 years versus 5 years), the higher the initial premium will be.

Decreasing term policies were developed for people with an insurance need that declines over time. It is most commonly used with home mortgages. With decreasing term insurance, the level of protection declines over time, but the premium remains constant.

Term insurance quotes are available online through www.insure.com, www.accuquote.com, and www.iquote.com. Some of these Web sites also have online calculators to determine the amount of insurance you should have.

Permanent life insurance combines protection for the life of the insured person with a savings component known as the **cash value**. Annual premiums are fixed for the life of the policy and are based on assumptions about interest and mortality rates. They may be payable

Life Insurance Needs

Name(s)_____ Date: _____

Item	Example	Your Amount

1. Income Replacement

Enter 75% of your current income. $30,000 $_____

2. Years Income Will Be Needed

Years	10	15	20	25	30	40
Factor	8.98	12.84	16.35	19.52	22.39	31.42

Enter the factor number.   x 22.39   x $_____

3. Subtotal (#1 x #2)   = 671,700   = $_____

4. Funeral Expenses

Enter the amount for funeral expenses
and other final-expense needs.   + 10,000   + $_____

5. Debt

Enter the total amount of all debt owed.   + 140,000   + $_____

6. Other

Consider other needs such as college expenses,
a readjustment period for a spouse, or day care.   + 0   + $_____

7. Total Expenses

Add lines 3, 4, 5, and 6.   = 821,700   = $_____

8. Government Benefits

Take the monthly amount of Social Security survivor benefits
and other benefits and multiply by 12, and then multiply by
the number of years they will be received. Subtract that
amount from line 7 (e.g., $1,237 x 12 mos. x 14 yrs).   – 207,816   – $_____

9. Other

Subtract other items such as current assets or income from
other family members for the same time period as above
(e.g., 14 years).   – 300,000   – $_____

10. Total

This is an estimate of how much insurance is needed to
cover the needs of your survivors.   = $313,884   = $_____

for life or for a limited period and are generally higher than term insurance premiums.

Common forms of cash value life insurance include **whole life**, **variable life**, and **universal life**. The main difference among these different forms is in the method of cash value buildup. These policies are often sold more for their investment returns than for death protection. However, you'll generally get a higher return and more flexibility with noninsurance investments (e.g., stocks and mutual funds). Thus, many financial experts advise buying 20- or 30-year level premium term life insurance and "investing the difference" between premiums for term and cash value policies.

Over time, your need for life insurance will change. For example, if you leave a job to start a business, you will probably lose company life insurance benefits and need to purchase an individual policy. If you get married or have a baby, you may need to buy your first policy or increase existing coverage. Once your children are grown and/or you've accumulated invested assets over several decades, your need for life insurance coverage should decrease. Below are some general tips for purchasing life insurance.

- Avoid simplistic formulas (e.g., four or five times your income) for determining how much life insurance you need. Instead, use a worksheet or online financial calculator and do an analysis based on your family's personal needs.
- Never cancel an existing policy until you've been approved for a new one and have the new policy in hand. Otherwise, you run the risk of lapsed coverage and/or difficulty obtaining a new policy.
- Compare administrative costs and evaluate fees and agents' commissions before switching policies. The costs might outweigh the benefits.
- Review your beneficiary and contingent beneficiary designations periodically and adjust as needed.
- Buy credit life insurance (to repay debts if a borrower dies) only if you cannot obtain life insurance elsewhere.
- Ask your agent about the interest-adjusted net cost. This is the most widely accepted method of comparing cash value life insurance policies. Cost comparisons should be made only between similar types of policies, however (e.g., universal life).

Health Insurance

An unexpected health crisis can easily wipe out a family's savings. Staying in a hospital for only 2 or 3 days can cost thousands of dollars. Many people rely on an employer group policy (theirs or their spouse's) to pay at least part of their medical expenses. Because of rising health costs, however, many employers are shifting some of the cost to their employees by requiring higher deductibles, copayments, and payroll deductions for insurance premiums. In addition, increasing numbers of employers are adopting **managed care health insurance** plans, such as health maintenance organizations (HMOs) and preferred provider organizations (PPOs), which require using doctors and hospitals within the plan's network. If you choose to go "out of network," you'll be responsible for all or part of the cost.

There are two types of primary health insurance policies:

- indemnity or "traditional" plans, and
- managed care plans (e.g., HMOs and preferred provider organizations).

Indemnity plans usually start off with an annual deductible. This is the amount that an insured person must pay before their insurance company pays anything. Usually, the deductible is charged each year. With some plans, however, it is charged for each illness or injury. After the deductible comes coinsurance, through which the insured pays a percentage of bills, usually 20%, up to the stop-loss limit. The stop-loss limit is generally between $1,000 and $5,000.

Managed care plans come in many varieties. Thus, it is important to "read the fine print" about what is and is not covered. Managed care emphasizes wellness and preventive care, but controls the care that is given and limits the selection of medical providers.

If you are self-employed or have an employer that does not provide health benefits, shop around for coverage. Contact an insurance agent that represents many companies. You may also be eligible for group coverage through a trade or professional association, fraternal or civic organization, or state heath insurance program.

If you're under age 65, you should have a comprehensive health insurance policy that includes both basic protection (hospital, surgical, and medical benefits) and major medical coverage for large expenses. If you are over 65, you'll want to purchase a Medicare supplement (a.k.a., Medigap) policy for expenses not covered by Medicare. A good source of information about Medigap policies is the State Health Insurance Assistance Program (SHIP), affiliated with state and county aging/senior services offices, which provides free counseling and/or Medigap policy shopping guides (see www.shiptalk.org).

Below are some general tips for purchasing health insurance.

- Look for a policy that is **guaranteed renewable** or **noncancelable**. Both terms mean that a policy will continue for life or until a certain specified age, assuming no lapse in premium payments. Guaranteed renewable policy premiums will not increase unless they are raised for everyone with the same type of policy. Noncancelable policy premiums will not increase, period.

- Find out if your health care coverage, or your spouse's, can be continued after you retire (as a supplement to Medicare) and, if so, at what cost and with what conditions (e.g., you may need to work for an employer for a minimum of 20 or 25 years to receive retiree health benefits).

- Check to see that an indemnity-type policy has a stop-loss provision that limits the amount you must copay each year. For example, a stop-loss limit of $2,000 means that after you have paid $2,000, the insurance company will pay 100% of additional expenses, up to the policy limit.

- Note preexisting condition clauses. These clauses mean that medical conditions that you had when you bought an insurance policy will not be covered for a specified period of time.

- Be cautious about switching policies. A new policy may mean new waiting periods and exclusions.

- If you lose your job and, along with it, your health benefits, you may be able to extend group coverage through a federal law called **COBRA**. The law requires employers with 20 or more workers to offer continued coverage to departing workers for up to 18 months. Employees are responsible for paying the full cost of coverage, plus a 2% administrative fee.

- If you are between jobs and are not eligible for or cannot afford COBRA coverage, you may qualify for state health care benefits. You can also take advantage of free or low-cost public health programs such as immunizations, well-baby clinics, mammograms, and Pap tests.

Below are some tips for dealing with a family medical crisis.

Keep good records. Save every document related to your medical condition, including diagnostic reports, medical bills, "explanation of benefits" statements from health insurers, and receipts or canceled checks for out-of-pocket expenses. If you belong to an HMO, save a copy of each referral form and note the expiration date and number of authorized visits to avoid a denial of claims. If you're scheduled for surgery or diagnostic tests, always ask if the procedure has been precertified.

Don't pay medical bills automatically. Several recent published articles have reported that about 90% of hospital bills contain at least one error and that the majority of mistakes are made in the hospital's favor. Check all bills for medical services and ask for explanations about questionable items. Also beware of medical providers who agree to accept a contracted rate from a managed care plan and then bill patients for an additional amount. Some people pay bills for which they are actually not responsible. Review your health insurance and/or employee benefit documents. If certain expenses are supposed to be covered, call the medical provider and/or your insurance company and ask why you received a bill.

Consider family and medical leave. For employees of companies with 50 or more workers (within a 75-mile radius of each other) who lack employer-paid "sick days," family and medical leave can be used during a medical crisis to care for a family member or for oneself. Eligible employees can receive up to 12 weeks of unpaid leave per year and return to their previous (or a similar) job and maintain health coverage while they're away. This leave can be taken in small increments. For example, cancer patients can take a few days or a week off after each chemotherapy treatment. You do not need to use the 12 weeks all at once. Employees must generally provide their employers with 30 days' advance notice when their leave is "foreseeable."

Disability Insurance

Disability insurance, or rather, the lack of it, is the biggest gap in family insurance coverage. Many people have life insurance to protect their family if they were to die and health insurance to pay their medical bills. Relatively few people, however, have disability insurance, which helps to cover the loss of income due to an inability to work.

Disability insurance provides a source of income to people who are unable to work because of an accident or illness. The maximum amount of coverage is usually limited to about two-thirds (60–70%) of a worker's gross income to encourage him or her to return to work instead of living on disability payments. Disability insurance is especially critical for single people whose paycheck provides their only means of support. It is also important for self-employed persons and employees who are not able to accrue employer-paid sick leave.

Some employers provide disability insurance, but it is generally short-term (2 years or less) and may replace only a small portion of a worker's salary. Social Security also provides disability benefits to qualified individuals, but there are strict guidelines and at least a 6-month waiting period. Worker's compensation provides benefits, but only for job-related disabilities. Since all of these disability income resources have limited benefits and restrictions, an individual policy is recommended.

A key feature of disability insurance is the definition of disability. **Own-occupation ("Own-Occ") policies** define disability as the inability to work in the particular field or trade for which you were trained. For example, bus drivers and flight attendants and surgeons all need to use their hands and sight to work. If they have difficulty seeing or lose the use of an arm, they cannot perform their job duties. **Any-occupation ("Any-Occ")** policies define disability as the inability to engage in any type of employment. It is a much more

restrictive definition because you are not considered disabled unless there is no type of work that you can do. Social Security uses the Any-Occ definition of disability to qualify people for benefits. Naturally, Own-Occ policies are more expensive than Any-Occ because they allow people to collect benefits when they could do a different type of job. Policies are also available with a split definition of disability (i.e., a certain number of years of Own-Occ, followed by a switch to Any-Occ) to keep premiums more affordable.

Another key feature of disability policies is the elimination period (a.k.a., "waiting period"). This is the number of days after a disability begins before benefits are paid. The longer the elimination period (e.g., 90 days versus 30 days), the lower the premium will be for a given amount (e.g., $1,000 per month) of disability insurance. Disability policy costs and features vary, however. Like life and health insurance, it is advisable to follow "The Rule of Three" and compare at least three competing policies before making a purchase.

Two key factors to consider when selecting an elimination period are the adequacy of emergency savings to replace lost income and the availability and accrual of employer-paid sick leave. For example, if you have a secure job, with no plans to leave, and have worked for 6 years and accumulated 60 sick days, you could easily choose a 60-day elimination period. On the other hand, if you have no savings or sick leave, you may want a shorter waiting period if you can afford it.

Below are some general tips for purchasing disability insurance.

- Look for a policy that provides protection until age 65 and is noncancelable. A noncancelable provision, as the name implies, guarantees continuation of a disability insurance policy until a specified age (e.g., 60 or 65). Of course, this assumes that premiums are paid in a timely manner. A noncancelable provision is better than a "guaranteed renewable" feature because it prevents premiums from being raised. Guaranteed renewable policies, on the other hand, can increase premiums for designated groups of policyholders (e.g., blue-collar workers or professionals and executives). The trade-off, of course, is that noncancelable policies are more costly than guaranteed renewable policies.

- Require that an ex-spouse purchase disability insurance if you are dependent upon his income for child support and/or alimony. Request this in your divorce decree.

- Try to purchase coverage equal to 100% of your after-tax income to avoid a reduction in lifestyle.

- Look for a policy that pays residual benefits to make up for income lost when the insured is unable to work at full capacity. In other words, your benefit is prorated to make up for the actual amount of income that is lost.

- Consider the costs and benefits of a cost-of-living rider to protect the purchasing power of your monthly benefit. Sometimes, the additional cost results in only a small allowable increase in coverage.

- Women should look for a policy that charges the same premium for both sexes. Gender-based policies generally charge women more.

- If you don't qualify for disability insurance (e.g., if you recently had a heart attack or treatment for depression), invest the amount you would have paid monthly for premiums to build up your emergency reserves.

- Purchase a "waiver of premium" rider. This means that if an insured is disabled for 90 days, the insurance company waives further premium payments for as long as the person remains disabled.

- Look for a "recurrent disability" clause. This means that if a person recovers from a disability but becomes disabled again from the same cause within 6 months of returning to work, the company does not start the policy elimination period all over again.

Remember, your earning power is one of your greatest financial assets. Protect it with disability insurance. Not convinced? Then consider this: Mortgage lenders report that foreclosures due to disability occur 16 times as often as they do for death. Your chance of being disabled for 3 months or longer prior to age 65 is about three times your chance of dying.

Long-Term Care Insurance

With longer average life expectancies being reported for both men and women, the cost of long-term care is an increasing financial risk. The term "long-term care" refers to a wide range of services ranging from limited assistance at home with daily activities to admission to a nursing home for intensive medical care and support. The risk of long-term care can be dealt with in three ways: retain it (people with a sufficient net worth can self-insure), avoid it (staying healthy is the best method but, unfortunately, there are no guarantees), or transfer it (pay an insurance company to handle the risk).

Do you need **long-term care (LTC) insurance**? Below are some guidelines to consider.

- A good rule of thumb, according to *Kiplinger's Retirement Report,* is that no more than 8% to 10% of your annual income should be spent on long-term care premiums (e.g., $3,200 to $4,000 premium with a $40,000 income).

- Should read as follows: Many long-term care experts say that if you have more than $150,000 to $250,000 in assets per person in your household (excluding your residence) and an annual income of $35,000 to $50,000 or more per person, you are a good candidate to buy a policy. You should also be able to afford the premium without a lifestyle change, as well as a potential 20–30% future increase. If your net worth is over $1 million to $3 million, you can often self-insure.

- Couples often need long-term care insurance more than singles because, if one spouse ends up in a nursing home, it can greatly reduce the amount of assets left for the well spouse.

- The best time to purchase a policy is generally around age 60. If you wait too long, premiums increase significantly and/or you could become uninsurable through a medical diagnosis or pre-existing condition. If you buy in your 40s or 50s, however, you could pay premiums for a long time before coverage is actually needed.

Below are some additional tips for purchasing long-term care insurance.

- Understand how you qualify for benefits. Coverage generally begins when a person is unable to perform a certain number of "activities of daily living" (e.g., bathing, dressing, toileting, continence, moving to and from a bed or chair, and eating).

- Insist on inflation protection to increase the amount of benefits over time. A "compound" inflation rider results in a larger benefit increase than a "simple" inflation rider, but it also costs more. The difference is that a simple inflation rider is calculated on the original benefit amount, while the compound inflation rider is based on the inflation-adjusted amount paid the previous year.

- Choose an appropriate elimination period (the amount of time between when care begins and when benefits are paid) based on the number of days of care you can afford to pay for out-of-pocket. Elimination periods can range from zero to 90 to 365 days for people who can afford to pay for a full year of care themselves in exchange for a lower premium.

- Two additional key decisions are the length of time you'll receive benefits (the range is 1 year to an insured's lifetime) and the benefit amount (often a specific number of dollars per day). The longer the benefit period and the higher the policy benefit, the higher the cost.

- Contact your county SHIP office for information and counseling about available LTC policies.

Auto Insurance

One of the largest items in many household budgets is auto insurance. The premium you pay for auto insurance depends upon a number of personal factors, including your state of residence, your driving record, where you live (e.g., city versus rural area), your marital status, and your credit history. That's right, some insurers are now checking credit reports as a factor to determine insurance premiums. In addition, driving an expensive, high-performance car, putting a lot of miles on your car, and having a young driver at home will run up your insurance bill.

Automobile insurance has two parts:

Liability coverage. This covers liability for bodily injuries, property damage, and medical expenses to others when you are at fault and coverage to pay for injuries caused by an unidentified "hit and run" driver or a motorist who is uninsured or underinsured (i.e., someone with liability limits less than the cost of damages).

Physical damage coverage (collision and comprehensive). This covers damage done to your vehicle from a collision (e.g., with another car or a telephone pole) or by fire, theft, flood, falling objects, or hitting an animal.

Liability coverage can be stated as either a single-limit or a split-limit. A single limit (e.g., $300,000) means that an insurance company will pay up to that amount for damages and injuries from a single accident. More commonly, though, liability limits are expressed as split limits (e.g., 100/300/50). This means that in a single accident the insurance company will pay up to $100,000 for each person injured, $300,000 for the total accident, and $50,000 for property damage. In light of today's high medical costs and the tendency of accident victims to sue, liability limits of 100/300/50 or higher are recommended. You can also increase your liability coverage further with an umbrella liability policy.

Umbrella liability insurance. Excess liability insurance that supplements the liability limits of a homeowner's or renter's policy and an automobile insurance policy (see Lesson 9, Umbrella Liability Insurance, for more information).

Liability coverage is the most important part of an auto insurance policy. It is important to remember that there is no upper limit on a potential liability judgment. It can be whatever the results of a lawsuit are if you are in an auto accident and a court decides that you are at fault. Awards in the millions of dollars are not unheard of. On the other hand, the cost of fixing physical damage to a car is limited to its replacement value. If you total a car valued at $8,000, for example, that is the maximum amount that you can lose. Although this loss is high, it isn't anywhere near the cost of court-ordered damages.

The minimum required amount of liability coverage is set by individual states and is generally much lower than 100/300/50. If someone had only $5,000 of minimum property coverage, for example, and was held responsible for totaling a $40,000 luxury car, their coverage would not even begin to cover the damages. Ditto for liability for an injured person's medical bills (e.g., $60,000 of expenses − $30,000 of coverage = $30,000 for which an underinsured motorist is responsible).

Below are some general tips for purchasing automobile insurance.

Increase liability coverage to at least 100/300/50. Limits of $200,000 per person and $500,000 per accident are even better (unless you carry an umbrella liability policy). In addition, raise your "uninsured motorist" coverage (which covers you if a driver with no liability insurance or inadequate liability insurance hits you) to 100/300/50 or higher. The extra cost is usually minimal.

Raise the deductibles on your policy (e.g., collision) to the highest level that you can afford to pay in case of an accident. Make sure that you have this amount (e.g., $1,000) saved in your emergency fund.

If you drive an older (7+ years) car, evaluate the cost and payoff for collision and comprehensive coverage on that vehicle. Check the Kelly Blue Book web site (www. kbb.com) to find out what your car is worth. If it got totaled, that is approximately how much you would get from your insurance company, after the deductible. Canceling collision and comprehensive coverage for older cars is a way to keep premiums down.

Buy a make and model of car that is less costly to insure and equip it with money-saving features such as air bags and alarms. High-performance sports cars are naturals for high-priced coverage. Standard sedans are usually the cheapest to insure.

Take advantage of available discounts. For example, combine two or more cars on one policy or purchase homeowners and auto insurance from the same insurance company. Discounts may also be available for short-distance drivers, part-time drivers (e.g.,

students away at school), drivers with a clean driving record (i.e., no "at fault" accidents), cars with antitheft devices, female drivers age 30–60, and students with a B average or better.

Keep your driving record clean and consider taking a defensive driving course. Make sure that teen divers in your family take driver's education training and maintain a good academic record.

Avoid duplication of insurance. An example is coverage for auto-related medical expenses if you already have a good comprehensive health insurance policy. However, if you drive a lot of nonfamily members around (e.g., carpooling), you may want to keep medical payments coverage. Otherwise, an injured passenger who does not have health insurance must sue you for negligence to get coverage under your liability.

Shop around. Get information about rates, coverage, and claims service from a number of companies or agents. A few phone calls could save $50–$100 per year (or more).

Notify your insurance company if you or an insured household member substantially increase or decrease your driving; move to a different city or state; buy or sell a car; or marry.

Homeowner's Insurance

For many people, their home is the single largest purchase they will ever make. Household furnishings and personal possessions represent another sizable investment. A lawsuit for a dwelling-related injury could seriously jeopardize the average homeowner's financial future. The risk of damage to a home and/or personal possessions and the possibility of home-related liability are covered in a single package called a homeowner's policy, which protects against the following specific risks:

- damages to a house or other structures (e.g., a freestanding shed or garage)
- loss of personal property
- living expenses while your home is being repaired
- personal liability
- medical payments to others injured on your property.

Specific types of homeowner's insurance policies are often referred to with an "HO" number. HO-1, HO-2, and HO-3 policies are specifically for homeowners. HO-4 policies are for renters and provide personal property and liability coverage. HO-6 policies are for condominium owners and insure the interior of a condo owner's unit, personal possessions, and liability to others. A special type of homeowners coverage, called HO-8, covers owners of older homes.

Take the time to photograph or videotape the contents of your home or apartment. For major items (e.g., electronic equipment), make a list of the brands and serial numbers as well. Store this documentation away from home, preferably in a safe deposit box at a bank. You could also use a digital camera to produce pictures for proof of ownership. Store the computer files and/or printed photos with a written inventory of major possessions. Documenting personal property shouldn't take a lot of time and is good "insurance" in the event of fire, flood, or theft.

Another wise move is to check the adequacy of your homeowner's insurance policy. The most important figure is the amount of insurance carried on a dwelling because other property loss limits are usually stated as percentages of it. Most insurers require that a home be insured for at least 80% of its full replacement cost to be considered fully insured. Replacement cost is the amount that you would have to spend today to rebuild a home, excluding the value of its land and foundation.

The 80% rule applies to losses on a home (dwelling) only, not to personal property. There are restrictions, however. Like all insurance, losses will be covered only up to the limits of the policy. Here is a specific example. A homeowner with a house having a replacement cost of $200,000 should carry at least $160,000 (80%) of coverage. If a fire caused $50,000 of damage (floods and mudslides are generally excluded), the insured would be paid the full $50,000 with no deduction for depreciation. However, if the house were totally destroyed, the insured would be able to collect up to $160,000, which is the face value of the policy. Covering the risk of loss of the full replacement value would require buying $200,000 of dwelling coverage.

If you have less than 80% replacement coverage and a partial loss, you will receive only partial payment to repair the damage. Insurance companies use a formula to determine prorated benefits for homes that are not fully insured. If your home is insured for less than 80% of its replacement value, you'll receive the greater of the actual cash value of the portion of the house that was destroyed (actual cash value = replacement cost minus depreciation) or a prorated amount as a result of the following formula:

$$\frac{\text{amount of insurance purchased}}{80\% \text{ of replacement cost}} \times \text{amount of loss}$$

To use the same example as before, if a homeowner had $150,000 of coverage on a $200,000 home (75%), instead of $160,000 (80%), their coverage for a $50,000 loss would be prorated to $46,875 (150,000 ÷ 160,000 or 0.9375 x $50,000 = $46,875).

It is a big mistake not to insure your home for at least 80% of replacement cost. Having 80% coverage means that repairs are fully funded up to the policy limit. Ideally, dwelling coverage should increase periodically for inflation when your policy is renewed. If not, check with your property and casualty insurance agent to make sure that the amount of coverage is still adequate.

As a general rule, the contents of a home are insured for no more than half of the coverage on the home. A much better choice is to add a **guaranteed replacement cost** endorsement to your policy to cover both the home (if available; many insurers no longer offer this option) and its contents.

For personal property, buy coverage that will replace items at current prices, up to a specified limit, rather than at their actual cash value (after depreciation). Often, the extra premium for replacement-cost coverage is very moderate (e.g., 10–15% more than the amount charged for actual cash-value coverage). Renters should purchase replacement cost coverage also. If you own expensive items, such as jewelry or silver coins, floater policies to insure their full value are also advisable.

Below are some additional tips for purchasing homeowner's insurance.

Pay your premium annually to reduce the cost. Generally speaking, the less bookkeeping for an insurance company, the lower the premium.

Installing safety devices, such as a burglar alarm and smoke detectors, might also reduce your insurance premium. Check with your agent to see what devices qualify for discounts.

Don't overinsure for small losses by selecting a low (e.g., $250) deductible. In addition to raising your premium, several low deductible claims within a few years could result in cancellation of your policy.

Consider purchasing flood insurance, even if you're in a low-risk area. According to the Federal Emergency Management Agency, the average premium is approximately $500 per year for $100,000 worth of coverage, depending on where you live and what coverage you choose. Federally backed flood insurance is the only kind of policy that is available. Check to see if your insurance company sells it. For additional information about flood insurance, visit www.floodsmart.gov.

If your home is damaged, let your insurance company know that you've suffered damages, make a list of all damaged or destroyed personal property, take photographs of damages, and make temporary repairs (if necessary) to prevent further damage.

Umbrella Liability Insurance

What if one of the neighborhood children fell while climbing a tree in your yard and suffered a severe, permanent injury? Or your dog bit a neighborhood child? Or you accidentally hit a swimmer with your motorboat? Or a houseguest fell and broke a hip near your pool? Or your neighbor took offense at a joke and sued you? Harsh examples, yes, but so are the realities of today's legal environment. Too often, people are involved in lawsuits for events beyond their control. People injured on your property or by your actions may be able to prove that you were negligent and collect damages.

Dollar amounts and the frequency of settlements for all sorts of liability cases have skyrocketed in recent years. Thus, one of the biggest financial risks that people face is the risk of being brought before a jury and sued for hundreds of thousands, even millions, of dollars. Fortunately, there is insurance to protect against this risk and it is relatively inexpensive.

Umbrella liability (a.k.a., "excess liability") insurance supplements the liability limits (e.g., $300,000) of a homeowner's or renter's policy and an automobile insurance policy. In addition, it covers situations excluded by other insurance, such as lawsuits for libel and slander, defamation of character, false arrest or false imprisonment, liability due to boat or aircraft accidents, and damages you cause while on someone else's property. Activities related to an insured's business or business property are not covered, however. Umbrella liability policies provide at least $1 million in additional liability protection over and above what policyowners already have with their existing home and auto policies.

Here's an example of how umbrella liability insurance works. Assume an accident takes place on your property and you are successfully sued for $650,000. You carry $300,000 of underlying liability on your homeowner's insurance, along with a $1 million umbrella policy. The first $300,000 of the settlement would be paid under the homeowner's policy and the umbrella policy would pick up the $350,000 difference. If you were held liable for $1,300,000, you would be covered for the full amount—a combination of $300,000 from the homeowner's coverage and the $1 million umbrella liability limit.

Relatively few people file large liability claims so the cost of umbrella coverage is reasonable. An estimated 80% of suits against individuals are settled for less than $300,000. Policies generally cost between $250 and $300 annually for the first $1 million of coverage and just under $500 for $2 million of coverage. Large amounts of coverage can also be purchased for increasingly higher premiums.

Below are some tips for purchasing umbrella liability insurance.

- Be sure to purchase the underlying amounts (e.g., $300,000) of auto and homeowner's insurance required by the policy issuer. Otherwise, there will be a gap in coverage because umbrella liability policies pay only damages that exceed this amount. Some insurers will also require that you purchase both your homeowners and auto policy from them before they will issue an umbrella policy.

- If you are active in the community, check to see if protection from liability for service on nonprofit boards is covered.

- Check at least three competing umbrella policies and compare coverage and exclusions (e.g., damages by pets, overseas coverage, definition of covered family members).

Insurance Checklist

Check "yes" or "no" for each question. Items for which "no" is checked indicate actions that should be taken in the future to improve your household insurance coverage.

	Yes	No
Can you locate your insurance policies, such as life, health, homeowner's or renter's, automotive, and disability?	☐	☐
Do you know the type and amount of life insurance protection you have?	☐	☐
Is your life insurance coverage adequate to protect dependents and assets?	☐	☐
Do you know the names of the beneficiaries and contingent beneficiaries of your life insurance policies?	☐	☐
Do you know the type of health insurance protection you have and the provisions of the policy?	☐	☐
Do you have major medical insurance with high lifetime limits?	☐	☐
Do you have adequate disability insurance?	☐	☐
Is your automobile liability insurance sufficient?	☐	☐
Is your automobile adequately insured for collision, yet not overinsured?	☐	☐
Are your home and personal property insured for today's replacement values?	☐	☐
Do you know the limits in your homeowner's policy on loss of silver, furs, collectibles, computers, and stereo equipment?	☐	☐
Have you appraised and insured valuables such as jewelry, silver, and collectibles?	☐	☐
Have you made a personal property inventory?	☐	☐
If you are not a homeowner, do you have renter's insurance that will cover your personal belongings?	☐	☐

Adapted from: Cude, Brenda. 1989. "Insurance Decisions." University of Illinois Cooperative Extension. © Board of Trustees of the University of Illinois.

Insurance Evaluation and Goals

Today's date _____/_____/_____   Review in 6 months on _____/_____/_____

To help you evaluate insurance coverage and plan for future needs, complete the forms on the following pages using your current policies as the source of the information. You may wish to confirm your findings with your agent(s).

Homeowner's Insurance

Name of insurance agency_____ Telephone _____

Address _____

Agent_____ Name of company insuring your property_____

Date of policy_____ Annual premium $_____ Policy number_____

Type of policy: ☐ HO-1   ☐ HO-2   ☐ HO-3   ☐ Home business

☐ HO-4 (renters)   ☐ HO-6 (condominium) ☐ HO-8 (older home)

Estimated replacement value of your home: $_____

Estimated value of home's contents: $_____

Building is insured for: $_____

Contents are insured for: $_____

Is your home insured for at least 80% of its replacement cost: ☐ yes   ☐ no

What is the deductible amount you must pay? $_____

Medical coverage per person is: $_____

Check the type of insurance, amount of coverage, and special riders or floaters.

Yes	Amount	Cost/year ($/yr)
☐ full replacement value	$_____	$_____
☐ actual cash value	$_____	$_____
☐ flood damage	$_____	$_____
☐ earthquake damage	$_____	$_____
☐ loss of use limits	$_____	$_____
☐ credit card protection	$_____	$_____
☐ sewer backup	$_____	$_____
☐ other riders	$_____	$_____

Insurance Evaluation and Goals

(continued)

What are your insured dollar limits, by category, on the following:

- money, gold, silver, coins, bank notes, medals $_____
- securities, deeds, manuscripts, stamps, valuable financial papers $_____
- watercraft and their trailers, furnishings, equipment, and outboard motors $_____
- trailers not used with watercraft $_____
- jewelry, precious and semiprecious stones, watches, and furs $_____
- silverware, silver plate, gold-ware, gold-plated ware, pewter-ware $_____
- guns and firearms $_____
- computers, special stereo equipment $_____

Disability Insurance

I have disability insurance ☐ through my employer ☐ purchased by me.

Name of company that insures me _____

Yearly premium $_____ Agent_____ Telephone _____

Amount I would receive per month if unable to work $_____

Length of time I must wait before receiving benefits _____

Can the policy be renewed? ☐ yes ☐ no   Can it be canceled? ☐ yes ☐ no

How is disability defined and what does it include? _____

_____

_____

How long can I receive benefits? _____

Health Insurance

My health insurance is provided ☐ through my employer ☐ by me ☐ by spouse

Monthly or yearly premium is $_____

The amount of copayment for each is $_____ for office visits, $_____ for prescription drugs,

and/or a $_____ annual deductible.

The policy ☐ can ☐ cannot be canceled.   It contains ☐ vision ☐ dental coverage.

The policy contains a stop-loss limit of $_____ and a lifetime limit of $_____.

Insurance Evaluation and Goals

(continued)

Automobile Insurance

Name of insurance agency_____ Telephone_____

Address _____ Agent_____

Name of company insuring your vehicles_____

Policy number_____

What are your liability limits? (written, e.g., 100/300/50) _____

Each person in the accident $_____

Total bodily injury per accident $_____

Total property damage per accident $_____

What is your uninsured motorist coverage? $_____

Each person per accident $_____ Total bodily injury per accident $_____

What is your comprehensive coverage limit? $_____ Your deductible $_____

What is your collision limit? $_____ What is your deductible? $_____

Does your policy cover a rental car ☐ when on vacation? ☐ due to an accident?

Life Insurance

I have the following term life insurance ☐ from my employer ☐ purchased on my own.

☐ Individual term $_____ (amount) from _____ (company)

☐ Group term $_____ (amount) from _____ (company)

☐ Other $_____ (amount) from _____ (company)

I have the following cash value life insurance (whole life, variable life, etc.):

Agency purchased from_____ Company insuring me_____

Type of insurance_____ Policy number_____

Amount $_____

The current cash value of all my life insurance as of today _____/_____/_____ is $_____

The total amount of life insurance listing me as a beneficiary from my spouse or partner is $_____

Insurance Evaluation and Goals

(continued)

To Do List

To be fully aware of the insurance coverage that I have and to ensure adequate coverage at the most reasonable cost, I should (check all that apply):

☐   prepare an inventory and take photographs or make a video of personal property.

☐   add smoke alarm(s), radon detector(s), and fire extinguisher(s) to my home.

☐   increase/decrease amount of dwelling cost coverage to at least 80% of replacement value.

☐   increase/decrease the deductible on homeowner's policy.

☐   increase/decrease coverage of personal property on homeowner's policy.

☐   add a rider to my homeowner's policy to cover special items.

☐   insure my home/apartment and automobile(s) with the same company.

☐   increase the deductible on my automobile policy for comprehensive and collision.

☐   increase/decrease medical coverage on automobile policy.

☐   increase/decrease liability coverage on automobile policy.

☐   increase/decrease collision coverage on automobile(s).

☐   increase/decrease comprehensive coverage for automobile(s).

☐   increase/decrease uninsured/underinsured motorist coverage.

☐   investigate term life insurance.

☐   increase/decrease amount of life insurance on my life and that of my spouse/companion.

☐   review life insurance beneficiary designations to ensure they reflect my current situation.

☐   investigate cost and coverage for disability insurance.

☐   investigate the following changes in health insurance coverage (list).

_____

_____

☐   investigate cost and advantages of an umbrella policy.

☐   other (list).

_____

_____

Exercise II-3 adapted with permission from: Dahl, B. (1996). *A Working Woman's Guide to Financial Security*. Urbana, Ill.: University of Illinois Cooperative Extension. ©Board of Trustees of the University of Illinois.

Your Minimum "Need To Knows" about Insurance

- A periodic review of insurance coverage is necessary to determine if present coverage is adequate. Use the questions on the *Insurance Checklist* (Exercise II-2) on page 64 to assess your present coverage and the *Insurance Evaluation and Goals* worksheet (Exercise II-3) on pages 65–68 to record key details about your current policies. Review the "to do list" for improved insurance coverage at the end of Exercise II-3.

- There are five ways to manage life's financial risks: do nothing and hope for the best, risk avoidance, risk reduction, risk acceptance, and risk transfer (insurance).

- The size (amount) of a potential loss—rather than its frequency—should be the determining factor in purchasing insurance. This is called the "large-loss principle."

- Major large-loss risks are disability, liability, large medical bills, loss of a household earner's income, and destruction of one's home.

- Some insurance is unnecessary for most people, including credit insurance, life insurance for children and people without dependents, cancer insurance, flight insurance, hospital indemnity policies, and "double indemnity" clauses in life insurance for accidental deaths.

- Consumers should check the financial stability of an insurance company before purchasing a policy.

- All insurance policies have features that limit coverage, including benefit coordination clauses, deductibles, copayments, coinsurance, elimination periods, and policy limits.

- Life insurance makes sense if you have dependents that would suffer financially in the event of your death. This includes both family earners and full-time homemakers.

- Term life insurance provides protection only for a specific period; cash value life insurance contains a savings component.

- Disability insurance provides a source of income to people who are unable to work because of an accident or illness.

- The longer the elimination (waiting) period on an insurance policy, the lower the premium for a specific amount of coverage will be.

- Liability coverage is the most important part of an auto insurance policy and should be at least 100/300/50.

- A home should be insured for at least 80% of its replacement cost, and a "guaranteed replacement cost" rider should be purchased for both a home (if available) and its contents.

- Umbrella liability insurance provides coverage above underlying auto and home liability limits.

Action Steps

SESSION II: **Insurance Basics**

☐ Review existing insurance policies and identify weaknesses, such as low liability limits.

☐ Identify "big ticket" insurance gaps (e.g., lack of disability and LTC coverage).

☐ Use the *Life Insurance Needs* worksheet (page 52) or ask an agent to determine policy needs.

☐ Read the coverage limits and exclusions of your health insurance policy.

☐ Determine if you receive any disability insurance (DI) through your employer.

☐ Contact an insurance agent for three price quotes for an individual DI policy.

☐ If you have an individual DI policy, read the coverage limits and exclusions.

☐ Read the coverage limits of your auto and homeowner's policy.

☐ Ask your property/casualty agent for ideas to reduce premiums and improve coverage.

☐ Get a price quote for umbrella liability coverage from your auto or homeowner's agent.

☐ Get three price quotes for long-term care coverage and consider buying a policy if you are about age 60.

References

A Money Management Workbook (1999). Washington, D.C.: American Association of Retired Persons (Women's Financial Information Program).

Basler, P. (2006, December). Pursuing Peace of Mind. *AARP Bulletin,* 47(11), 10–11.

Clements, J. (2007, October 17). Protecting Your Assets in Case You Find Yourself in Court. *The Wall Street Journal,* D1.

Dahl, B. (1996). *A Working Woman's Guide to Financial Security.* Urbana, Ill.: University of Illinois Cooperative Extension.

Flood Insurance: Why You Might Need It (2008, June). *Consumer Reports,* 47.

Garman, E.T., and Forgue, R.E. (2008). *Personal Finance.* Boston, Mass.: Houghton Mifflin Company.

Greene, K. (2007, April 24). Buying Old-Age Insurance. *The Wall Street Journal,* D2.

High School Financial Planning Program (2007). Denver, Colo.: National Endowment for Financial Education.

Johnson, A. (2000). *The Financial Check-Up.* Providence, Utah: Watkins Printing.

Keating, P. (2008, May). Take (Long-Term) Care. *Smart Money,* 48–49.

Keown, A.J. (2001). *Personal Finance: Turning Money into Wealth.* Upper Saddle River, N.J.: Prentice-Hall.

When It Rains, It Pours: How to Protect Your Assets. (2005, June). *AAII Journal,* 27(5), 3.

Investing Basics

Mary had a little cash
In fives and tens and such
And every dollar Mary saved
Made her retirement fund more flush.

What will be covered in Session III

Investment Lessons

1. Setting Goals and Finding Solutions
2. Understanding and Accepting Risk
3. Investment Choices—Stocks, Bonds, and Mutual Funds
4. What Are Stocks and Why Should You Own Them?
5. What Are Bonds and Why Should You Own Them?
6. What Are Mutual Funds and Why Should You Own Them?

Terms to Learn (bolded in the text)

Bond	Maturity
Diversification	Mutual fund
Dividend reinvestment plan	No-load
Expense ratio	Stock
Load	Taxable distribution

Exercises

1. $mart Financial Goal Setting
2. What Kind of Investor Are You?
3. Finding Your Comfort Zone
4. Comparing Stock Investments
5. Comparing Fixed-Income Investments
6. Mutual Funds with a Growth Objective
7. Mutual Funds with an Income Objective
8. Mutual Funds with Both Growth and Income Objectives
9. Mutual Funds with a Preservation of Capital Objective
10. Mutual Funds with All Four Objectives
11. Comparing Mutual Fund Investments
12. Your Personal Investment Statement

Setting Goals and Finding Solutions

Mary is a 57-year-old human resource manager who plans to retire in 5 years, yet she has no idea (1) how much money she will need to supplement her employer benefits and maintain her current standard of living and (2) how long her savings must last.

In Session I, financial goal setting was introduced. The topic is further expanded below as it relates to investment decisions.

"Not setting measurable goals" is the biggest error Americans make with their money, according to a survey by the Certified Financial Planner Board of Standards. Even among people who have sought out professional financial help, less than one-third actually know what they'd like their money to accomplish.

Why should goal setting be important to you? The answer: research shows that it works. Setting milestones for your money is similar to setting goals for your career (promotion to manager in 2 years), your health (lose 10 pounds in 3 months and exercise 1 hour, three times a week). If you don't set goals, you'll have no way to measure your success.

To establish financial goals, learn how to create $MART goals using the following criteria:

$ Goals must be **specific** and indicate dollar amounts, dates, and resources to be used in reaching the goals.

M Goals must be **measurable**. Determine regular amounts to set aside weekly, biweekly, or monthly. Another good "M" word to consider is mutual. Goals that are mutual, or shared with other family members, will be easier to achieve. It also is important to think about how you will keep yourself and other family members motivated to achieve goals, especially long-term goals.

A Your goals must be **attainable** given your financial situation.

R It is important that your goals be **realistic**. What resources are available for you to use in achieving

your goals? Review and revise your goals periodically as necessary.

T You must indicate a specific **time** period for accomplishing your goals. You must also be willing to make trade offs in your financial life. Know the difference between "needs" and "wants." Prioritize your goals because there is never enough money to fund all of your financial goals at one time.

Take the time to put your goals in writing. Use the worksheet *$MART Financial Goal Setting,* (Exercise III-1, page 73) to help you list short- and long-term financial goals. Then, to stay motivated, visualize how you will feel when you accomplish your goals. Last, regularly set aside a predetermined sum of money for each specific financial goal.

Depending upon your goals and time frame, you can select investments that provide income, growth, or tax savings, or preserve your capital (the amount initially invested).

- If you don't require additional income to meet your everyday expenses or you are looking to fund your retirement 30 years from now, long-term growth would be your primary objective. You would choose investments that can offer growth over a long period. Because of the longer time frame, you could afford some risk.
- You may be planning to replace your car in 3 years, so your objective would be preservation of capital. You need to know the money will be there when you need it.
- You may be looking for tax savings to help you shelter as much money as possible.
- If you are nearing retirement, you might begin converting some growth or tax-sheltered investments into those that produce income.

You may find that a combination of objectives, such as growth and income, is best for you because no single investment will provide all four benefits.

$MART Financial Goal Setting

$ = Specific; **M** = Measurable; **A** = Attainable; **R** = Realistic; and **T** =Time period.

Directions: $MART goals need to be written down on paper to reinforce their importance. Use the worksheet below to set some short- and long-term financial goals that follow the $MART goal format. To keep the calculations simple, a 0% interest rate and inflation rate are assumed and taxes are excluded. A sample goal for each category is provided.

To get where you want to go in life, decide in advance how you will get there. Goals are signposts on the highway of the future. They serve as your road map to personal, career, and financial success.

By keeping specific goals in view, you can direct your energies toward achieving your goals.

Short-term goals (less than 3 years)

Goal	Total cost	Target date	Amount to save/month
House down payment	$15,000	3 years	$417.00*

* $15,000 ÷ 36 months = $417.00/month

Intermediate-term goals (3–10 years)

Goal	Total cost	Target date	Amount to save/month
New car	$20,000	5 years	$333.33

Long-term goals (longer than 10 years)

Goal	Total cost	Target date	Amount to save/month
College tuition	$75,000	15 years	$417.00*

Understanding and Accepting Risk

Investments come with varying degrees of risk, as shown on the Risk Ladder on page 75. Table III-1 shows combinations of stocks, bonds, and cash in the best and worst years from 1926 to 2007. Note the greater average annual return—and greater chance of loss—as the percentage of stock increases.

Any investment involves some risk. But if you have taught yourself to recognize and evaluate the risks you may incur, you will be better able to balance your investment objectives and tolerance for risk.

The Major Investment Risks

Market risk. This refers to the risk that prices of individual investments will be affected by the volatility of financial markets in general. This means a stock's price may fall simply because the overall stock market has dropped.

> Higher risks (more stock) generally equate with higher long-term average returns; a long time horizon helps to lower risk.

Business risk. This is the risk caused by events that affect only a specific company or industry, thereby influencing the value of an investment. Some examples are a class action lawsuit against a company, the death or firing of a company's chief executive officer, or the failure to get expected U.S. Food and Drug Administration approval for a company's new drug.

Interest rate risk. An inverse relationship usually exists between bond and stock prices and interest rates. When interest rates rise, stock prices usually fall. Bond values will also fall. Some investments, such as

TABLE III-1

Asset Mixes and Their Past Performance: 1926–2007

Portfolio Allocation Stock%/Bond %	Average Annual Return (%)	Worst One-Year Loss (%)	Number of Years Out of 82 With Losses
100% bonds	5.5%	-8.1% (1969)	13 of 82
20% stocks and 80% bonds	6.8%	-10.3% (1974)	11 of 82
30% stocks and 70% bonds	7.4%	-14.2 % (1931)	13 of 82
40% stocks and 60% bonds	7.9%	-18.4% (1931)	15 of 82
50% stocks and 50% bonds	8.4%	-22.5% (1931)	16 of 82
60% stocks and 40% bonds	8.9%	-26.6% (1931)	20 of 82
70% stocks and 30% bonds	9.3%	-30.7% (1931)	21 of 82
80% stock and 20% bonds	9.7%	-34.9% (1931)	22 of 82
100% stock	10.4%	-43.1% (1931)	24 of 82

* Stock returns are based on the Standard and Poor's 500 Index (S&P 500), which is a benchmark of the performance of the 500 largest U.S. companies. Bond returns are based on high-quality corporate bond indexes. Cash returns are based on the Citigroup 3-month Treasury Bill Index.

Source: The Vanguard Group https://personal.vanguard.com/us/planningeducation/general/PEdGPCreateTheRightMixContent.jsp

Risk Ladder

Which Investments Match Your Risk Tolerance?

RUNG 4: HIGH RISK
Small-cap, sector, international, emerging market, and precious metal mutual funds; Penny stocks; Commodities

RUNG 3: MODERATE TO HIGH RISK
Stocks (income, blue chip, growth, value); Stock mutual funds; Index funds; High-yield bond funds; Variable annuities

RUNG 2: LOW TO MODERATE RISK
Municipal and corporate bonds; Bond mutual funds; Ginny Maes; Zero-coupon bonds

RUNG 1: LOW RISK
T-bills, T-notes, and T-bonds; Money market funds; CDs; FDIC-insured money market and savings accounts; EE and I bonds; Fixed-rate annuities

certificates of deposit (CDs) and bonds, have a fixed rate of return. This can be to your benefit if interest rates fall, but to your disadvantage if rates rise.

Inflation risk. Inflation risk refers to a loss of buying power, which can occur if the rate of inflation is higher than the rate of return on an investment. The rate of inflation averaged 3.1% over an 82-year period (1926–2007). Had you invested in long-term government bonds averaging 5.5% during that time,

> There's no such thing as a perfect, risk-free investment.

your after-inflation return would have been only 2.4% (5.5–3.1%).

Reinvestment risk. This is the risk of having to re-invest existing funds at a lower return than previously earned, resulting in a decline in income. Example: A high-interest CD matures and you can only renew it at a lower rate because interest rates have dropped.

Complete Exercise III-2, *What Kind of Investor Are You?* (page 76), and Exercise III-3, *Finding Your Comfort Zone* (page 77), to evaluate your tolerance for risk in your investments.

Loanership vs. Ownership

You can invest money in two basic ways. You can loan it to pay for a company's or the government's debt, OR you can own the investment yourself. When you loan your money to a company or the government, you receive income based upon a set interest rate for a set period of time. The entity promises to pay back your original principal plus interest. Loanership, or debt investments, include savings accounts and bonds; money market accounts and funds; Treasury bills, bonds, and notes; and certificates of deposit.

On the other hand...

When you own an investment or equity, you purchase part or all of it. The value of ownership assets will fluctuate with market conditions, potentially giving you a higher return than you might receive from loaning money. Ownership investments include stocks, stock-owning mutual funds, real estate, commodities, collectibles, and precious metals (gold coins).

EXERCISE III-2
What Kind of Investor Are You?

By understanding and coming to grips with your risk tolerance, you can eliminate or limit any type of investment that doesn't fit your criteria. Check those statements that apply.

You are a conservative investor if:

- ☐ You want your money safe at all times, and you don't want to lose any of it.

- ☐ Any decline in the value of your investment concerns you.

- ☐ You are uncomfortable with price volatility.

- ☐ You want to minimize losses and fluctuation in the value of your investments.

- ☐ You would invest in something safe that offers a fixed rate of return.

- ☐ You are willing to give up higher rates of return to keep most of your principal intact.

- ☐ You prefer investments that offer income opportunities without much exposure to principal loss.

You are a moderate investor if:

- ☐ You want your investment return to beat inflation by at least 2%.

- ☐ You select investments that have a moderate amount of volatility yet offer the opportunity to earn a higher rate of return than CDs or government bonds.

- ☐ Although a decline in the value of your investments is a concern, you can accept temporary market volatility in return for growth opportunities.

- ☐ You would like to moderately increase the value of your investments with limited exposure to risk.

- ☐ You want a balanced investment mix and are willing to tolerate some short-term fluctuation in value.

You are an aggressive investor if:

- ☐ You like to pursue substantial appreciation opportunities, even though it puts your capital at high risk.

- ☐ Temporary market fluctuations do not concern you because maximum appreciation is your primary long-term goal.

- ☐ You expect a return greater than the S&P 500 Index from your investments.

- ☐ You are financially able to accept lower liquidity in your investment portfolio.

- ☐ You can take calculated risks to ensure a potential for the highest return over time.

- ☐ You have the conviction necessary to hold on to your investment during those years when it could drop in value by 25% or more.

Conclusion: Based on my needs, concerns, and risk tolerance,

I consider myself to be a(n) _____ investor.

Adapted with permission from: Dahl, B. (1996). *A Working Woman's Guide to Financial Security*. Urbana, Ill.: University of Illinois Cooperative Extension. ©Board of Trustees of the University of Illinois.

EXERCISE III-3

Finding Your Comfort Zone

Answer the following questions to determine your comfort with risk or market volatility.

1. Based on the investment return over the last 82 years through 2007, it is reasonable to expect the following long-term market performance in excess of inflation:

Stocks	4–6%
Long-term bonds	2–3%
Treasury bills	0–1%

   With your investment philosophy in mind, what is your rate of return objective? Inflation plus _____%.

2. To reach your long-term investment goals, how much risk or decline in your investment portfolio would you be willing to tolerate in a given year?

   ___ None   ___ 10–14%

   ___ 1–4%   ___ 15–19%

   ___ 5–9%   ___ 20% or more

3. If a $10,000 investment you made for a goal 5 years away lost value during the first year, at what dollar amount would you want to sell and move to a less volatile investment, rather than wait for a market turnaround?

   ___ $9,500   ___ Less than $8,000

   ___ $9,000   ___ I would not sell

   ___ $8,500

4. If you are investing for retirement in 20 years and the stock market drops 20% or more in a given year, would you:

   ___ Stop investing   ___ Put new contributions into fixed income

   ___ Move equities to a money market or CDs   ___ Buy more stocks

   ___ Continue to invest into equities predetermined amounts on a regular basis (dollar-cost-averaging)

Adapted with permission from: Dahl, B. (1996). *A Working Woman's Guide to Financial Security*. Urbana, Ill.: University of Illinois Cooperative Extension. ©Board of Trustees of the University of Illinois.

Investment Choices—Stocks, Bonds, and Mutual Funds

Mary, like many women, struggles with the risk vs. reward tradeoff that is a part of investing. She tends to choose investments so conservative that her money does not grow once taxes and inflation are factored in. For example, over the last 82 years, Treasury bills have paid an average annual return of 3.7%. If you subtract out 3.1% inflation, this leaves you with 0.6%, and you still haven't paid income taxes yet! You may find, after ongoing study of the different investments available, that you can gradually become more comfortable with risk and thus gain potentially more growth.

As shown on page 75, investments can be placed on a risk ladder for better understanding of their relative risks and rewards.

Rung 1—
Low-Risk (Conservative) Investments

Cash and Cash Equivalents

Savings accounts (regular passbook or statement). Easily opened at commercial banks, savings and loan (S&L) associations, and credit unions. Frequency of compounding of interest varies; accounts are usually government-insured and liquid (quickly converted to cash without loss of value).

Money market deposit accounts. Bank and credit union accounts that typically provide a slightly higher rate of return than savings accounts. **Money market deposit accounts** carry Federal Deposit Insurance Corporation (FDIC) or National Credit Union Administration insurance for balances of up to $100,000. You have slightly less access to your money (limited number of checks and withdrawals per month) than with a savings account.

Money market mutual funds. Unlike money market deposit accounts (bank products), **money market mutual funds** are mutual funds available in taxable and tax-free versions. They invest in the lowest risk,

TABLE III-2

What Returns Can You Expect from Your Investments?

Investor profile	Type of investments	Expected return before inflation and taxes (%)
Conservative (low risk)	Significant allocation to fixed income (bonds, money markets, CDs, and savings accounts)	2–8
Moderate (medium risk)	Significant allocation to equities (stocks and mutual funds)	8–11
Aggressive (high risk)	Significant allocation to equities, including foreign, small cap, and sector funds	10–15

shortest term, most highly rated debt securities such as Treasury bills and certificates of deposit and short-term municipal debt instruments (such as municipal bonds). Maturities (the date on which the principal amount of a bond or loan must be paid) are less than 90 days to provide safety from a change in short-term interest rates. Shares are worth $1.00 apiece. These funds are not federally insured, but are extremely safe and liquid and generally yield a bit more than money market deposit accounts.

Certificates of deposit. **CDs** are deposit accounts with strings attached. Depositors select the number of days, months, or years to fit their goals and needs. Available at banks, savings and loan associations, credit unions, and brokerage firms, the rate of return, depending on maturity, can be higher than what's available from money market funds. If you should withdraw your money early, you'll pay a 3–6-month interest penalty. Bank CDs are insured. However, CDs sold by brokerage firms may not be.

U.S. Treasury Securities

"Treasury securities" is an umbrella term for three groups of securities with differing maturities.

Treasury bills (T-bills). These are types of short-term federal debt securities with maturities ranging from a few days to 52 weeks (1 year). You can buy a T-bill for a minimum of $100, with increments of $100. T-bills are purchased at a discount. For example, depending on the prevailing interest rate, you might buy a 6-month T-bill for $940. At maturity you get back $1,000. (In this example, your profit is approximately $60 or 6.4% ([$60 ÷ $940] x 100). Interest is exempt from state and local income tax.

U.S. Treasury notes and bonds. These kinds of investments are popular because of their safety and competitive interest rates. Interest on both kinds of investments is paid semiannually. This interest is subject to federal taxes but is free from state or local taxes. Treasury notes are issued with maturities of 2, 3, 5, and 10 years. Treasury bonds are long-term federal debt securities that mature in 30 years.

Treasury securities are available by phone without a sales fee from the Bureau of Public Debt, over the Internet using a plan called Treasury Direct, or for a small fee (about $50) from financial institutions. For more information about Treasury Direct, call 800-722-2678 or visit www.treasurydirect.gov.

U.S. Series EE bonds and I bonds. Series EE bonds are the lowest denomination securities issued by the federal government with the income earned exempt from state and local taxes. Federal taxes can be deferred for up to 30 years or until the owner cashes in the bond. Both the Series EE and inflation-adjusted I bonds are available at most banks and other financial institutions, as well as through payroll deduction, in

> Note: Earnings on both bond series are subject to federal tax but may be tax-free if cashed during a year in which the owner pays qualified education expenses and meets income guidelines (see Internal Revenue Service (IRS) publication 970, Tax Benefits for Education, for details).

denominations ranging from $50 to $5,000 (I bonds) or $10,000 (E bonds). The purchase price of EE bonds is one-half of their face value (e.g., $50 for a $100 bond). I Bonds are sold at face value in the same denominations as Series EE. The accrued interest on both series is paid when the bonds are redeemed. Bonds can be redeemed at most financial institutions. For further information, visit www.savingbonds.gov.

Effective May 1, 2005, investors who buy Series EE savings bonds will receive whatever rate is in effect at the time of purchase for the life of the bond. Prior to this date, interest rates on Series EE bonds changed every six months based on current interest rates. The change to a fixed rate does not affect holders of Series EE bonds purchased before May 1, 2005, nor does it affect those holding Series I bonds, which are adjusted every six months for inflation.

Fixed-Rate Annuities

An **annuity** is a contract between an investor and a life insurance company. You invest in the contract by making a lump sum or periodic deposits in exchange for tax-deferred growth of principal. A guaranteed lifetime income is available if you "annuitize"—meaning you convert your annuity account into a monthly income stream. The investor is guaranteed a fixed rate of return while the savings grow. The income received is based on the amount invested, the length of time it grows, and the interest rate paid on savings.

Annuities are popular retirement investments for two reasons: they are tax-deferred, and the rate of return is usually better than that of CDs. The disadvantages include:

- Withdrawals before age 59½ may trigger an IRS penalty of 10%.
- Fixed-rate annuities normally carry a declining surrender fee (a type of commission whereby fees are gradually reduced over time) for 5–10 years.
- High expenses, including an annual contract maintenance fee and mortality charge (1.30% on average) to cover insurance company overhead and death benefits.

Buy annuities only from companies rated A or better (AAA is the top rating, then AA and A) by the recognized rating services for insurance companies (Table III-3) so you can ensure that the money you invest will be there when you want it.

Variable annuities invest in mutual funds and are explained in greater detail on page 82.

explained in greater detail on page 82.

TABLE III-3

Rating Services of Insurance Companies

Rating company	Web site
Standard & Poor's	www.standardandpoors.com
Duff & Phelps	www.duffllc.com
Moody's	www.moodys.com
Weiss Research	www.weissratings.com
A.M. Best	www.ambest.com

Rung 2— Low- to Moderate-Risk Investments

Bonds

A bond promises the return of your capital, plus interest, if you hold it to its maturity date. When you buy a bond, you are loaning your money to the issuer.

The safest bonds in the low- to moderate-risk category (after the federally secured bonds described in the Rung 1 section) are those rated A or better by Moody's or Standard and Poor's rating services (see page 89). Bonds rated BBB are considered medium grade and those rated BB or lower are considered below investment grade or "junk" bonds.

Municipal bonds. "Munis" are loans by investors to a state or local government or related agency for the purpose of building schools, hospitals, roads, bridges, or other municipal projects. In turn, the government or agency must honor the repayment of the bonds. However, all munis are not equal in quality. The higher the rating (and safer the bond), the lower the yield. Interest earned is federally tax-free and, if issued in your state, state tax exempt. Generally, the yields on municipal bonds are lower than what corporate bonds pay.

Corporate bonds. Companies issue bonds to pay for all sorts of activities, from research and development to acquisitions. The risk in corporate bonds is higher than in Treasuries—but the return is higher, too. It is generally 1–4% higher than a comparable Treasury bond, depending on the credit risk of the company. Available through brokerage firms, the minimum investment is $1,000. The interest you earn on corporate bonds is taxable by both the state and federal governments.

Ginnie Mae funds (GNMAs). **GNMAs** are mortgage-backed securities issued by the Government National Mortgage Association. Investment is in repackaged debt from 30-year government-funded home mortgages issued by the Federal Housing Authority and by the Veterans Administration. GNMAs are considered a "pass through" security because mortgage principal and interest payments are distributed proportionately to investors. As homeowners pay their monthly mortgage, their money is passed through to Ginnie Mae investors—partly in interest and partly in return of principal. GNMAs offer the full faith and credit backing of the federal government and require a minimum investment of $25,000. They can be purchased through banks and brokerage firms. They can also be purchased for a lot less ($1,000–3,000) through a mutual fund or unit investment trust.

The major risk with GNMAs is that when interest rates fall people tend to refinance their mortgages. This causes larger amounts of principal to be returned to investors when interest rates drop, thus lowering the expected rate of return.

Bond funds. All types of bonds are available in mutual funds. Their value fluctuates according to business, market, and economic conditions and can be as unpredictable as stock funds. Since bond funds don't mature (the fund manager is constantly buying and selling the bonds), an investor's principal and income stream is always subject to interest rate risk. To preserve principal and earn a set amount of income for a particular period of time, investors should probably choose individual bonds if possible. The advantages of bond funds, however, are the diversification you get (the manager may buy hundreds of bonds), low investment minimums, the ability to reinvest dividends (the share of profits or earnings that a company passes on to its shareholders), ongoing professional management, and a monthly check if you decide not to reinvest in additional shares.

> Note: Mutual funds consisting of junk bonds, called high-yield bond funds, belong on Rung 3. Because they are lower quality, their share value fluctuates more like a stock.

Zero-coupon bonds. With **zero-coupon bonds**, the investor collects no (zero) interest during the life of the bond. Instead, the bond sells at a deep discount and each year the value of the bond increases. You get all your money at maturity instead of collecting a little each year. Corporations, municipalities, and the U.S. Treasury issue zero-coupon bonds. The downside is that you have to pay taxes on the interest earned each year even though you never put it in your pocket. Those taxes can be deferred or eliminated if the bond is put in an individual retirement account (IRA) or if you purchase a municipal zero-coupon bond. Interest on Treasury zero-coupon bonds is not subject to state or local taxes, and interest on municipal zeros is federally and/or state tax-exempt.

Rung 3—
Moderate- to High-Risk Investments

Ownership investments are assets that you buy and own as property. As a stockholder (partial owner) of a corporation or real estate, there is potential for growth if the value of the asset increases and a potential for loss if the value declines.

Stocks (a.k.a., equities) are the heart of a well-managed portfolio and the best hedge against inflation over the long run. Rung 3 investments are for long-term money only—goals with deadlines more than 5 years in the future.

Stock Types

Income stocks are issued by companies that expect to pay regular, relatively high (compared to other companies) dividends (e.g., utilities).

Blue-chip stocks are issued by large, stable companies with a record of profitability over many years; they generally pay a dividend.

Growth stocks are issued by successful companies with above-average earnings and tend to rise in value every year. Growth stocks have a higher price relative to earnings than stocks on average. The major risk is that price declines are inevitable. Many growth stock companies pay little or no dividends.

Value stocks can be issued by large or small companies and trade at prices that are low compared to their true worth or future prospects. Often these stocks are cheap because the companies have fallen out of favor. They are generally less risky to own than growth stocks because they have less to lose in a declining market and have room to rise if company earnings improve. They also carry lower price-earnings ratios and usually pay bigger dividends than growth stocks.

Stock mutual funds are investment companies that pool money from shareholders and invest in a variety of stocks, including large, small, value, growth, sector, and international. The investment company sells shares to investors. The shares provide investment returns in the form of dividends and capital gains (an investment's increase in value).

Because mutual funds contain many investments, they tend to be safer than individual stocks or bonds. The price per share will fluctuate with business, market, and economic conditions. Minimum investments range from $500 to $5,000, in most cases, but can be lower if payments are made automatically from your checking account.

Mutual funds are available through full-service brokerage firms for a sales charge ("load") or directly from discount brokers (fund "supermarkets" such as Charles Schwab's OneSource). You can also buy mutual funds directly through the fund companies themselves for lower sales charges or none at all ("low-load funds" or "no-load funds"). History shows that no-load funds perform as well as load funds.

Many mutual fund companies have good educational materials available on the Web or by mail.

Stock funds exist for every type of stock listed above.

Other popular types of stock funds are *index funds*, which aim to match a particular market index (e.g., Standard & Poor's 500) by investing in the securities found in the index, *balanced funds*, which mix stocks and bonds; and *global funds*, which invest in foreign companies as well as U.S. companies.

Variable Annuities

In addition to fixed-rate annuities, there are also variable annuities, which belong on Rung 3 or Rung 4 of the Risk Ladder, depending on the investments in the account. A variable annuity is the same kind of insurance contract (available through an insurance company) as a fixed-rate annuity, except that the investor has the responsibility of managing the account and choosing investments from an array of mutual fund sub-accounts. The value of the annuity fluctuates based on market performance of the underlying mutual funds. Some variable annuities are offered without surrender fees and sales charges through mutual fund companies. However, all companies charge an annual management fee of 0.25–2%. The assets grow tax-deferred and earnings are taxed at ordinary income tax rates rather than at lower capital gains rates. Low expenses are absolutely critical here.

Rung 4—High-Risk Investments

Only aggressive mutual funds are included on Rung 4 of the Risk Ladder. The underlying individual securities would also belong in the high-risk category. These mutual funds are appropriate for investors who have a long time frame and can tolerate the most risk; these funds can experience dramatic price changes.

Small company (small cap) funds tend to make stellar gains in a rising market. Small companies are young and growing fast, and their dramatic gains are sometimes followed by sudden drops. Over time, however, these funds tend to return more than Rung 3 funds—if you can tolerate the volatility.

Sector funds focus on particular industries, such as technology, natural resources, health care, or financial services, and purchase only stocks in one industry.

Emerging markets funds focus on companies in developing countries. The funds are vulnerable to currency fluctuations and political conditions in those areas.

Gold and precious metals funds invest in the stock of companies related to gold and precious metals (e.g., mining).

International funds invest in stocks and bonds of companies located outside the United States.

Penny stocks are sold for $5 per share or less. If you invest in them, be prepared to lose all of your money. However, they can occasionally produce good returns.

Commodities are bulk goods, such as food, coffee, grain, livestock, and metals, that are traded on the Commodities Exchange.

Checking Up on Quality

If you are going to buy stocks, corporate bonds, shares in a mutual fund, or an annuity, you should first research their quality using the tools below. You want to verify that the company is financially stable and profitable. The authoritative ratings for each type of investment are available in most libraries or on the Internet.

Ranking Services and Sources

Bonds: *Standard & Poor's* and *Moody's*. Ratings are also available from brokers.

Annuities: *Standard & Poor's, Moody's,* and the other rating services listed on page 80.

Stocks: *Value Line Investment Survey* and *Standard & Poor's Stock Guide.*

Mutual Funds: *Morningstar* and *Value Line Mutual Fund Survey*

What Are Stocks and Why Should You Own Them?

Stock is an ownership asset. If you buy stock in a company, you are a partial owner of that company, even if it is only a minuscule piece.

> **Stock.** A security that represents a unit of ownership in a corporation.

How Does an Investor Make Money?

You can make money in two ways by owning stock in a company.

1. *Price appreciation (capital gain)*

Example: You buy a stock at $25 a share and sell it at $39 a share, which is $14 more than you paid for it. Multiply the number of shares you bought by $14 to figure your profit (capital gain).

2. *Dividends.* Dividends are the share of profits or earnings a company makes that it passes on to its shareholders.

Example: A company earned $15 million and had 10 million shares of stock outstanding. Divide $15 million by 10 million shares to get $1.50 per share of earnings. The company decides to distribute 80 cents of the earnings per share to shareholders as a dividend. If you owned 100 shares, you would receive $20 ($0.20 x 100) each quarter, for a total of $80 for the year.

In addition to ownership, the possibility for price appreciation, and dividends, a stock investor also gets a chance to help make corporate decisions by voting her proxy (giving authorization to vote on company business). An investor also has an opportunity to see company management at work at the annual meeting.

There are two types of stock: preferred and common.

Preferred stock has an established dividend that does not move up or down based on how well the company is doing. Preferred stockholders always get paid their dividends before common shareholders and, if a company should fail, would be paid off first.

Common stock offers voting rights and any dividends the company decides to pay. Dividends will fluctuate depending on the company's success or failure. These are the shares that most investors own.

Where to Buy and Sell Stocks

You can buy or sell stock through full-service brokerage firms, discount brokers, deep discount brokers, directly from a company, and online. A commission is charged for every purchase and sale.

All publicly traded stocks are listed on one or more exchanges or on the over-the-counter (OTC) market.

The three primary exchanges in the United States where investors trade stock are:

The New York Stock Exchange (NYSE). This is the largest and oldest of the U.S. stock exchanges (located in New York City); trades the shares of many large and well-established companies.

The American Stock Exchange. Also located in New York City, this exchange has less rigorous standards than the NYSE and lists smaller companies.

The National Association of Securities Dealers Automated Quotation System (NASDAQ or OTC). NASDAQ is sometimes called the OTC (over-the-counter) market because there is no actual trading floor as there is at the other exchanges. The NASDAQ is made up of brokers networked together around the country who trade stocks back and forth with computers. A lot of high-tech companies trade here, and volatility is generally the highest of the stock exchanges.

Stocks by Size

The size of a company is described in "market lingo" as market capitalization, a.k.a., market cap. Market cap is determined by multiplying the current price of a share of stock by the number of outstanding shares.

> **Capitalization (Cap).** The total market value of all shares of a company's stock; calculated by multiplying the share price by the number of outstanding shares.

While exact definitions of market capitalization vary somewhat according to various sources, all companies can be classified into one of the following market cap ranges:

Mega-cap	Over $1 trillion
Large-cap	Over $10 billion
Mid-cap	Between $1 or $2 billion and $10 billion
Small-cap	Between $250 million and $1 billion or $2 billion
Micro-cap	Between $50 million and $250 million
Nano-cap	Below $50 million

How Stocks Measure Up— What to Look For

For investors, the best way to evaluate and learn about a stock is to use fundamental analysis, the study of information about a corporation's financial health and likelihood of success. By examining a company's management, its growth rate, how much it earns, and how much it spends to run its business, you can determine if it is a good buy or overpriced. This information can be found in company annual reports and the Value Line Investment Survey (available in library reference areas).

The most common stock measurements can reveal valuable information:

Cash flow per share. Cash flow is the stream of cash through a business. Bills need to be paid on time.

Cash flow per share is simply a company's cash flow divided by the number of shares outstanding. It tells you what you are paying for a share of the company's cash flow.

Current ratio. This is one of the best measures of whether a company can pay its bills. It is calculated by dividing current assets by current liabilities. Current assets are items that are used up and replaced often, such as cash or inventory. Current liabilities are debt payments that are due usually within 1 year. Look for companies with a current ratio of at least 2:1.

Earnings per share. This is the most important of growth measures. It's the proverbial "bottom line" on a company's income statement and is calculated by dividing what the company earned last quarter (or last year) by the number of shares outstanding. Earnings reports can often cause a stock to rise or fall sharply.

Dividend yield. A stock's dividend yield is the annual cash dividend divided by the current stock price (this is always found in the newspaper). Usually the larger, well-established companies offer higher dividend yields and are considered to be safer stocks.

Price/book ratio. This ratio compares a stock's price to how much the stock is worth at that very moment if a company had to be sold. To arrive at the book value, the value of the company's belongings would be added up and then divided by the number of shares outstanding. Then the current price of the stock is divided by the book value to get the price/book ratio. If the ratio is less than 1, buyers pay less for the stock than its liquidation value, which is good.

Price/earnings ratio (PE). This is the most important measure of a stock's value. The price/earnings ratio of a stock is calculated by dividing the price of a stock by the earnings per share. It is riskier to invest in a stock with a high PE because of the greater difficulty of meeting the higher earnings expectations of analysts and investors. Companies with lower PEs generally pay dividends and are usually in slower growth industries. You'll often find very high PE ratios in the newer and riskier technology companies.

Winning Stock Market Strategies

Even though stocks have shown an upward trend since 1802, there have been lots of time periods when an investor's patience has been tried. But, in any case, there are several strategies that will reduce your risk and increase the possibility of higher growth.

Buy and hold. This is an investment strategy that involves long-term ownership of high quality securities. Don't try to time the markets. Market prices go up as well as down. Be prepared to keep your money in for the long haul, at least 5 years, and ignore the temporary ups and downs in the stock market. Trying to second-guess the market is about as sure as betting on a horse race. It is impossible to know what the market will do next week, next quarter, or next year. A buy-and-hold strategy minimizes taxes (you are taxed only when you finally sell) and transaction costs (multiple commissions) and eases tax preparation (you have only dividends to report). Over the long term, a sound stock investment should rise in value, dividends should increase, and the stock may split, giving you more shares.

Dollar-cost-averaging. This is a regular (e.g., monthly) investment of a predetermined amount (e.g., $50) of money regardless of whether securities markets are moving up or down. Dollar-cost-averaging is a disciplined way to invest in the stock market because you are making a commitment to yourself to add to your investments on a regular basis, regardless of market conditions. It takes the emotions out of investing. The set dollar amount you decide to invest periodically will buy more shares when the prices are down and fewer when the prices are high. When you average the cost of your shares over time, you will find that this method results in ownership of more shares at a lower average price per share. Dollar-cost- averaging is very easy to do with mutual fund automatic investment

and stock dividend reinvestment plans (DRIPs). Table III-4 illustrates how regular investments lead to lower average share prices.

TABLE III-4

Dollar-Cost-Averaging Illustration

Month	Regular investment	Share price	Shares acquired
1	$100	$10.00	10.0
2	100	7.50	13.3
3	100	5.00	20.0
4	100	7.50	13.3
5	100	10.00	10.0
Total	$500	$40.00	66.6
Your average share cost: $500 ÷ 66.6 = $7.50			

Reinvest your dividends and capital gains—A DRIP is the easiest and least expensive way to buy new stock. By taking advantage of a direct investment plan, you can purchase additional shares of stock directly from a company without paying brokerage fees.

> *Dividend reinvestment plan (DRIP).* A stock or mutual fund purchase option that allows investors to automatically reinvest any dividends their stock or mutual fund pays in additional shares, as well as to invest optional lump sum cash payments.

Use Exercise III-4, *Comparing Stock Investments* (page 86), to determine the best deal among three stocks in which you are considering investing.

EXERCISE III-4

Comparing Stock Investments

Characteristic	Stock investment #1	Stock investment #2	Stock investment #3
Name			
Earnings per share			
Dividend yield			
Price/earnings ratio			
Stock category			
Stock size			
Long-term debt			
Cost per share			
Other features			

Your Minimum "Need to Knows" about Stocks

- Stocks are ownership investments. The value of your stocks will fluctuate with market conditions, potentially giving you a higher return than you might receive from loaned money (bonds).

- It is possible for an individual investor to build real wealth over time in the stock market.

- Buying the stock of a company allows you to profit from that company's future growth and earnings.

- Buy and hold stocks long-term—at least 5 years.

- Stocks are worth only as much as a buyer will pay.

- Don't invest more than 5% of your total portfolio in an individual company's stock.

- Do your homework. Don't skip research just to get in quickly.

- Earnings per share is the most important measure of a stock's quality.

- The best yardstick for a company's value is its price/earnings ratio.

- Investing a set amount of money in the same stock each month results in dollar-cost-averaging—a good way to buy stock over time.

- DRIPs permit you to buy a small number of shares of stock and to reinvest dividends directly into company shares.

What Are Bonds and Why Should You Own Them?

Bonds are a very different type of investment from stock, but equally important. When you are younger, you'll focus less on bonds than you will when you are older. If you are in your 30s, you might have only 20% of your portfolio in bonds, but as a 65 year-old you might have 50–60% in bonds.

> *Bond.* A debt instrument or IOU issued by a corporation or government entity.

Why are bonds important? **Fixed-income investments**—ranging from long-term corporate bonds, Treasury notes and bills, CDs, and money market mutual funds—address certain financial goals better than others do (such as stocks or real estate). Being able to tap the money you need when you need it is the name of the game. Bonds also cushion your stock portfolio. In years when the stock market is moving down rather than up, a bond portfolio can often temper your overall losses.

Decision Time— Individual Bonds or Bond Funds?

Individual bonds will give you:

- a set income stream (payable twice a year) over the period of the loan (when you invest in a bond, you're loaning your money to the holder of the bond).
- all of your principal back at the end (when the bond matures).

Bond mutual funds give you:

- a portfolio composed of bonds that has no maturity date. At no point in time are you guaranteed your full investment back. On the other hand, you are getting diversification. Instead of owning just one bond, you own pieces of many bonds, perhaps 100 or more.
- dividends that are paid out monthly instead of semiannually.
- the ability to cash out whenever you want.

> *Diversification.* The policy of spreading assets among different investments to reduce risk of a decline in the overall portfolio as well as a decline in any one investment.

The trade-off between owning bonds vs. bond funds is:

- you can lose principal in a bond fund, but you (usually) can't with an individual bond, as long as you hold it until maturity.
- you can purchase bond funds with no sales charge (commission). Not so with individual bonds (unless they are new issue). You'll pay a commission to buy, as well as to sell, if you redeem early.

> *Maturity.* The date on which the principal amount of a bond or loan must be paid.

> Advice: If you have less than $50,000 to invest in bonds, choose quality bond funds that have low management fees. They come in many varieties, as described earlier on page 80. It is difficult to build a diversified bond portfolio with less money.

If you have $50,000 or more to invest, create a bond portfolio with a combination of assets with different maturity dates. This is called **laddering** (Table III-5, page 88). As each bond matures, reinvest the proceeds at the longest time interval to maintain the ladder.

TABLE III-5

Example of Laddering

Year 1			
Amount ($)	Yield (%)	Maturity (years)	Annual interest ($)
10,000	5.00	1	500
10,000	5.25	2	525
10,000	5.50	3	550
10,000	5.75	4	575
10,000	6.00	5	600
		Total	$2,750

How Bonds Work

Bonds are issued with a face value of $1,000 but are usually sold in increments of five (e.g., $5,000, $10,000). The length of time between when a bond is issued and when it matures varies significantly (e.g., short-term bonds mature in 2 years or less, intermediate bonds mature in 3–10 years, and long-term bonds mature up to 30 years after issue).

Some bonds are sold at face or "par" value ($1,000) and pay investors interest over the term of the bond. Others, such as Series EE U.S. savings bonds and zero-coupon bonds, are sold at a discount to their stated value. They return nothing until they mature, and at that time, give an investor the full face value.

Bond interest can be described in two ways. You'll need to understand the distinctions to avoid confusion when you actually begin to invest.

Coupon rate, a.k.a., the stated interest rate, is used to compute the interest payment in dollars that you will receive from the bond as a percentage of the bond's face value, e.g., $1,000.

Example: A newly issued bond for $1,000 has a coupon rate of 8%, meaning that you receive a total of $80 of interest income for that year (payable in two $40 payments). Every year, you will collect $80 from the bond until it matures. At that point, you get back your $1,000.

Current yield is based on the current market price of the bond rather than the "par" or face value.

Example: A bond with a face value of $1,000 drops in value to $900. You still earn your $80 of interest income based on the bond's stated rate of interest. Thus, the current yield of the bond is ([$80 ÷ $900] x 100) or 8.9%.

What Should You Look Out For?

The five major risks of bonds and bond funds are:

Call risk, which relates to the fact that the issuer of a bond can buy it back, or call it, from an investor prior to maturity. "Yield-to-call" is similar to "yield-to-maturity," but it assumes the bond issuer will stop paying interest on the call date. This is quite common with municipal and corporate bonds. Investors are forced to redeem their bonds at this point, as they will no longer earn interest.

Credit (or default) risk, which relates to the financial strength of the company that is issuing the bond and is based on the ability of the company to repay principal and interest on time. Look for highest quality as rated by Standard & Poor's and Moody's (Table III-6).

Interest rate risk, which confirms that interest rates and bond prices move in opposite directions. Think of this movement like a seesaw. When bond prices rise, interest rates go down. Conversely, when interest rates rise, bond prices fall. In the latter case, it means that your bond is losing value because new bonds are being issued at a higher interest rate (see figure on page 89).

Example: If you could buy a newly issued $1,000 bond paying a stated interest rate of 9%, you certainly wouldn't offer your friend $1,000 for her bond paying 8%. So unless you can buy your friend's bond for less money, it's a bad deal.

Time risk, which means that the volatility of bond prices increases as their length of maturity increases. The risk is that you will be stuck with a lower pay-

TABLE III-6

Credit Quality Ratings and What They Mean

Moody's	Standard & Poor's	Fitch	Interpretation
Aaa	AAA	AAA	Outstanding quality. If everything that can go wrong goes wrong, the bond issuer can still service debt.
AA	AA	AA	Very high quality by all standards.
A	A	A	Investment grade; good quality.
Baa	BBB	BBB	Lowest investment-grade rating; satisfactory, but needs to be monitored.
Ba	BB	BB	Somewhat speculative; low grade.
B	B	B	Very speculative.
Caa	CCC	CCC	Even more speculative. Substantial risk.
Ca	CC	CC	Widely speculative. May be in default.
C	C	C	In default. Junk. No interest being paid or bankruptcy petition filed.
	D	D	In default

Adapted with permission from: Thau, A. (2000). *The Bond Book.* McGraw-Hill Trade.

Additional source: www.InvestinginBonds.com.

ing bond until maturity when new ones are paying a higher interest rate.

Example: If interest rates rise 1%, a 2-year Treasury note (or short-term bond) loses nearly 2% in value. On the other hand, a 30-year Treasury loses about 12% in value.

Reinvestment risk, which can be experienced since bond issuers have the right to call back their bonds and return the bondholder's principal. The risk is that you generally have to reinvest your principal at lower rates than you were receiving and counting on.

Exercise III-5, *Comparing Fixed-Income Investments* (page 90), will help you compare three bond investment vehicles and choose the one best suited to your needs.

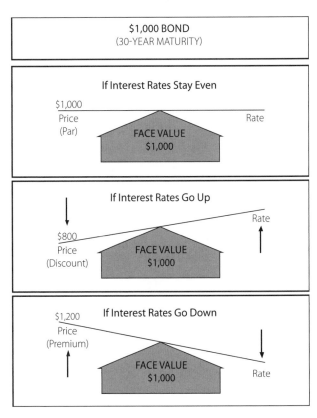

Comparing Fixed-Income Investments

Characteristic	Fixed-income investment #1	Fixed-income investment #2	Fixed-income investment #3
Name			
Return			
Maturity date, if any			
Minimum investment amount			
Subsequent investment amount			
Tax advantages, if any			
Frequency of interest payments			
Quality rating			
Other features			

Your Minimum "Need to Knows" about Bonds

- A bond is an interest-bearing security with a maturity date.

- A bond is a loan to a corporation, the federal government, or a state or local government or government agency.

- Compared to stocks, bonds offer higher current income with less volatility, but don't grow in value.

- Bonds are given ratings from AAA to C or D (depending on the rating firm), denoting their issuers' ability to repay principal and interest owed to holders.

- Low expenses are critical to bond fund returns.

- Mutual funds that invest in bonds are generally more risky than individual bonds, all things being equal (for the same quality of bonds).

- Bonds and bond funds are frequently recommended as a low-risk way to balance or stabilize a portfolio and for short-term goals.

- It can be wise to limit bond maturities to 5 years to reduce interest rate risk.

- It is best not to sacrifice quality. Investing in lower-rated junk bonds (or junk bond funds) can be high risk.

What Are Mutual Funds and Why Should You Own Them?

Every mutual fund has specific investment criteria that are spelled out in its prospectus, the official booklet that describes a mutual fund. Investors then know what they are getting and can match their investment objective to that of a fund.

> **Mutual fund.** A portfolio of stocks, bonds, or other securities that is collectively owned by thousands of investors and managed by a professional investment company. The shareholders are people who have similar investment goals.

In a nutshell, this is how mutual funds work . . .

- A large number of people with a common objective put money in a pot (a mutual fund) with other people's money.
- They pool their money for more buying power.
- The fund manager invests all of the money in a collection of stocks, bonds, or other securities.
- In exchange, investors are given shares in the fund. The number they own is proportionate to the amount they invest.
- Investors receive or reinvest dividends and capital gains distributed by the fund.

What Are the Advantages of Mutual Funds?

- You get full-time professional money management. Most people do not have the time or skill to select and monitor individual stocks and bonds.

- You get reduced risk through diversification because a mutual fund owns many stocks or bonds. You can also pick your level of market risk by choosing particular types of funds.

- You don't need a lot of money to get started. Many funds require only $1,000 to open an account, and some funds require minimum initial investments as low as $500. Subsequent deposits can be as small as $25–100 if an automatic investment plan (AIP) is adopted.

- You retain ready access to your money. A mutual fund is required to buy back your shares, which makes withdrawals easy. The management company will mail your check within 7 days of the request at the closing price (the net asset value, or NAV) on the day it is received. The NAV is calculated as follows:

$$\frac{\text{value of fund securities} - \text{expenses}}{\text{number of shares outstanding}}$$

> **Automatic investment plan.** An arrangement in which you agree to have money automatically withdrawn from your bank account on a regular basis (e.g., once a month or every quarter) and used to purchase individual stock or mutual fund shares.

- Mutual funds are often a less expensive way to invest than individual stocks because the thousands of shareholders share research and operating costs. The most efficiently run funds have an expense ratio of less than 1% per year. Some well-established funds charge annual fees as low as 0.10–0.50%. Also, many funds are sold directly through their sponsors with no sales charge; these are known as no-load funds.

- Mutual funds are convenient. They can be purchased (and sold) directly from a mutual fund company by mail, by telephone, and from full-service brokers, financial planners, banks, or insurance companies.

- Automatic withdrawal plans are available, making it possible to have a steady stream of income for retirement (e.g., withdrawals of $250 per month).

> **Expense ratio.** The percentage of fund assets deducted for management and operating expenses.
> **"No-load" funds.** Require no up-front fees to purchase shares and have no marketing fees.
> **"Low-load" funds.** Carry a sales commission of 1–3% of the amount invested.
> **"Load" funds.** Carry a sales commission of up to 8.5% of the amount invested.

- Monitoring mutual funds and stocks is simple. Prices are reported daily in the financial section of many newspapers.

Now for the Downside . . .

- If there is a broad market drop, your fund's value will dip with it. The diversification of most mutual funds protects you when one or several securities fall, but not when the whole market takes a downturn.

- Mutual funds have no guaranteed rate of return, as there is with CDs and Treasury securities.

> **Taxable distributions.** Payments to investors of profits (capital gains) realized upon the sale of securities within a mutual fund.

- Unwanted taxable distributions could also be a disadvantage. Funds are required to pay out 98% of their dividends, interest, and capital gains annually. Taxes must be paid on these distributions, even if you never received them but instead reinvested them in additional shares. Unfortunately, sometimes you can also owe taxes even if your fund lost money for the year. This is a non-issue if funds are held in a tax-deferred account such as a 401(k) or IRA.

Where to Buy and Sell Mutual Funds

The issue isn't whether you can find someone to sell you a mutual fund, but the best way for you to buy.

The decision will depend mainly on how much of the research you are willing to do, whether it bothers you to see some of your investment dollars go into sales commissions, rather than into the funds themselves, and how high a premium you place on convenience.

The four main avenues by which to own or redeem funds are:

- directly from the mutual fund company
- financial planners and full-service brokers
- banks with associated investment firms
- discount brokers including mutual fund supermarkets such as Charles Schwab, Fidelity, TD Ameritrade, and Vanguard.

Types of Mutual Funds

Mutual funds fall into three main categories:

- stock (or equity) funds
- bond funds
- money market funds.

Stock Funds

Stock funds invest primarily in stocks. But stock fund portfolios vary, depending on the fund's investment objective. The major distinction is that some stress growth, some income, and some a combination of the two. The profits on all stock fund distributions are taxable (if held in a taxable account), but there is no tax on the increase in value until shares are sold.

Bond Funds

Just like bonds, bond funds produce regular income. However, unlike bonds, bond funds have no maturity date and no guaranteed repayment of the amount you invest. Dividends can be reinvested in the fund to increase the principal. Buyers can invest a much smaller amount of money than would be needed to buy an individual bond and still get a diversified portfolio.

Bond funds come in many varieties with different investment strategies, goals, and maturities. They include investment-grade corporate bonds, Treasuries, junk bonds, long-term, short-term, taxable, and tax-free (municipals). Interest earned on corporate and

U.S. government funds is taxed. There is no federal tax on municipals and no state and local taxes for investors who live in the state and/or municipality that issued them.

Money Market Funds

These funds resemble savings accounts. For every dollar you put in, you get a dollar back, plus interest.

- Investors can write checks against their account, but there is usually a per-check minimum (e.g., $250 or $500).

- Money market funds come in taxable and tax-free varieties—taxables buy the best short-term corporate or government issues available. Tax-frees buy municipal debt.

- A money market fund usually pays a little more interest than a bank money market or CD, but always compare.

- Check yields and management fees.

- Use a money market fund as a place to stash money you'll need soon, as a parking place for cash you'll invest later, and as a place for your emergency fund.

Mutual Fund Objectives

A fund's objective should correspond with an investor's objective. Every mutual fund—stock, bond, or money market—is established with a specific investment objective that fits into one of these basic goals:

- future growth
- current income
- both income and growth
- preservation of capital.

Use the following worksheets (Exercises III-6 to III-11, pages 94–97) to help match your goals with the appropriate mutual funds. Examples for each category are provided. Any of the sample objectives could be met by any of the mutual fund types in each category. Write in your goals under "Your Objective" in each worksheet.

Mutual Funds with a Growth Objective

Your objective	Mutual funds with a growth objective
Examples: Retirement in 25 years College fund for a newborn _____ _____ _____ _____	**Growth funds** invest for the long term, and share prices can fluctuate considerably. They buy profitable, well-established companies that expect above-average earnings growth. Income is secondary; they pay very small dividends, if any. **Aggressive growth funds** (also called maximum capital appreciation funds) use riskier investment techniques and/or invest in stocks of smaller, less proven companies. They can be very volatile, but the trade-off is a high potential for capital appreciation. **Small capitalization funds** invest in stocks of small companies with assets less than $1 billion and are riskier than larger capitalization stock funds (more than $5 billion in assets). (Capitalization means number of shares outstanding multiplied by the price per share. See page 84 for details.) **Specialty or sector funds** limit investments to a specific industry (e.g., health care, biotechnology, financial services). **International funds** invest in securities of countries outside of the United States. **Global funds** invest in securities worldwide, including the United States. **Index funds** invest in stocks of one of the major broadly based market indexes such as the S&P 500 (large companies), Russell 2000 (small companies), or EAFE (Europe, Australia, Far East—an international index). Generally, these are passively managed funds with low expenses (meaning there is no manager deciding when to buy or sell securities).

Mutual Funds with an Income Objective

Your objective	Mutual funds with an income objective
Examples: Additional income for high tax-bracket retiree Supplement Social Security and pension for living expenses Lower risk in a stock-rich portfolio _____ _____ _____ _____	**Income funds** usually include a combination of bonds and utility stocks to produce steady income and lower investment risk. **Corporate bond funds** are available in short-, intermediate-, or long-term maturities. They invest in investment-grade bonds (debt) of seasoned companies. Investment-grade bonds have ratings of AAA, AA, A, or BBB by Moody's or Standard and Poor's. **Municipal bond funds** (short-, intermediate-, long-term) invest in tax-exempt municipal issues of state and local governments. They are generally sought by investors in the 25% and higher tax brackets. **High-yield (junk) bond funds** buy bonds with less than a BBB rating, thereby increasing risk to seek a higher return (not suitable for the risk-averse). **Government bond funds** invest in safe government-backed securities (e.g., Treasury notes and bonds). **GNMA funds** hold securities backed by a pool of government-insured mortgages. **Global bond funds** invest in bonds of overseas companies.

Mutual Funds with Both Growth and Income Objectives

Your objective	Mutual funds with both growth & income objectives
Examples: College tuition in 7 years Retirement in 10 years _____ _____	**Equity-income funds** aim for moderate income and some growth, investing primarily in blue-chip companies and utilities that pay current income and higher dividends. **Growth and income funds** aim for more long-term growth and a little less income than equity-income funds. They invest in large well-known firms that pay dividends. **Balanced funds** combine stocks and bonds in one portfolio to earn a reasonable income with reasonable growth. They usually contain a fixed ratio of 60% stocks to 40% bonds.

Mutual Funds with a Preservation of Capital Objective

Your objective	Mutual funds with a preservation of capital objective
Example: Down payment on a house in 1 year _____ _____	**Taxable and tax-free money market funds** invest in very short-term debt securities such as Treasury bills and corporate IOUs known as commercial paper. **Tax-free money market funds** invest in very short-term securities issued by state and local governments.

Mutual Funds with All Four Objectives

Your Objective	Mutual funds with all four objectives
Examples: Invest for retirement in 5 years in one-fund portfolio (e.g., a fund with multiple objectives) New graduate starting from scratch _____ _____ _____	**Lifestyle funds** typically offer three to four static portfolios from which to select. Different mixes of stocks, bonds, and cash are offered to fit people at different stages of life, with different tolerances for risk, or those getting started with a limited amount of money (e.g., T. Rowe Price Personal Strategy funds and Vanguard Life-Strategy funds). **Target Date Funds** (a.k.a., Target Retirement Funds and Life Cycle Funds) are a variation of lifestyle funds. Popular in 401(k) plans, they are one-decision funds for retirement investing. Investors simply pick a fund with a date close to their expected retirement (e.g., 2020, 2030) or other long-term goal and fund managers do the rest—allocate deposits around a broad spectrum of stocks, bonds, and cash and automatically adjust asset weightings over time so that the fund portfolio gets more conservative as the target date approaches. T. Rowe Price, Vanguard, and Fidelity are well-respected choices. **Asset allocation funds** aim for good returns with relatively low risk by combining changing amounts of the three asset classes—stocks, bonds, and cash. Managers of the fund shift the investments among the categories at their own discretion. **Funds of funds** are mutual funds that buy shares of their funds. In some instances these funds are run by a mutual fund family (e.g., Vanguard STAR and T. Rowe Price Spectrum-Income).

EXERCISE III-11

Comparing Mutual Fund Investments

Read the prospectus from three different mutual funds and complete the worksheet below.

	A	B	C
Name of fund			
Type of fund			
Your objective(s)			
Fund's investment objective(s)			
Performance over 1 year			
over 3 years			
over 5 years			
(Optional) over 10 years			
Minimum investment			
Maximum cost (fees)			
Commission/sales charge			
Redemption fee			
12b-1 fee*			
Expense ratio			
Manager tenure			
Portfolio turnover rate			
Other features			

* A fee charged by mutual funds for advertising and distribution costs.

Your Personal Investment Statement

Fill in the blanks to finalize your investment goals and plans.

1. I can best describe myself as a _____ investor (conservative, moderate, or aggressive).

2. I feel most comfortable investing in (e.g., CDs, stocks, mutual funds)_____, _____, _____, and _____.

3. Possible alternative investments might be (e.g., real estate) _____.

4. I feel I will be able to get a real (after-inflation) return of _____% from my investments.

5. Within the next month I will do the following to learn more about investing:

   _____

   _____

6. Within the next year I will do the following to educate myself about investing:

   _____

   _____

   _____

7. By the year _____, I wish to have $_____ invested so I can

   _____

   _____

8. By the time I plan to retire at age _____ in _____ years, I want to have accumulated $_____ in assets.

9. I will accomplish these goals by: _____

   _____

   _____

10. The following circumstances might make me change my goals: _____

    _____

    _____

Adapted with permission from: Dahl, B. (1996). *A Working Woman's Guide to Financial Security*. Urbana, Ill.: University of Illinois Cooperative Extension. ©Board of Trustees of the University of Illinois.

Your Minimum "Need to Knows" about Mutual Funds

- Mutual fund investing is simpler than investing in individual stocks and bonds.

- Mutual funds give you the benefit of instant broad diversification and professional management, usually at a low cost.

- Mutual funds vary greatly according to investment objective and what they invest in (e.g., stocks, bonds).

- Buying (and selling) mutual funds is an easy process, whether you do it directly through the fund company itself or through a broker/financial planner, bank, or mutual fund supermarket.

- All mutual funds are established with a specific investment objective that corresponds to one of these goals: growth, income, growth and income, preservation of capital, or a combination of all four.

- Funds can be purchased directly without a sales commission (no-load) or with a sales charge (load) through a broker/financial planner.

- All mutual funds charge management fees. Low-cost funds are critical to better returns.

- Look for mutual funds that have good performance records, not just for 1 year, but for 3, 5, and 10 years.

- With mutual funds and other investments, the higher the risk, the greater the potential return.

- Consider only no-load funds so that you'll have all your money working for you. There is no need to pay a commission for a fund or to pay high expenses.

Money Talk: A Financial Guide For Women

Action Steps

SESSION III: **Investing Basics**

☐ Identify your risk tolerance with the *What Kind of Investor Are You?* worksheet (page 76) and the *Finding Your Comfort Zone* worksheet (page 77).

☐ Review the list of Rung 1 investments (page 78) and select those appropriate for your goals.

☐ Review the list of Rung 2 investments (page 80) and select those appropriate for your goals.

☐ Review the list of Rung 3 investments (page 81) and select those appropriate for your goals.

☐ Review the list of Rung 4 investments (page 82) and select those appropriate for your goals.

☐ Automate your investments with payroll deductions and/or automated deposits.

☐ Use the *Comparing Stock Investments* worksheet (page 86) to compare several possible stock investments.

☐ Use the *Comparing Fixed-Income Investments* worksheet (page 90) to compare fixed-income securities.

☐ Determine the type(s) of mutual funds that best match your investment objective.

☐ Use the *Comparing Mutual Fund Investments* worksheet (page 97) to compare mutual funds.

References

A Money Management Workbook (1999). Washington, D.C.: American Association of Retired Persons (Woman's Financial Information Program).

Bach, D. (1999). *Smart Woman Finish Rich*. New York: Broadway Books.

Bertrand, M. (1998). *A Woman's Guide to Savvy Investing*. New York: AMACOM.

Boston, K.E. (2006). *Who's Afraid to Be a Millionnaire?* Hoboken, NJ: John Wiley & Sons.

Chatzky, J. (2001). *Talking Money*. New York: Warner Books, Inc.

Dahl, B. (1996). *A Working Woman's Guide to Financial Security*. Urbana, Ill.: University of Illinois Cooperative Extension.

Garman, E.T., and Forgue, R.E. (2008). *Personal Finance*. Boston, Mass.: Houghton Mifflin Company.

Goodman, J. (2000). *Everyone's Money Book*. Chicago, Ill.: Dearborn Press.

Investing for Your Future (2002). Publication E227. New Brunswick, N.J.: Rutgers Cooperative Extension.

Kelly, J. (1996). *The Neatest Little Guide to Mutual Fund Investing*. New York: Penguin Books.

Kelly, J. (1998). *The Neatest Little Guide to Stock Market Investing*. New York: Penguin Books.

Kristof, K. (2000). *Investing 101*. Princeton, N.J.: Bloomberg Press.

Market Capitalization (2005). A to Z Investments. Available online at: http://www.atozinvestments.com/market-capitalization.html.

Market Capitalization (2008). Wikipedia. Available online at: http://en.wikipedia.org/wiki/Market_capitalization.

Morris, V., and Morris, K. (1997). *A Woman's Guide to Investing*. New York: Lightbulb Press.

O'Neill, B. (1999). *Investing on a Shoestring*. Chicago, Ill.: Dearborn Financial Publishing.

Quinn, J.B. (1997). *Making the Most of Your Money*. New York: Simon & Schuster.

Quinn, J.B. (2006). *Smart and Simple Financial Strategies for Busy People*. New York: Simon and Schuster.

Sander, J., Boutin, A., and Brown, J. (1999). *The Complete Idiot's Guide to Investing for Women*. New York: Alpha Book.

Schwab, C. (1998). *Charles Schwab's Guide to Financial Independence*. New York: Three Rivers Press.

Stocks, Bonds, Bills, and Inflation 1926–2007. Chicago, IL: Morningstar Inc.

Thau, A. (2001). *The Bond Book*. New York: McGraw-Hill.

Treasury Securities and Programs (2008). Washington, DC: Treasury Direct. Available online at: http://www.easysaver.gov/indiv/products/products.htm.

Updegrave, W. (1999). *Investing for the Financially Challenged*. New York: Warner Books, Inc.

The Value Line Mutual Fund Survey (2008). New York: Value Line. Available online at: https://www.ec-server.valueline.com/products/print3.html.

Vanguard Model Portfolio Allocations (2008). Valley Forge, PA: The Vanguard Group. Available at: https://personal.vanguard.com/us/planningeducation/general/PEdGP-CreateTheRightMixContent.jsp.

Investing for Retirement

Mary has a lot of time
so she needs a little money
but...
If Mary had a little time
she'd need a lot of money

What will be covered in Session IV

Retirement Planning Lessons

1. Asset Allocation and Diversification
2. Building an Investment Portfolio for Retirement
3. Investment Returns
4. Taking the Guesswork out of Retirement
5. Keeping Your Financial Records in Order
6. Withdrawals—How to Make Your Money Last
7. How to Choose Financial Professionals

Terms to Learn (bolded in the text)

Asset allocation	Defined contribution plan
Core investment	Equity investing
Cost basis	Return
Defined benefit plan	Rules of 72 and 115

Exercises

1. Your Asset Allocation Formula
2. Your Investment Portfolio
3. Estimating Your Investment Return
4. Draw Your Retirement Dreams
5. How Much Money Will You Need for Retirement?
6. Looking Ahead to Retirement
7. Estimated Cost of Living
8. Estimating Your Retirement Income
9. Ballpark Estimate
10. How $10 a Month Will Grow
11. Purchase and Sale of Assets
12. Comparison of Financial Professionals

2007 statistics from the Women's Bureau of the Department of Labor showed that women made up 46% of the labor force. This percentage is expected to increase to 47% by the year 2015. Many women are responsible for a sizable proportion of their families' income. They are also very busy—in addition to jobs, women often have the major share of raising kids and keeping the household going. So it's no wonder that many women don't want the added responsibility of investing money. But we have to get over that. According to Marsha Bertrand in *A Women's Guide to Savvy Investing*, "Without money in this world, you are in trouble. You have to know how to take care of what you have and make it grow."

An estimated 80–90% of women will be solely responsible for their own finances at some point in their lives. The bottom line is since most poor seniors are women who have been widowed, separated, or divorced, women of all ages need to understand investing and plan for their futures.

Many women of the baby-boom generation live independently, not by design, but because of divorce after being married for 15–30 years. Investing for their future is sometimes a new responsibility; many are without the 20 years or so of investing experience that their spouses possess.

Lots of women of retirement age find themselves suddenly single because of the death of their spouse. They must cope with trying to figure out just what investments their husbands left, where they are, and how they work. The teachable moment shouldn't have to be a life crisis to get us to learn the basics of investing.

Why are women behind in retirement planning?

1. Many women don't have as much money to work with as men do.
2. Women often have shorter work histories, e.g., men are out of the work force an average of 1.6% of potential work years, while, for women, it's 14.7%.

3. A shorter work history means lower Social Security benefits.
4. Less than half (47.2%) of working-age women participate in an employment-based retirement plan, compared to 49.4% of men, according to the Employee Benefit Research Institute.
5. Women earn only 80 cents for every dollar men make, according to the Women's Bureau of the Department of Labor, and only 6% of women working in year-round full-time jobs make over $75,000 annually, compared to about 16% of men.
6. Women often do not fare as well as men in divorce settlements.

So whether you are 22, 42, or 72, single or married, understanding how to invest your money so that you can take charge of your financial life should be a high priority.

The most important step toward guaranteeing future financial security is early planning for retirement. Although the best time to start planning is when you start working, few people are disciplined enough to do this and/or they don't understand the importance of compound interest over time. You have already taken an important first step, however, by educating yourself on how to become financially secure.

Studies show that many retirees will need to replace between 70 and 90% of their preretirement income to maintain their current standard of living, and their savings will have to keep pace with inflation. Whether you will be able to live on 70–90% of your preretirement income depends on your current and planned retirement lifestyle.

Financial planners such as Michael Stein, Certified Financial Planner (CFP®), author of *The Prosperous Retirement,* find that many people need 100–110% of their preretirement income in the early years of retirement, especially if they plan expensive activities, such as more travel. In midretirement, spending often declines to 70–80% but may increase again later with health and long-term care expenses.

Asset Allocation and Diversification

In Session III, various types of investments were described. This session extends what you've already learned by discussing specific investment strategies for retirement.

You can't turn on a financial talk radio show or read a personal finance magazine without coming across the word "diversification." That is Wall Street's word for not putting all your eggs in one basket. What it means is that there are three basic baskets of assets you want to own—stocks, bonds, and cash equivalents. **Asset allocation** involves the placement of a certain percentage of investment capital within different types of assets (e.g., 50% in stocks, 30% in bonds, and 20% in cash).

> *Note:* Mutual funds are not a separate asset class—they are collections of stocks, bonds, cash investments, or some combination of them picked by a professional manager to match an investment objective. By buying a mutual fund, you get built-in diversification.

When your portfolio is diversified, you don't just own one stock, bond, or cash investment, but a mix of several or more of one or more asset types. Generally speaking, stocks are riskier than bonds, which are, in turn, riskier than cash.

We can expect stocks and bonds to move up and down in price each year. Prices move at different rates at different times, so spread your money around. Because nobody knows when the market will go up or down, it is important to diversify in different industries and types of investments to spread your risk.

The percentage of your money you want to allocate to each investment type depends upon how far away you are from actually needing that money. The longer your time frame, the more years you have to weather the ups and downs of the stock market and the more you can put in stocks. The other factor that weighs

on how much risk to take is your tolerance for it. It's called the "sleep at night" factor.

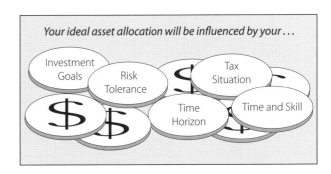

Your ideal asset allocation will be influenced by your . . .

Investment Goals · Risk Tolerance · Tax Situation · Time Horizon · Time and Skill

The younger you are, the more stocks (equities) you should own in your retirement portfolio to allow your money to grow. As your goals and age change, you may choose to put more funds into income-producing (fixed-asset) investments and less into growth. Be sure you don't have too much duplication (for instance, you probably don't need two growth and income funds).

Most people use a mathematical method to determine what portion of their portfolio should be devoted to various types of investments. The securities you select will be determined by your age, income, job security, marital status, loss aversion, general financial needs, and current economic conditions of the country. Think of your portfolio as a pie. The stocks, bonds, mutual funds, and savings you choose are the filling. Although there is no right portfolio for everyone, a general guideline is:

Stocks and/or stock mutual funds	40–90% (for growth and/or income)
Bonds	5–50% (for income)
Cash equivalents	10–25% (for liquidity)

Here's another guideline to help you with your asset allocation decision.

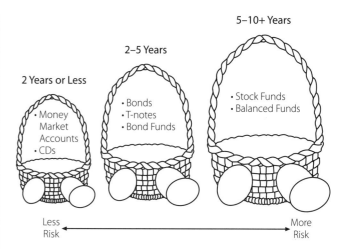

This concept of asset allocation is designed to help you reach your goals regardless of whether those goals are 30 years off or in the next few years. Choose a mix of investments that won't keep you awake at night or your stomach churning. Remember, patience is imperative. Successful investing is as much a factor of time as anything else. Completing Exercise IV-1, *Your Asset Allocation Formula,* will help you come up with an asset allocation formula that works for your needs.

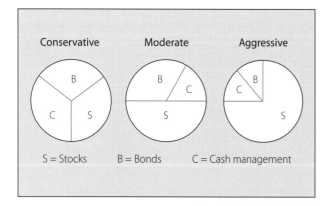

By setting up a personal allocation of assets in your portfolio from the three baskets and letting time work its magic, you should get where you want to go.

An investment in stocks should be made with an understanding of the risks these securities entail. These include the risk that the financial condition of the issuers of the securities in the portfolio, or the condition of the stock market in general, may worsen.

No one knows what the future holds. All we have is what history shows us. The more history we can view—meaning the further back we look—the safer projections about the future can be. **But, and it is a big BUT,** past returns are no guarantee of future returns. Table III-1 on page 74 shows sample asset allocations (portfolio mixes) and the best, worst, and the average annual return and worst one-year loss from January 1926 to December 2007.

Once you have determined your asset mix, to maintain the balance in your portfolio, you'll need to periodically adjust your holdings. For example, if your stocks (or stock mutual funds) have been increasing in value faster than your bonds and T-bills, it won't be long before they represent a lot more than 50% of the value of your portfolio. At that point, you'll need to sell enough of your stocks (or add new money to bonds and T-bills) to get the percentage back to the percentage you started with. This is called **portfolio rebalancing.** You should consider rebalancing any time your investment percentages get 5–10% out of whack from their original weightings.

Your Asset Allocation Formula

Following is a sample asset allocation model that is based on age and life cycle and can be used as a starting point in customizing your portfolio on the worksheet below. Total percentages should add up to 100% in each column.

Asset allocation formula				
	Age 20 single (%)	Age 40 married with children (%)	Age 60 preretiree (%)	Age 80 retired (%)
Cash (money market fund)	5	10	10	20
Certificates of deposit (CDs)/short-term bonds or funds	5	10	10	25
Intermediate bonds (laddered) or funds	0	10	20	35
Large-cap domestic stocks	45	35	40	20
Small-cap domestic stocks	30	20	10	0
International stocks	15	15	10	0
Total	100	100	100	100
Your desired asset allocation				
	Your age _____			
Cash (money market fund)	%			
CDs/short-term bonds or funds	%			
Intermediate bonds (laddered) or funds	%			
Large-cap domestic stocks	%			
Small-cap domestic stocks	%			
International stocks	%			
Total	100			

Building an Investment Portfolio for Retirement

Before you can decide on specific investments to fund your retirement goals, you need to have a blueprint—a plan for dividing your retirement savings among the three categories of investments, stocks, bonds, and cash equivalents—that will get you there. Selecting investments does not have to be a complicated process. You just have to take one step at a time and focus on your goal. It may not be practical or financially feasible to implement your plan all at once, but you will have the master plan.

The investment portfolio example on page 107 will illustrate how to construct a portfolio and help you visualize your asset allocation strategy to meet your predetermined retirement savings goal.

Working your way down, the top slot of the pyramid holds your financial goal, e.g., "accumulate $500,000 in 25 years." The section below contains your monthly investment ($492/month) in a tax-deferred (if possible) account at a particular interest rate (e.g., a rate of 9%). Next, we do the broad asset class division—how much in equity and how much in fixed income (e.g., 60% equity (stocks), 40% fixed income).

> *Equity investing.* Becoming an owner or partial owner of a company or a piece of property through the purchase of investments such as individual stocks, stock mutual funds, and real estate.

We next break down the equity and fixed income blocks further. In equities, we choose 50% stocks and 10% real estate. On the fixed income side, we choose 30% bonds and 10% money market. Moving down another block, we get more specific. On the equity side, we select 30% in a large company stock fund, 10% in a small company stock fund, 10% in an international stock fund, and 10% in a real estate fund. On the fixed income side, we select 10% short-term bonds or bond funds, 10% intermediate-term bonds or bond funds,

10% GNMA funds, and 10% in money market funds. The final step of the process is to actually identify the specific mutual funds (or individual securities) for each asset class. Notice that various investment strategies form the base of the pyramid—all of which were discussed earlier. Exercise IV-2 (page 108) will allow you to draw out your own investment portfolio.

Table IV-1 gives you some other estimates of what you would need, depending on your age, to set aside to reach a goal of $500,000 by age 65, assuming a 9% average annual rate of return. For example, at age 40, you would have to deposit a lump sum of $57,984 or make monthly investments of $492 to accumulate this nest egg. For simplicity, taxes are excluded from this illustration.

TABLE IV-1

Amount Required to Have a $500,000 Retirement Fund @ 9%

Years to age 65	Your age	Lump-sum amount ($)	Monthly investment amount ($/mo.)
40	25	15,918	123
35	30	24,493	193
30	35	37,685	306
25	40	57,984	492
20	45	89,215	814
15	50	137,269	1,419
10	55	211,205	2,743

Index funds could be used as a core of your investment portfolio in each category because of their low expenses. You could then add additional actively managed funds to complement them.

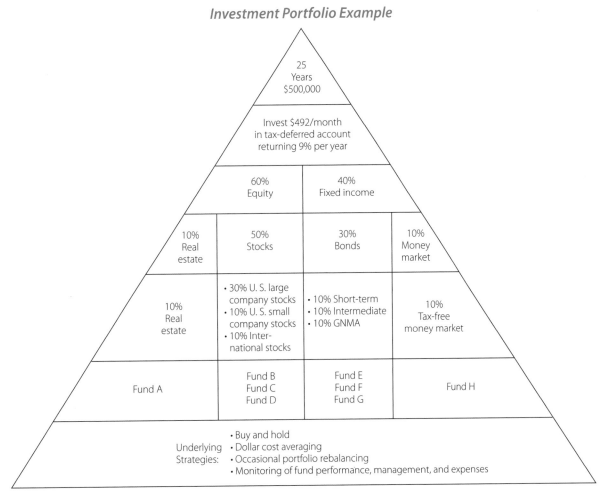

Investment Portfolio Example

25
Years
$500,000

Invest $492/month
in tax-deferred account
returning 9% per year

| 60%
Equity | 40%
Fixed income |

| 10%
Real
estate | 50%
Stocks | 30%
Bonds | 10%
Money
market |

| 10%
Real
estate | • 30% U. S. large
company stocks
• 10% U. S. small
company stocks
• 10% Inter-
national stocks | • 10% Short-term
• 10% Intermediate
• 10% GNMA | 10%
Tax-free
money market |

| Fund A | Fund B
Fund C
Fund D | Fund E
Fund F
Fund G | Fund H |

Underlying
Strategies:
• Buy and hold
• Dollar cost averaging
• Occasional portfolio rebalancing
• Monitoring of fund performance, management, and expenses

Adapted from: Taylor, J. (1993). *Building Wealth with Mutual Funds.*

Core investment. The foundation of a portfolio (e.g., a stock index fund) to which an investor might add additional securities.

Index funds track a specific market index such as the Standard & Poor's 500. Actively managed funds provide the opportunity to outperform the market and to, therefore, potentially raise your investment returns. You can make investing very simple and just choose index funds in each category and at least be assured of market-matching returns (minus expenses). This is a more conservative approach than choosing actively managed funds.

If you choose to combine index funds and actively managed funds, here's one way you could build a portfolio. The percentages in Table IV-2 are merely guidelines.

TABLE IV-2

Portfolio Illustration

Component	Large-cap stock funds	Small-cap stock funds	International stock funds	Real estate
Core	70% index funds	50% index	40% index	50% index
Beyond	30% actively managed	50% active	60% active	50% active

Table IV-3 shows what the above proportions would look like in dollars. Suppose you had $10,000 to invest. Let's say you want 60% of your money in stock mutual funds, 30% in bond mutual funds, and 10% in

TABLE IV-3

Stock Portion of Portfolio

Type of fund	Total for this class of fund (%)	Equivalent amount ($)	Index/ nonindex (%/%)	Equivalent amount ($/$)
Large-cap	30	3,000	70/30	2,100/900
Small-cap	10	1,000	50/50	500/500
International	15	1,500	40/60	600/900
Real estate	5	500	50/50	250/250

money market (cash) funds. The cash portion would be $1,000, and the bond portion would be $3,000. The remaining $6,000 would be divided between index and actively managed funds according to the guidelines in the previous table.

To summarize, build a core with one broad-based index fund each in the large-cap, small-cap, international, and real estate (optional) categories. Add to these no more than two actively managed funds in each stock asset class. In the fixed-income area, choose short- and intermediate-term index funds, plus an actively managed low expense fund (e.g., GNMA fund). Throw in a money market fund, and your portfolio is complete.

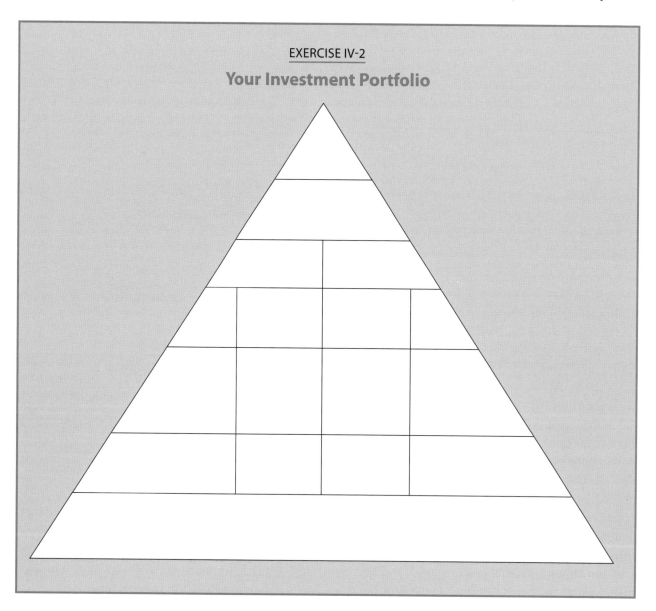

EXERCISE IV-2

Your Investment Portfolio

Investment Returns

An investment gain or loss is referred to as the **return**. This may include the receipt of income (interest, dividends, or rent) or capital gains. The combination of income and capital gains or losses is the **total return** from an investment.

Obviously, if the value of an investment has fallen, a negative rate of return may result (depending upon whether income received from the investment exceeds the loss in value). However, if an investor doesn't actually sell or liquidate the investment (rather, she holds on to it) and the value of the investment goes down, the loss may only be a "paper" one because the value may rise again before she sells it.

Most investors measure return on a "yield" or "rate of return" basis—that is, as a percentage of the amount invested on an annualized basis—rather than in dollars. That way, you can compare the yields on different investments and find out how much you earned per dollar invested. Remember that the rate of inflation and your tax bracket reduce the rate of return on any investment.

Minimum Rate of Return (RR)

You can estimate the minimum rate of return (RR) you need to break even with inflation and federal taxes.

Divide the inflation rate by 1 minus your marginal tax bracket (the tax rate you would pay on the last dollar of income earned) expressed as a decimal. For example, imagine that the inflation rate is 4% and you are in the 25% marginal tax bracket.

$$RR = \frac{.04}{1 - .25} = 0.053 \text{ or } 5.3\%$$

The minimum rate of return needed to break even is 5.3%. In the 15% bracket, the rate needed with a 4% rate is 4.7% (.04 ÷ (1 − .15)).

Table IV-4 lists the marginal tax rates for 2009. Table IV-5 will give you an idea of what type of return you will need to achieve to at least keep up with inflation and taxes depending on your own marginal tax rate at various inflation rates. For annual marginal tax bracket updates, see http://njaes.rutgers.edu/money/taxinfo/.

TABLE IV-4

Individual Tax Rate Schedules for 2009

	Taxable income ($)	Marginal tax bracket rate (%)
Married filing jointly	0–16,700	10
	16,701–67,900	15
	67,901–137,050	25
	137,051–208,850	28
	208,851–372,950	33
	over $372,950	35
Head of household	0–11,950	10
	11,951–45,500	15
	45,501–117,450	25
	117,451–190,200	28
	190,201–372,950	33
	over 372,950	35
Single	0–8,350	10
	8,351–33,950	15
	33,951–82,250	25
	82,251–171,550	28
	171,551–372,950	33
	over $372,950	35
Married filing separately	0–8,350	10
	8,351–33,950	15
	33,951–68,525	25
	68,526–104,425	28
	104,426–186,475	33
	over 186,475	35

TABLE IV-5

The Challenge of Earning a Break-Even Rate of Return

If inflation is this much (%)	You must earn this much (%) to break even after inflation & federal taxes		
	Marginal income tax rate		
	15%	25%	28%
0	0.0	0.0	0.0
3	3.5	4.0	4.2
4	4.7	5.3	5.6
5	5.9	6.6	6.9
6	7.1	8.0	8.3
7	8.2	9.3	9.7
8	9.4	10.7	11.1
9	10.6	12.0	12.5
10	11.8	13.3	13.9

Rules of 72 and 115

Want to double your money? Triple your money? Of course you do. Can anyone show you how to do it? Of course they can't. However, with the Rule of 72, you can calculate how long it will take for your investments to double. The Rule of 72 assumes that your investments are tax-deferred and earning compound interest.

$$72 \div \begin{array}{c} \text{Rate of return} \\ \text{you receive} \\ \text{per year} \end{array} = \begin{array}{c} \text{Number of years} \\ \text{for your money} \\ \text{to double} \end{array}$$

Let's put this formula to work. If you have a 9% investment return, your money will double in 8 years—72 divided by 9.

$$\text{Rate of return } 9\% \overline{\left) \frac{\text{8 years to double}}{72} \right.}$$

Maybe you would rather do more than double your money. You'd prefer to triple it. Let's move on to the Rule of 115. Instead of using the number 72, use the number 115. Now the money you have invested at 9% will triple in 12.8 years (115 ÷ 9 = 12.8 years).

$$\text{Rate of return } 9\% \overline{\left) \frac{\text{12.8 years to triple}}{115} \right.}$$

Rates of return on both are examples only and are not meant to represent any specific investments.

These formulas can't guide you to investments that pay you the rate of interest you need, but they can at least tell you at what rate you need to invest your money to double or triple it within a certain time frame. However, whether an investment can double or triple your money is of less importance than the safety and the appropriateness of the investment.

Determining Your "Real" Return

When a mutual fund touts its performance from last year, it is saying how the fund did, not how you did in the fund. There's a difference. Calculating your precise personal rate of return is difficult, but not impossible. It's the kind of data a financial advisor should provide (although not all do). In any case, you can also estimate your personal return using a reasonably simple formula. An example is given below, followed by a worksheet (Exercise IV-3) to help you determine your own real return.

Here's what you will need:

- the balance in your account (or portfolio) at the start of the year.
- the value of that account, including any dividends, capital gains, or interest that you took in cash, at year's end.
- the total value of additional investments made during the year (e.g., biweekly 401(k) plan contributions).
- a calculator.

Now, put that calculator through the following paces.

Step 1) Write down the beginning balance of your portfolio at the start of the year and your ending balance at year's end.

Step 2) Add to your beginning balance one-half of your total additional investments.

Step 3) Subtract from your ending balance one-half of your total additions over the year.

Step 4) Divide the result in Step 3 by the result in Step 2.

Step 5) To turn the number into a percentage, subtract 1 and multiply by 100.

Estimating Your Return
Using Simple Arithmetic

Invest $200 per month or $2,400 over the year.

Step 1

    January 1—Account balance $15,368
    December 31—Account balance $19,627

Step 2

	$15,368	Beginning balance
Add	$ 1,200	½ of $2,400 added
	$16,568	

Step 3

	$19,627	Ending balance
Subtract	$ 1,200	½ of $2,400 added
	$18,427	

Step 4

$$\frac{\$18,427}{\$16,568} = 1.11$$

Step 5

To turn the number into a percentage, subtract 1 and multiply by 100. The return in this example is 11.1%.

EXERCISE IV-3

Estimating Your Investment Return

Step 1

Write down the beginning balance of your portfolio at the start of the year and your ending balance at year's end.

  $_____   Beginning account balance

  $_____   Ending account balance

Step 2

Add to your beginning balance one-half of your total additional investments during the year.

    $_____   Beginning balance

+ $_____   Add ½ of additions made
                       to the account over the year

= $_____

Step 3

Subtract from your ending balance one-half of your total additions over the year.

    $_____   Ending balance

− $_____   Subtract ½ of additions made to
                       the account over the year

= $_____

Step 4

Divide the result in Step 3 by the result in Step 2.

    $_____   Result of Step 3

÷ $_____   Result of Step 2

= $_____

Step 5

To turn the number into a percentage, subtract 1 and multiply by 100.

_____ %

Your Minimum "Need to Knows" about
Asset Allocation, Diversification, and Investment Returns

- Asset allocation is the biggest factor in determining your overall return. Choose your asset allocation carefully.

- Select investments based on your age, income, job security, marital status, tolerance for risk, and the general economic conditions of the country.

- Consider investing primarily for growth if you are in your prime earning years.

- Have a healthy sense of caution when investing, but don't be paralyzed by fear. Time and experience will help.

- Evaluate your investment returns annually.

- Reevaluate your investment strategies periodically to see if they're keeping you on the path to your goals.

Taking the Guesswork out of Retirement

We all have a certain number of days until retirement. That number will be different for each person.

If you are like many people, retirement is always something you put off thinking about until tomorrow. But sooner than you think, tomorrow will be today. You could be in for a rude awakening if you wait until the last few years of work to plan for retirement.

These are some of the harsh realities:

- Americans aren't saving enough. Our personal savings rate in the United States today is less than 1–2% of our income.

- Baby Boomers, the largest population group in U.S. history, are starting to retire, further straining the Social Security system.

- Most experts agree you'll need between 70 and 100% of your preretirement income to retire comfortably.

- Social Security currently pays average 65-year-olds 25–40% of what they will actually need to maintain their preretirement lifestyle.

- People are living longer. Although you'll likely have more years of retirement to enjoy, you'll also have to pay for those extra years.

You can't control the passing of time, but you can take action when it comes to planning for your financial future. To help you get started, complete Exercises IV-4 and IV-5.

Only 22,283 days until retirement.

EXERCISE IV-4

Draw Your Retirement Dreams

EXERCISE IV-5

How Much Money Will You Need for Retirement?

The preretirement planning decisions you make or don't make now will determine your ability to realize your retirement goals. Because you will probably live longer than you expect, proper financial planning now will determine the standard of living you will enjoy throughout your retired life.

How much money will you need for retirement?

This is a difficult but crucial question to ask. Because many factors must be considered, the answer is, "It depends." Answer the following questions to begin to formulate a retirement plan:

• What is your current age? _____

• At what age do you intend to retire? _____

• Do you plan to work during retirement? _____

• How many years might you live in retirement? (How long might you live?) _____

• How much are you currently earning? _____

• What will be your main source of income during retirement? _____

• How much money do you need (or want) to spend each month in retirement to achieve your goals and maintain your lifestyle? _____

• How much have you already accumulated in employer benefits? _____

• How much have you already saved or invested for retirement? _____

• How comfortable are you taking risks with your investment dollars? _____

• How many people must you support (financially) now and in the future? _____

Adapted with permission from: Dahl, B. (1996). *A Working Woman's Guide to Financial Security.* Urbana, Ill.: University of Illinois Cooperative Extension. © Board of Trustees of the University of Illinois.

Steps to Successful Retirement Planning

You will feel a sense of control over the retirement process if you follow these financial planning steps:

• identify and set preretirement and postretirement goals.
• estimate the length of your retirement.
• determine your net worth.
• estimate your retirement expenses.
• estimate your retirement income.
• balance expenses and income.

• plan for the effects of inflation.
• evaluate and revise your plan.

Identify and Set Goals

Putting realistic, attainable goals in writing will help crystallize your thoughts about what you want your money to do for you in retirement. The more specific you can make your goals, the more likely you are to be committed to them. Your goals may change, and that's OK.

Take a few minutes now to think ahead, prioritize your goals, and complete Exercise IV-6. You may wish

EXERCISE IV-6

Looking Ahead to Retirement

(Consider your answers from the previous exercise.)

	Example	Your situation
Your age today	42	
Age you plan to retire	62	
Number of years until retirement	20	
Where do you plan to live?	Madison, same home.	
Will you work part-time?	Yes	
What hobbies/activities will you do in your free time?	Volunteer at library, church choir,	
Will you be caring for any family members?	Don't know.	
Goals to accomplish before retiring	Pay off mortgage. Buy a new car. Have $100,000 in savings/investments. Finish B.A. degree.	
Goals to accomplish after retiring	Trip for two to Ireland. Minor kitchen remodeling. Start part-time business.	

Adapted with permission from: Dahl, B. (1996). *A Working Woman's Guide to Financial Security.* Urbana, Ill.: University of Illinois Cooperative Extension. ©Board of Trustees of the University of Illinois.

to review your goals each year when you complete your annual review.

How Long Will You Live?

There was a time when you weren't expected to live much past your 65th birthday. Now studies show that by 2015, 5% of the population will live to 100+ years. Therefore, to be safe, most women should plan for a retirement period of 30–40 years (age 95).

If you retire at age 65, will you be able to maintain your current standard of living for another 30 years based on what you plan to receive in employee retirement and Social Security benefits and what you have already saved?

Determine Your Net Worth

This was done as part of Session I and should be updated and evaluated each year.

How Will Your Spending Plan Change in Retirement?

Some expenses in retirement *may be lower* than in preretirement:

- Housing costs could decrease as home equity loans and mortgages are paid off.
- Work-related expenses such as lunches away from home, union or professional dues, transportation, and wardrobe maintenance are reduced.
- Educational expenses for children are paid.
- Most large household improvements and home furnishings expenses are decreased.
- Deductions for Social Security and contributions to a pension plan cease.
- Savings and investments usually decrease but hopefully do not stop.
- Disability insurance will no longer be needed, and you may choose to stop life insurance payments.
- Discounts are available for a lot of goods and services after age 55, 60, 62, or 65.
- Federal and state income taxes are lower if you are living on less.

Some expenses *may remain the same* or perhaps decrease in retirement:

- Food prepared at home
- Personal care
- Automobile expenses, including insurance
- Utilities
- Homeowner's/renter's insurance (if you move)
- Taxes (Some states don't tax pension benefits.)

Other expenses *may increase* when you retire:

- Medical and dental expenses and health insurance premiums
- Long-term care expenses
- If you're taking early retirement (before age 65), you will need to purchase medical and dental insurance. The cost for this period, until age 65, when Medicare begins, may well be $6,000 to $10,000 or more per year.
- Expenditures for leisure, travel, and entertainment may increase, especially in early retirement years.

Anticipating Your Costs of Retirement Living

To know how much money you will need during retirement, estimate your anticipated expenses. Base this estimate on your current living expenses. Most people want a standard of living in retirement similar to their preretirement level. A written spending plan and record of household expenses gives important information for projecting retirement living costs. Use Exercise IV-7, *Estimated Cost of Living,* on pages 118–119 to indicate your costs now and after retirement.

- Enter your current expenses for each category in the "Now" column. Annual, semiannual, and quarterly expenses should be broken down into monthly amounts.
- Decide if you will spend less, the same, or more in each category after retirement. This will be simple to do if you decide to remain in the same home you lived in before retirement since many of your expenses will remain the same.
- If you think the expense will increase or decrease, put the new amount in the "After Retirement" column based on the approximate dollar amount in today's dollars.

Where Will You Get Your Retirement Income?

Traditionally, retirement funds came from what is called the three-legged stool: *Social Security, employer-sponsored plans,* and *personal savings and investments.* Unfortunately, many women's "stools" aren't supported by three strong legs or, in some cases, even by two.

LEG 1—Social Security

Social Security is the foundation of most women's retirement income. This leg is paid for in equal amounts by both you and your employer if you are an employee and totally by you if you are self-employed.

Your eligibility for Social Security benefits is generally based on your lifetime earnings record (or your spouse's earnings record) and your age. Eligibility for Social Security benefits requires meeting the work requirement yourself or being married for at least 10 years to someone

Age	Annual limit*	Reduction
< full retirement age	$14,160	$1 for every $2 earned
> full retirement age	none	none

* 2009 limit. The Social Security earnings limit is adjusted annually for inflation. Consult www.ssa.gov for current information.

A special earnings limit calculation is done for the year in which a person reaches full retirement age. Benefits are permanently reduced when received between age 62 and full retirement age.

- Social Security retirement rules have changed for people born after 1937. Full retirement age increases in 2-month increments until it reaches 67 for people born in 1960 and later, as Table IV-6 shows.

TABLE IV-6

Full Retirement Age Depends on Year of Birth

Year of birth	Full retirement age
1937 or earlier	65
1938	65 and 2 months
1939	65 and 4 months
1940	65 and 6 months
1941	65 and 8 months
1942	65 and 10 months
1943–1954	66
1955	66 and 2 months
1956	66 and 4 months
1957	66 and 6 months
1958	66 and 8 months
1959	66 and 10 months
1960 and later	67

Adapted from: *Social Security Retirement Benefits* (2003). Social Security Administration, Publication No. 05-10035.

Retirement Income Sources

- The government: Social Security, federal and state pensions, veteran's benefits.
- Your employer: pension, profit-sharing, and tax-deferred savings plans.
- Your savings and investments: individual retirement accounts (IRAs), Keoghs, SEPs (retirement plans for self-employed workers), insurance, stocks, bonds, mutual funds, money market accounts or funds, rental real estate, savings accounts, commissions, fees, or business income.
- Your assets: your home, vehicles, collections (coins, art, and antiques) when sold, anticipated gifts and/or inheritances.
- Additional earnings: full- or part-time employment after you and/or your spouse retire.

---

who does. If you are older than 25, have paid into Social Security, and are not currently receiving benefits, you will annually receive a Social Security benefit estimate about 2–3 months prior to your birth date. Reviewing this statement every year helps ensure its accuracy.

Currently, the average retiree receives under $14,000 per year and relies on Social Security for more than 40% of his or her income.

The approximately top third of retirees and retired couples, those with $32,000 or more in annual income, depend far less on Social Security—it is about a quarter of their income.

Some points to consider:

- Employed women who are married, widowed, or divorced after at least 10 years of marriage are said to be "dually entitled" and are eligible to collect Social Security benefits on the higher of their own work record or their husband's. Many receive higher benefits based on their husband's (rather than their own) records. Just under half of dually entitled women draw benefits based on their own work record.
- Earned income in retirement may reduce your Social Security benefits.

Estimated Cost of Living

	Now per month	Expected change in retirement (+ or –)	After retirement per month
Housing			
Electricity, heat (gas or oil)	_____	_____	_____
Floor covering, window treatments	_____	_____	_____
Furniture, appliances	_____	_____	_____
House cleaning, repair, yard care	_____	_____	_____
Internet service provider	_____	_____	_____
Phone, cellular phone	_____	_____	_____
Property taxes	_____	_____	_____
Rent or mortgage payments	_____	_____	_____
Water, sewer, garbage, recycling	_____	_____	_____
Insurance			
Automobile	_____	_____	_____
Disability	_____	_____	_____
Flood	_____	_____	_____
Health	_____	_____	_____
Homeowner's or renter's	_____	_____	_____
Life	_____	_____	_____
Long-term care	_____	_____	_____
Umbrella liability	_____	_____	_____
Transportation			
Bus/taxi/train/tolls/parking	_____	_____	_____
Gasoline	_____	_____	_____
License and vehicle registration	_____	_____	_____
Maintenance and repairs	_____	_____	_____
Monthly car payment(s)	_____	_____	_____
Clothing			
Clothing for entire household	_____	_____	_____
Laundry/dry cleaning	_____	_____	_____

Adapted with permission from: Dahl, B. (1996). *A Working Woman's Guide to Financial Security*. Urbana, Ill.: University of Illinois Cooperative Extension. ©Board of Trustees of the University of Illinois.

	Now per month	Expected change in retirement (+ or −)	After retirement per month
Food			
At home (groceries)	_____	_____	_____
Away from home	_____	_____	_____
Entertainment			
Cable TV, computer	_____	_____	_____
Memberships/dues	_____	_____	_____
Music, movies	_____	_____	_____
Sports	_____	_____	_____
Vacations, trips	_____	_____	_____
Donations			
Charitable/political	_____	_____	_____
Gifts	_____	_____	_____
Religious	_____	_____	_____
Savings, investments			
Banks, credit unions, money market funds	_____	_____	_____
Employer retirement plans:			
Profit sharing, 401(k)s, 403(b)s	_____	_____	_____
Investments (taxable)	_____	_____	_____
Retirement: IRA, Keogh, SEP	_____	_____	_____
Health care			
Deductibles/copayments	_____	_____	_____
Eye glasses, hearing aids	_____	_____	_____
Medications	_____	_____	_____
Physicians, dentists	_____	_____	_____
Taxes			
Federal income tax	_____	_____	_____
Social Security (FICA)	_____	_____	_____
State income tax	_____	_____	_____
Other	_____	_____	_____
	_____	_____	_____
Total expenses	$_____	$_____	$_____

LEG 2—Pensions

Pension plans are usually either a **defined benefit plan** that guarantees a specified monthly amount that often is not adjusted for inflation, **OR**, a **defined contribution plan** that grows tax-deferred but does not guarantee a specific retirement benefit. The latter type of plan is typically paid to the employee in a lump sum upon retirement.

Some points to consider:

- The pension leg of the stool is missing for many women. You are more likely to have a defined benefit employer-provided pension if you work for a local, state, or federal government, a large company, or one that is unionized.
- The trend today is toward defined contribution plans that specify the amount of money employees can contribute annually to an employee

---

Major Types of Defined Contribution Plans

- **401(k) plans** (offered through corporations), **403(b) plans** (offered through nonprofit organizations), and **Section 457 plans** (offered through state and local governments)—allow an employee to make tax-deferred contributions by reducing his or her salary by up to $16,500 ($22,000 if age 50 and over) in 2009.
- **Profit-sharing plans**—contributions depend on the company's profits, so employer contributions can vary from year to year.
- **Money purchase pension plans**—require an employer to contribute a certain amount yearly for each employee, generally a percentage of earnings.
- **Stock bonus plans**—require an employer to buy stock in the company on behalf of the employee. It is usually held in trust until retirement when the employee can receive the shares or sell them at their fair market value.

---

retirement account. These plans are not insured, but they are portable, that is, the money in the plan may be taken out when you leave a job. To avoid taxes, however, the money must be transferred to another employer's plan or to a rollover IRA.

- Your rights to benefits from an employer-sponsored retirement plan are defined by the vesting schedule.

> **Vesting.** Refers to the date when you are entitled to the money that your employer has contributed to your retirement account.

If your pension rights are not vested, you will get back only your own contributions plus the earnings on them. If you are fully vested because you have worked at least the required number of years for your employer, you probably will be eligible for full benefits. Be sure to check your employer's vesting schedule.

LEG 3—Savings and Investments

Even if you receive benefits from Social Security and an employer-sponsored retirement plan, your stool will have only two legs and you will probably not have enough income to live comfortably at your preretirement level. Your personal retirement savings program should be the strongest leg on your stool because it supports the other two. Besides employer plans, you may also have private savings sources such as IRAs, Keoghs, SEPs, and annuities. These are the types of plans that YOU originate and control. You may also have other investments in taxable accounts.

Few people find it easy to save for retirement. Many people have trouble putting away money that they won't use for 20 years or more. Many women find it difficult to save because current needs consume most or all of their income and unexpected emergencies frequently occur. Every dollar set aside today can more than double, or even quadruple, if it can grow tax-deferred or is invested wisely.

Use Exercise IV-8, *Estimating Your Retirement Income*, to review all the sources of money to determine what your potential retirement income will be.

Estimating Your Retirement Income

		Monthly income ($)	Annual income ($)
Government benefits	Federal, state, and/or municipal government pension	_____	_____
	Social Security	_____	_____
	Social Security on your spouse's or former spouse's earnings or widow's benefit	_____	_____
	Veteran's benefits	_____	_____
Employer benefits	401(k), 403(b), or Section 457 plans	_____	_____
	Company pension plan(s)	_____	_____
	Profit sharing	_____	_____
	Stock purchase/ownership plan	_____	_____
Individual savings and investment income	Annuities (income)	_____	_____
	Bonds (dividends)	_____	_____
	Certificates of deposit (interest)	_____	_____
	IRA	_____	_____
	Money markets (interest)	_____	_____
	Mutual funds (dividends, capital gains)	_____	_____
	Pension/annuity from former spouse	_____	_____
	Savings accounts (interest)	_____	_____
	Stocks (dividends)	_____	_____
	Treasury securities	_____	_____
Your earnings	Commissions, royalties, consultant fees	_____	_____
	Salary, wages, tips	_____	_____
Other	_____	_____	_____
	_____	_____	_____
	Total estimated income	_____	_____

Make Sure You'll Reach Your Goal

To determine whether or not you are on track to reach your retirement plan goals, you need to find out if you have a "retirement income gap"—the difference between how much you estimate you need in retirement and how much you'll actually have, based on current savings, pension, and Social Security resources. The last thing you want to discover after you retire is that you don't have enough money. Too many people learn too late that the only available solution is to keep working. Contact your human resources/benefits office at work to get a pension estimate and the local Social Security office for the *Request for Earnings and Benefits Estimate Statement*. (Note: This form is also sent automatically prior to your birthday each year until you're 65.)

Use this information to complete the *Ballpark Estimate* worksheet (Exercise IV-9). This form is also available on the American Savings Education Council's Web site at www.asec.org and can be completed online.

This exercise simplifies issues that seem complicated, such as the future value of current savings, and can be completed with a calculator in a matter of minutes. *The Ballpark Estimate* assumes that you'll realize a constant real (after inflation) return of 3%.

Jonathan Pond, financial planner and author, has counseled "conservatively speaking, your retirement savings should be equal to between 20 and 25 times your [individual or combined (if married)] pretax income (your shortfall after Social Security and pension) in your first year of retirement."

David Bach, in *Smart Women Finish Rich,* argues that if the experts say that everyone (but they really mean men) should be putting away 10% of their pretax income for retirement, that's not necessarily good enough for women. After all, women live longer than men, and as a result, need to put more away for retirement. If women's retirements tend to last 20% longer than mens', then women's nest eggs need to be 20% larger. In other words, as a woman, you should be saving 12% of your annual gross income.

Further analysis to determine how much you need to save for retirement can be done either by using computer software from sources such as T. Rowe Price, Fidelity, and Vanguard or by consulting a financial professional.

Balance Your Expenses and Your Income

Now that you know what your anticipated income and your retirement expenses might be, you may have discovered there is more anticipated expense than income. Don't give up. You have several alternatives to help close the gap.

Save more money. Surveys show that most American workers know their retirement savings and investments will not be enough to provide a comfortable retirement. Use Exercise IV-10 on page 126 to see how an extra $10 a month will grow. If you can save more, multiply the result by $10 units.

Increase your income. By working overtime or taking a part-time job in addition to your full-time job, you can add to your savings program. You might wish to work part-time after retirement.

Boost your retirement contributions. Completely fund your IRA each year and contribute as much as possible to tax-deferred programs such as 401(k)s, 403(b)s, Keoghs, or SEPs. Automatic deductions from your paycheck make it easier to save. Try to max out your contributions limitation, e.g., $16,500 in 2009, to a 401(k), or at least up to your employer's match. If you are already doing that, then kick your contribution up 1% more, especially after receiving a raise.

One percent of a $35,000 salary, for example, is $350. According to the investing tool the *401(k) Booster Calculator,* produced by Advantage Publications, for a 40-year-old with 25 years to go to retirement, this would mean $39,474 of additional savings at age 65, assuming an 8% average return and 4% average annual pay increases.

Put off retirement. By delaying retirement, you will build additional Social Security, pension, and retirement plan benefits. You will also reduce the number of years you will have to provide for. For example, by working an extra 3 years and factoring in compound interest on your assets that are not being withdrawn,

Ballpark E$timate®

Planning for retirement is not a one-size-fits-all exercise. The purpose of *Ballpark* is simply to give you a basic idea of the savings you'll need when you retire. So let's play ball!

If you are married, you and your spouse should each fill out your own *Ballpark Estimate®* worksheet, taking your marital status into account when entering your Social Security benefit in number 2 below.

1. How much annual income will you want in retirement? (Figure at least 70% of your current annual gross income just to maintain your current standard of living; however, you may want to enter a larger number. See the tips to help you select a goal at www.choosetosave.org.) $_____

2. Subtract the income you expect to receive annually from:

• Social Security—If you make less than $25,000, enter $8,000; between $25,000 and $40,000, enter $12,000; over $40,000, enter $14,500. (For married couples—the lower-earning spouse should enter either their own benefit based on their income or 50% of the higher-earning spouse's benefit, whichever is higher.)

For a more personalized estimate, enter the appropriate benefit figure from your Social Security statement from the Social Security Administration (1-800-772-1213, www.ssa.gov). *Ballpark* assumes you will begin receiving Social Security benefits at age 65, however, the age for full benefits is rising to 67. Your Social Security statement will provide a personalized benefit estimate based on your actual earning history.   – $_____

• Traditional employer pension—a plan that pays a set dollar amount for life, where the dollar amount depends on salary and years of service (in today's dollars)   .– $_____

• Part-time income   – $_____

• Other (reverse annuity mortgage payments, earnings on assets, etc.)   – $_____

This is how much you need to make up for each retirement year: = $_____

Now you want a ballpark estimate of how much money you'll need in the bank the day you retire. So the accountants went to work and devised this simple formula. For the record, they figure you'll realize a constant real rate of return of 3% after inflation, you'll live to age 87, and you'll begin to receive income from Social Security at age 65. If you anticipate living longer than age 87 or earning less than 3% real rate of return on your savings, you'll want to consider using a higher percentage of your current annual gross income as a goal on line 1.

3. To determine the amount you'll need to save, multiply the amount you need to make up by the factor below. $_____

Age you expect to retire	Choose your factor based on life expectancy (at age 65):					
	Male, 50th percentile (age 82)	Femaile, 50th percentile (age 86)	Male, 75th percentile (age 89)	Female, 75th percentile (age 92)	Male, 90th percentile (age 94)	Female, 90th percentile (age 97)
55	18.79	20.53	21.71	22.79	23.46	24.40
60	16.31	18.32	19.68	20.93	21.71	22.27
65	13.45	15.77	17.35	18.79	19.68	20.93
70	10.15	12.83	14.65	16.31	17.35	18.79

Ballpark E$timate®

(continued)

4. If you expect to retire before age 65, multiply your Social Security benefit from line 2 by the factor below.   + $_____

Age you expect to retire:	55	Your factor is:	8.8
	60		4.7

5. Multiply your savings to date by the factor below (include money accumulated in a 401(k), IRA, or similar retirement plan).   – $_____

If you want to retire in	10 years	Your factor is:	1.3
	15 years		1.6
	20 years		1.8
	25 years		2.1
	30 years		2.4
	35 years		2.8
	40 years		3.3

Total additional savings needed at retirement: = $_____

Don't panic. Those same accountants devised another formula to show you how much to save each year in order to reach your goal amount. They factor in compounding. That's where your money not only makes interest, your interest starts making interest as well, creating a snowball effect.

6. To determine the ANNUAL amount you'll need to save, multiply the TOTAL amount by the factor below.   = $_____

If you want to retire in	10 years	Your factor is:	.085
	15 years		.052
	20 years		.036
	25 years		.027
	30 years		.020
	35 years		.016
	40 years		.013

See? It's not impossible or even particularly painful. It just takes planning. And the sooner you start, the better off you'll be.

The *Ballpark Estimate®* is designed to provide a rough estimate of what you will need to save annually to fund a comfortable retirement. It provides an approximation of projected Social Security benefits and utilizes only one of many possible rates of return on your savings. *Ballpark* reflects today's dollars and does not account for inflation; therefore, you should recalculate your savings needs on a regular basis and as your salary and circumstances change. You don't want to stop with the *Ballpark Estimate®*; it is only a first step in the retirement planning process. You will need to do further analysis, either yourself using a more detailed worksheet or computer software, or with the assistance of a financial professional.

Reprinted with the permission of the American Savings Education Council, www.asec.org   Revised 10/05

your nest egg might be able to last another 7–10 years, depending on the rates of return and withdrawal.

Cut down on retirement expenses. You may decide to move to a smaller home or apartment or to relocate to a less expensive part of the country. Reevaluate keeping your life insurance, particularly if your mortgage is repaid or nearly repaid and the children are out of the house and nobody is financially dependent on you.

Tap into your home equity (the value of your home minus loans against it). Sell your existing home and purchase a smaller, less expensive home and invest the proceeds or rent and invest the proceeds of the sale. Are you aware that a 1997 tax law allows you to take advantage of up to a $500,000 (if married), $250,000 (if single) capital gains tax break without any age restriction?

Another way to tap equity in a home is to consider a reverse mortgage, which will allow you to stay in your home and receive either a lump-sum payment, a line of credit, or periodic payments based on your home's equity, prevailing interest rates, and your life expectancy.

Earn a higher rate of return. The more you earn on your investments, the less you will need to accumulate. If you can earn even one or two extra percentage points per year both before and after retirement, it can have a sizable impact on the total assets that are accumulated.

For a more detailed description of retirement catch-up strategies, download the *Guidebook to Help Late Savers Prepare for Retirement* at http://www.smart-aboutmoney.org/.

Inflation, the Silent Thief

The expenses you calculated in Exercise IV-7 (pages 118–119) are based upon today's prices. But we all know that today's prices will not be accurate next year, and certainly not 5, 10, 20, or 30 years from now when you plan to retire.

Inflation, even if it is a low rate, will erode the value of your retirement savings. The longer the period you plan to be retired, the greater the potential erosion. Long-term projections are difficult to make but should still be attempted. Many of your financial decisions will be greatly affected by inflation.

To estimate your income needs at retirement more accurately, you need to:

- know how long it will be before you retire.
- estimate what the rate of inflation will be (the average from 1926–2007 was 3.1%).
- adjust your estimated expenses for different categories.
- begin with estimates based on current prices.

1. Choose the number of years until your retirement starts from the left-hand column of Table IV-7 (page 127).

2. Select an inflation rate from the row across the top of the table. Inflation cannot be predicted from year to year, so estimate an average annual rate.

3. Read across and down to find the appropriate inflation factor corresponding to your predicted rate of inflation (for example, 10 years at 4% inflation yields a factor of 1.48).

4. Refer back to Exercise IV-7 (pages 118–119). Multiply your answer for total monthly expenses by the inflation adjustment factor to get an idea of how much you will need for your living expenses in the first year of retirement, taking inflation into account.

How $10 a Month Will Grow

Number of years	Interest rate earned						
	4%	5%	6%	7%	8%	9%	10%
1	$122	$123	$124	$125	$125	$126	$127
2	249	253	256	258	261	264	267
3	382	389	395	402	408	415	421
4	520	532	544	555	567	580	592
5	663	683	701	720	740	760	781
6	812	841	868	897	926	957	989
7	968	1,008	1,046	1,086	1,129	1,173	1,220
8	1,129	1,182	1,234	1,289	1,348	1,409	1,474
9	1,297	1,366	1,435	1,507	1,585	1,667	1,755
10	1,472	1,559	1,647	1,741	1,842	1,950	2,066
15	2,461	2,684	2,923	3,188	3,483	3,812	4,179
20	3,668	4,128	4,644	5,240	5,929	6,729	7,657
25	5,152	5,980	6,965	8,148	9,574	11,295	13,379
30	6,940	8,357	10,095	12,271	15,003	18,445	22,793

Adapted from: Matejic, D., and Pankow, D. (1995). *How to Save $1,000 or More a Year.* Rutgers Cooperative Extension. http://njaes.rutgers.edu/pubs/publication.asp?pid=FS539

Once you have studied the table above, use it to answer the following questions:

1. How much can I set aside each month? $ _____

2. What is my investment time frame?   _____ years

3. What rate of return do I expect to earn?   _____ %

4. How much money will I have in the future? $ _____

TABLE IV-7

Inflation Factors

Years to retirement	Annual rate of inflation									
	3%	4%	5%	6%	7%	8%	9%	10%	11%	12%
1	1.03	1.04	1.05	1.06	1.07	1.08	1.09	1.10	1.11	1.12
2	1.06	1.08	1.10	1.12	1.15	1.17	1.19	1.21	1.23	1.25
3	1.09	1.13	1.16	1.19	1.23	1.26	1.30	1.33	1.37	1.41
4	1.13	1.17	1.22	1.26	1.31	1.36	1.41	1.46	1.52	1.57
5	1.16	1.22	1.28	1.34	1.40	1.47	1.54	1.61	1.69	1.76
6	1.19	1.27	1.34	1.42	1.50	1.59	1.68	1.77	1.87	1.97
7	1.23	1.32	1.41	1.50	1.61	1.71	1.83	1.95	2.08	2.21
8	1.27	1.37	1.48	1.59	1.72	1.85	1.99	2.14	2.30	2.48
9	1.31	1.42	1.55	1.69	1.84	2.00	2.17	2.36	2.56	2.77
10	1.34	1.48	1.63	1.79	1.97	2.16	2.37	2.59	2.84	3.11
11	1.38	1.54	1.71	1.90	2.11	2.33	2.58	2.85	3.15	3.48
12	1.43	1.60	1.80	2.01	2.25	2.52	2.81	3.14	3.50	3.90
13	1.47	1.67	1.89	2.13	2.41	2.72	3.07	3.45	3.88	4.36
14	1.51	1.73	1.98	2.26	2.58	2.94	3.34	3.80	4.31	4.89
15	1.56	1.80	2.08	2.40	2.76	3.17	3.64	4.18	4.78	5.47
16	1.61	1.87	2.18	2.54	2.95	3.43	3.97	4.60	5.31	6.13
17	1.65	1.95	2.29	2.69	3.16	3.70	4.33	5.05	5.90	6.87
18	1.70	2.03	2.41	2.85	3.38	4.00	4.72	5.56	6.54	7.69
19	1.75	2.11	2.53	3.03	3.62	4.32	5.14	6.12	7.26	8.61
20	1.81	2.19	2.65	3.21	3.87	4.66	5.60	6.73	8.06	9.65
21	1.86	2.28	2.79	3.40	4.14	5.03	6.02	7.40	8.95	10.80
22	1.92	2.37	2.93	3.60	4.43	5.44	6.66	8.14	9.93	12.10
23	1.97	2.47	3.07	3.82	4.74	5.87	7.26	8.95	11.03	13.55
24	2.03	2.56	3.23	4.05	5.07	6.34	7.91	9.85	12.24	15.18
25	2.09	2.67	3.39	4.29	5.43	6.85	8.62	10.83	13.59	17.00
26	2.16	2.77	3.56	4.45	5.81	7.40	9.40	11.92	15.08	19.04
27	2.22	2.88	3.73	4.82	6.21	7.99	10.25	13.11	16.74	21.32
28	2.29	3.00	3.92	5.11	6.65	8.63	11.17	14.42	18.58	23.88
29	2.36	3.12	4.12	5.42	7.11	9.32	12.17	15.86	20.62	26.75
30	2.43	3.24	4.32	5.74	7.61	10.06	13.27	17.45	22.89	29.96

Example:
1. You would like to retire at age 63, 12 years from now.
2. You think the inflation rate will rise slowly and average about 4%.
3. 12 years at 4% = 1.60 inflation factor.
4. Your estimated retirement income of $20,400 x inflation factor of 1.60 = $32,640 income needed for the first year of retirement to live as you plan to.

10 Tips for Securing a Worry-Free Retirement

1. *Plan for inflation to be higher than you think, rather than lower.*

2. *Practice living on the income you expect to receive during retirement.* If you are saving/investing up to 20% of your income, you are already living at 80%.

3. *Live beneath your means.* Scale back your lifestyle now to make an easier adjustment later on. Make wise choices with your spending in favor of financial priorities. Remember that all the major purchases you make now will have retirement implications.

4. *"Pay yourself first" each payday.* Set aside at least 5% of your income, perhaps up to 20%. If money can be saved through payroll deductions or automatic investment plans, you won't see it or spend it. Think of saving and investing as your number-one financial obligation each month.

5. *Start planning and preparing early.* However, it's also never too late to get started.

6. *Save and invest wisely.* It's imperative that you keep ahead of inflation and shelter investment earnings from taxes, where possible.

7. *Explore career possibilities you can pursue later in life.* Many people have turned a hobby into a paying venture.

8. *Mentally prepare yourself for retirement.* Assess your goals and values and relate them to how you would like to live. Think about possibly relocating as you travel to different areas of the country.

9. *Carefully analyze early retirement incentive plans* if you don't have substantial savings and investments to rely on. Always compare the offer to what you could receive if you stayed until age 62 or 65. Seek professional help before making a decision.

10. *Stay invested.* Experts agree that while many of us can remember individual days in which the market moved wildly up or down, over the long term, it tends to rise. Historical data indicate that staying invested—riding out those highs and lows—is a valid long-term strategy. Market timing does not work. So the solution is "stay the course." It's a time-proven investment strategy.

Your Minimum "Need to Knows" about Planning for Retirement

- Women generally live longer than men, but many have far less money in retirement.

- Your preretirement decisions will affect your ability to realize your retirement goals.

- Social Security will probably still be there when you retire, but it will cover only 25–40% of your retirement needs.

- Your retirement income will come from a number of sources: the government, your employer, your savings and investments, and possibly, full- or part-time employment.

- Even a low rate of inflation will erode the value of your retirement nest egg.

- Traditional company pensions are rare—today you must manage your own pension, e.g., employer 401(k) and 403(b) plans.

- Always make the maximum allowable contributions to retirement plans if you can. It will make a big difference in 20 years.

- Throughout your working life, estimate where you are in your retirement savings goals and whether you are on target or need to make up for lost time.

- Although some expenses decrease in retirement, be prepared for others to increase. Most experts say you need between 70 and 100% of your preretirement income to live in retirement.

Keeping Your Financial Records in Order

If you are like many people, you have a collection of financial "stuff" that you don't know whether to keep or to toss out.

Keep your investment statements for two reasons:

- You can check for mistakes made by your broker or mutual fund company and reported to the IRS. If you sold any securities during the year (e.g., stocks, bonds) or received any dividends, your broker or mutual fund company will send you a 1099 form and a matching one to the IRS to report the income or loss.

- Your statements will help keep you from paying too much tax because they allow you to track reinvested dividends and capital gains. Each time you reinvest, it's equivalent to the broker sending you a check and your returning it to purchase additional shares of stock. At the time of sale, you are permitted to indicate exactly which shares you want sold (identified by date of purchase). Usually the shares with the highest cost basis will have a more tax-favorable status in a rising stock market. For mutual funds, you will be able to track the taxes paid every year on the dividends and capital gains the fund distributed. You will add them to your cost basis when you sell.

For income tax filing, it is necessary to have records of the date you acquired an asset, its purchase price, and your date of sale or transfer to another investment. Complete Exercise IV-11 and update it as necessary. If records are lost, try contacting the company, checking for prices in the business reference section of your library, or paying a professional advisor to do the digging for you.

> **Cost basis.** An investment's original cost. This number, which is used for tax purposes, also includes transaction costs plus reinvested dividends and capital gains.

These Items Are "Keepers"

1. Your tax returns. Copies from up to six previous years can be retrieved from the IRS for a charge. You need to keep the supporting documentation for your tax returns (e.g., 1099s or brokerage statements) for at least 3 years after you file. After that, you can be audited only if the IRS suspects fraud.

2. Your settlement documents on any house closings, including mortgage papers.

3. Retirement plan records. This includes records of contributions to plans, loans and distributions from the funds, conversions, and rollovers.

4. Records of purchase and sale of every investment you own, whether bought by you, received as a gift or inheritance, or given as a gift. The documentation should be kept for as long as you hold the asset, plus at least 3 years.

5. Regular statements from brokerage accounts, mutual funds, limited partnerships, bank CDs, etc. Once you have received your annual summary statement, the monthlies or quarterlies can be tossed.

Purchase and Sale of Assets

Date of purchase or inheritance	Type of security	Number of shares	Purchase price or inheritance value* ($)	Date of sale or transfer	Amount of sale** ($)

 * The purchase price plus cost of purchase, such as commission. For inherited assets, enter the value on the date of death.
** The amount received from the sale of an asset excluding commissions or fees.

Adapted from: *Planning Your Retirement—An Investment for Your Future* (1997). ©2004 Board of Regents of the University of Wisconsin System, doing business as Division of Cooperative Extension of the University of Wisconsin-Extension.

Your Minimum "Need to Knows" about Building a Portfolio and Keeping Your Investment House in Order

- Investing is not a one-time shot, but an ongoing lifelong process.

- Reinvesting dividends and capital gains is the best way to systematically grow your portfolio.

- Set up a plan in which you invest regularly, e.g., dollar-cost-averaging, and use a buy-and-hold strategy in your taxable accounts to minimize taxes.

- Index funds are a good choice for the core of both your tax-deferred and taxable accounts.

- Occasional rebalancing—generally not more than once or twice a year—may be necessary to keep your asset allocation at the correct proportions.

- Once you settle on a sensible investment plan that suits you, commit to it and believe in its logic. This will keep you going when markets are in a downturn.

- Good record keeping is essential to avoid overpayment of taxes at the time of sale.

Withdrawals—How to Make Your Money Last

No single withdrawal rate is "just right" for every individual. People have different goals and family situations. Some may want to spend down to the last dollar and others to leave a large inheritance. You may hear or read advice that advocates withdrawal rates of anywhere from 3 to 10% as "safe." The newer research however, using various asset allocation models and payout rates, suggests a first-year withdrawal rate of between 4 and 5% of your retirement assets (e.g., 4% of $100,000=$4,000). Thereafter, each year you would increase the withdrawal amount by the inflation rate for that year (e.g., 3% of $4,000=$120, for a second-year withdrawal of $4,120). The 4% rate is based on an asset allocation of 60% stock/40% fixed income. This gives you the best chance of not outliving your money, rather than the other way around.

If you're a very conservative investor, you'll need to withdraw less (e.g., 3%). These conservative withdrawal rates would be particularly important if you were to go into retirement when the stock market is in a downturn and stays there for a while. If you could be guaranteed a bull market, such as we experienced throughout the late 1990s, you could make withdrawals at a higher rate. The difference between 4 and 8% may not seem very significant, but it is. It could spell disaster, especially if you are planning an income stream for 30–40 years. Later on in your retirement, perhaps you could withdraw more.

Annuities

If you seek the comfort of knowing you'll have a guaranteed income, then you may wish to purchase an immediate annuity, through which you trade your lump sum principal for a lifetime income stream. The downside of this strategy is that your monthly payments will not keep up with inflation—they remain the same for life. Also, you don't get to leave an inheritance (what is left reverts to the insurance company) unless you choose certain options, all of which lower your payment.

Below are the common payout options from an annuity.

Life annuity. You get the largest checks with this choice, and payments will continue for your lifetime—and only your lifetime. Payments do not continue to your beneficiaries.

Joint and survivor annuity. This option provides a continuing income for your spouse should you die first—from 50 to 100% of what you were receiving. Monthly payments are lower than those for a single life annuity because they are extended over the lifetimes of two people instead of one.

Cost of living adjustments. With this option, your annuity would begin at a lower rate but would be increased each year for inflation.

Life-with-period-certain annuity. This option gives you a lifetime income plus a guarantee of payments for 10 years or more. If you should die within that time, your beneficiary collects the remaining payments.

Refund annuity. This plan guarantees a return of premiums paid to purchase an annuity to the beneficiary if the owner dies before sufficient payment.

When you purchase an annuity, two considerations are of great importance. First, buy only from companies rated A or better by the authoritative rating companies, such as Standard and Poor's, Duff and Phelps, and A.M. Best (see Session III, page 80, for Web sites). Second, shop around for the best terms. Each company may quote a different amount of income for the same amount of principal. Use the Web site www.annuityshopper.com to help with comparisons.

How to Choose Financial Professionals

It's time to take a good look at your needs, interests, and lifestyle. Over the course of your adult years, the minimum financial chores you will need to handle are your investments; securing and paying off loans; buying or selling a house; insuring your home, property, and health; and protecting yourself against catastrophic losses, as well as developing a plan to pass on your home and assets to your beneficiaries.

A lot of those jobs you can do on your own, if you have the interest and take the time to develop the expertise. The knowledge is available to you in personal finance classes, books, magazines, newspapers, newsletters, and via the Internet. However, more often than not, you will need some outside help, even if it is just someone who looks over your financial plan and gives you the confidence to proceed.

Even though professional help is frequently very important to personal money management, should you choose the wrong advisor, your financial security could be in jeopardy. So before you go out and sign on with a financial planner, attorney, accountant, or stockbroker, understand that the right way to pick advisors requires discipline and attention to detail. Here's a way to get started:

- Prepare a list of referrals from friends and other professionals.
- When possible, gather some preliminary information, such as number of years in practice and professional qualifications. Some professionals will send you a resume. You might also be able to get information from national professional associations by telephone or via their Web sites. For financial planners, check www.fpanet.org, www.napfa.org, or www.cfp.net.
- Remember the "Rule of Three": Interview at least three advisors. Use the *Comparison of Financial Professionals* interview form on page 134 to help you in your search.

Below are the generic questions that you would ask any professional. Then we'll move into special questions for each type of financial advisor.

1. *How many years have you been in practice?* At least 3 years' experience in dealing with financial issues such as yours is desirable.

2. *What are your qualifications?* Ask about formal education and certifications in the field and how he/she keeps his/her knowledge updated.

3. *Will there be a written contract?* Unless you pay for each visit, a contract is a must to confirm your fee and service agreements. The contract should list the tasks the professional is to perform, provide an estimate of fees or a statement of how charges are made, and explain how you will be billed, e.g., quarterly, annually.

4. *How do you calculate your fees* (e.g., hourly rate)? Do research to find out what the range of fees should be for the type of professional you are hiring.

5. *How long should the work take to complete?*

6. *Will you be delegating any of the work?* If so, at what rate and to whom?

7. *May I have references to contact?* (Ask about clients in similar circumstances to yours.)

Use the worksheet in Exercise IV-12 to compare the qualifications and fees of three financial professionals.

Hiring A Financial Planner

Qualified financial planners take a broad view of your financial situation and design an overall strategy to meet your personal financial goals. This necessitates an in-depth look at your entire financial situation, current

Comparison of Financial Professionals

	Professional 1	Professional 2	Professional 3
Specialty area			
Name			
Address			
Phone number			
Referred by			
Years of experience			
Degrees or certifications			
Verbal or written contact?			
Issues to cover			
Compensation: flat rate, hourly, retainer, commissions, etc.			
How many meetings?			
Delegation of work?			
References?			
Charge for telephone calls?			
Other questions			

cash flow, budget, net worth, savings, investments, taxes, insurance, and retirement and estate arrangements. You will want to look for financial planners who evaluate your entire financial picture rather than address only investments.

Just as you would with any person you pay for advice, you need to carefully check credentials. There is little regulation of the financial planning industry. In most states, anyone can claim to be a financial planner, regardless of training. Many of these individuals have professional experience as insurance agents or stockbrokers. Others have related professional careers such as bankers, accountants, and tax and estate planning lawyers. However, only some of these people have taken specialized courses and examinations in all aspects of financial planning and must complete ongoing education credits as well as ethics courses.

The most recognized credentials to look for are Certified Financial Planner® (CFP®) or Chartered Financial Consultant (ChFC). Beyond credentials, look for extensive financial planning experience. And remember, even with credentials and experience, there are still no absolute guarantees of ethical practice.

What Do the Letters Mean?

Below are professional designations established by self-regulatory membership organizations—not by state or federal regulatory agencies—that signify study in specific areas.

- *CFP®* licensees have to complete a course of study and pass examinations in risk management, investment, tax planning, retirement planning, and estate planning. They must also have a minimum of three years of work experience, continue to update their knowledge in the field, and adhere to a prescribed code of ethics. CFP® licensees are certified by the Certified Financial Planner Board of Standards, Inc. (CFP Board).

- People holding the *ChFC* designation complete courses in economics, investments, insurance, taxation, and related areas from the American College in Bryn Mawr, Pennsylvania. This designation is an outgrowth of the Chartered Life Underwriter program, which indicates extensive

study of insurance. Ethics requirements also apply to holders of this designation.

- Personal financial specialist (PFS) designations are obtained by some certified public accountants (CPAs). The designations call for additional specialized education, and other requirements established by the American Institute of CPAs must be met. CPAs with the PFS designation provide a broad range of personal financial services, which may include investment advice.

Locating Financial Planners

Interview several financial planners so that you will have choices to evaluate. Get references from friends and other professionals. For lists of financial planners in your areas, check with the following organizations:

> National Association of Personal Financial Advisors (NAPFA)
> 3250 North Arlington Heights Road, Ste. 109
> Arlington Heights, Illinois 60004
> 847-483-5400
> www.napfa.org
>
> Financial Planning Association (FPA)
> Suite 400
> 4100 E. Mississippi Avenue
> Denver, Colorado 80246-3053
> 800-322-4237
> www.fpanet.org
>
> Society of Financial Service Professionals
> 17 Campus Boulevard
> Suite 201
> Newtown Square, PA 19073-3230
> 610-526-2500
> www.financialpro.org

Know How Your Financial Planner Earns Income

Many financial planners make all or part of their income from commissions on the products they sell. One way to avoid any conflict of interest is to select a fee-only planner. However, you will find that there are many more commissioned planners than fee-only.

Check with NAPFA for the names of fee-only planners in your area.

Fee-only planners. Financial planners who are compensated from client fees only. They charge for gathering and analyzing your financial data and recommending a plan of action. They do not earn income from the financial products they might suggest you buy. Fees are typically from $125 to $250 per hour; flat fees for a plan are based on an estimate of the work involved. Ask if a fee-only planner is NAPFA-registered. This indicates a high level of continuing education and peer review.

Commission-only planners. Financial planners who earn their money through commissions paid by the sponsors of the investment products (e.g., annuities and mutual funds) they sell.

Fee and commission planners. Financial planners who are sometimes called "fee-based" or "fee-offset" planners usually are compensated by some combination of commissions for products sold, flat fees for financial plans, and "trailing fees" on assets under management. Sometimes the planner's commissions will reduce the initial planning fee that the planner quotes the client. This is known as "fee-offset" compensation.

Choose your financial planner wisely and be an informed consumer. Following is a five-page questionnaire to ask your prospective financial planner to complete. It was developed by NAPFA. Photocopy it, and if you like what you see in the answers, call and ask the planner for a free half-hour get-acquainted meeting. Select a planner on the basis of qualifications and rapport. You want someone you'll enjoy working with and trust.

Hiring an Accountant

Accountants may serve as a possible source of financial investment advice. Usually accountants provide relatively generic advice on investment information rather than recommending particular investments. They can help you evaluate the possible effects of investment alternatives on your overall financial condition, income taxes, and future taxes.

- Enrolled agents are tax preparers who have passed an IRS certification examination and are qualified tax advisors.
- Public accountants are licensed and trained in accounting. They cannot represent you before the IRS in an audit.
- CPAs obtain extensive education and experience in accounting, auditing, economics, finance, management, and taxes to become certified and licensed to practice. They must also take ongoing continuing education courses to maintain their certification.

Although anyone can be a paid tax preparer, only an enrolled agent, CPA, or tax attorney can represent you in an audit.

Questions to Ask a Tax Professional

1. Is doing tax returns a regular part of your business?
2. What kind of training do you have?
3. Are you available to answer tax questions throughout the year?
4. Are you experienced with tax situations like mine?
5. Are you conservative or aggressive in interpreting tax laws and regulations?
6. How much help would you provide if I were audited?
7. How much will preparing my return cost?

Hiring an attorney

Attorneys can provide information about legal and tax implications of a particular investment but do not generally advise you on which investments to make. They are the only professionals who can provide legal advice, resolve legal and property transfer issues, and prepare legal documents (e.g., wills and trusts).

Attorneys may charge a flat fee for a particular service, an hourly rate, or a combination of the two. Because attorney fees tend to be high, they are most often consulted for specific questions or issues (e.g., estate administration).

Financial Planner Interview Questionnaire

Background and Experience

The backgrounds of financial planners can vary as much as the services offered. A planner's education and experience should demonstrate a solid foundation in financial planning and a commitment to keeping current.

Note: A yes or no answer requiring explanation is not necessarily cause for concern. The National Association of Personal Financial Advisors (NAPFA) encourages you to give the advisor an opportunity to explain any response.

1. What is your educational background?

   ☐ College degree and area of study: _____

   ☐ Graduate degree and area of study: _____

2. What are your financial planning credentials/designations and affiliations?

   ☐ NAPFA-Registered Financial Advisor (60 hours continuing education every 2 years)

   ☐ Certified Financial Planner (CFP) (30 hours continuing education every 2 years)

   ☐ Chartered Financial Consultant (ChFC) (30 hours continuing education every 2 years)

   ☐ Certified Public Accountant/Personal Financial Specialist (CPA/PFS) (60 points every 3 years)

   ☐ Financial Planning Association (FPA) (continuing education not required)

   ☐ Other:

3. How long have you been offering financial planning services?

   ☐ Less than 2 years   ☐ 6–10 years

   ☐ 2–5 years   ☐ More than 10 years

4. Do you have clients who might be willing to speak with me about your services?   ☐ Yes   ☐ No

   If no, explain _____

5. Will you provide me with references from other professionals?   ☐ Yes   ☐ No If no, explain

   _____

   _____

6. Have you ever been cited by a professional or regulatory governing body for disciplinary reasons?

   ☐ Yes   ☐ No

   If yes, explain _____

   _____

Financial Planner Interview Questionnaire
(continued)

7. Describe your financial planning work experience or attach your resume.

_____

_____

_____

_____

_____

_____

Services

Financial planners provide a range of services. It is important to match client needs with services provided.

1. Do you offer advice on: (check all that apply)

   ☐ Goal setting

   ☐ Cash management and budgeting

   ☐ Tax planning

   ☐ Investment review and planning

   ☐ Estate planning

   ☐ Insurance needs in the areas of life, disability, long-term care, health, and property/casualty

   ☐ Education funding

   ☐ Retirement planning

   ☐ Other: _____

   _____

2. Do you provide a comprehensive written analysis of my financial situation and recommendations?
   ☐ Yes   ☐ No

3. Does your financial planning service include recommendations for specific investments or investment products?   ☐ Yes   ☐ No

4. Do you offer assistance with implementation of the plan?   ☐ Yes   ☐ No

5. Do you offer continuous, on-going advice regarding my financial affairs, including advice on non-investment-related financial issues?   ☐ Yes   ☐ No

6. Do you take possession of, or have access to, my assets?   ☐ Yes   ☐ No

7. If you were to provide me on-going investment advisory services, do you require "discretionary" trading authority over my investment accounts?   ☐ Yes   ☐ No

Business Practice

1. How many clients do you work with? _____

2. Are you currently engaged in any other business, as a sole proprietor, partner, officer, employee, trustee, agent, or otherwise? (Exclude non-investment-related activities which are exclusively charitable, civic, religious, or fraternal and are recognized as tax-exempt.)　☐ Yes　☐ No

   If yes, explain: _____

   _____

3. Will you or an associate of yours work with me?

   ☐ I will

   ☐ An associate will

   ☐ We have a team approach

   If an associate will be my primary contact, complete questions 1–7 in the Background and Experience section for each associate as well.

4. Will you sign the Fiduciary Oath below?　☐ Yes　☐ No

Fiduciary Oath

The advisor shall exercise his/her best efforts to act in good faith and in the best interests of the client. The advisor shall provide written disclosure to the client prior to the engagement of the advisor, and thereafter throughout the term of the engagement, of any conflicts of interest which will or reasonably may compromise the impartiality or independence of the advisor.

   The advisor, or any party in which the advisor has a financial interest, does not receive any compensation or other remuneration that is contingent on any client's purchase or sale of a financial product. The advisor does not receive a fee or other compensation from another party based on the referral of a client or the client's business.

5. Do you have a business continuity plan?

   ☐ Yes　☐ No

   _____

   If no, explain: _____

   _____

Financial Planner Interview Questionnaire
(continued)

Compensation

Financial planning costs include what a client pays in fees and commissions. Comparison between planners requires full information about potential total costs. It is important to have this information before entering into any agreement.

1. How is your firm compensated and how is your compensation calculated?

    ☐ Fee only (as calculated below)

    Hourly rate of $_____/hour

    Flat fee of $_____

    Percentage_____% to _____% of _____

    ☐ Commissions only; from securities, insurance, and/or other products that clients buy from a firm with which you are associated

    ☐ Fee and commissions (fee-based)

    ☐ Fee offset (charging a flat fee against which commissions are offset). If the commissions exceed the fee, is the balance credited to me?   ☐ Yes   ☐ No

2. Do you have an agreement describing your compensation and services that will be provided in advance of the engagement?   ☐ Yes   ☐ No

3. Do you have a minimum fee?   ☐ Yes   ☐ No

    If so, explain: _____

    _____

    _____

    _____

4. If you earn commissions, approximately what percentage of your firm's commission income comes from:

    _____% Insurance products

    _____% Annuities

    _____% Mutual funds

    _____% Limited partnerships

    _____% Stocks and bonds

    _____% Coins, tangibles, collectibles

    _____% Other: _____

    _____% Other: _____

    100 %

Financial Planner Interview Questionnaire
(continued)

5. Does any member of your firm act as a general partner to, participate in, or receive compensation from investment companies whose products you may recommend to me? ☐ Yes ☐ No

6. Do you receive referral fees from attorneys, accountants, insurance professionals, mortgage brokers, or others? ☐ Yes ☐ No

7. Do you receive on-going income from any of the mutual funds that you recommend in the form of "12(b)1" fees, "trailing" commissions, or other continuing payouts? ☐ Yes ☐ No

8. Are there financial incentives for you to recommend certain financial products? ☐ Yes ☐ No

   If so, explain: _____

   _____

   _____

Regulatory Compliance

Federal and state laws require that, under most circumstances, individuals or firms holding themselves out to the public as providing investment advisory services be registered with either the U.S. Securities & Exchange Commission (SEC) or the regulatory agency of the state in which the individual/firm conducts business.

1. I (or my firm) am registered as an Investment Advisor

   ☐ With the SEC

   ☐ With the state of _____

Please provide your Form ADV Part II or brochure being used in compliance with the Investment Advisors Act of 1940.

If not registered with either the SEC or any state, please indicate the allowable reason for non-registration.

_____

_____

_____

_____

Signature of Planner: _____

Firm Name: _____

Date: _____

Adapted with permission from the National Association of Personal Financial Advisors, Arlington Heights, IL. <www.napfa.org>

Hiring a Stockbroker

A registered representative (commonly called a stockbroker, but sometimes referred to as a financial consultant, account executive, or registered investment adviser) is someone who is employed by a registered broker-dealer firm and who is authorized to buy and sell stocks, bonds, mutual funds, or certain other securities for investors. Registered representatives must be licensed through the Financial Industry Regulatory Authority (FINRA), a self-regulatory organization, and registered in each state in which they conduct business. Registered representatives must pass a variety of securities examinations, depending upon the type of investments they are selling.

Full-service brokerage firms offer investment advice and usually have research departments that provide reports and other services to evaluate investment alternatives for their clients. One alternative to working with a full-service broker is to subscribe to an investment advisory newsletter or service. Then you would place your order with a discount stock-broker or directly with the source, such as a mutual fund company.

Discount brokers are useful when you know what investments you want to make and you don't need investment advice or help in examining investment strategies and alternatives. Some larger discount brokerage firms may provide some reports and other information services that investors can use in evaluating various investment choices. Commissions at discount brokers may be 30–70% less than at full-service brokers. However, there may be a minimum fee.

Hiring a Real Estate Broker

You can buy or sell real estate without a broker. However, before you list your property as "for sale by owner," review what a good real estate broker can do for you:

- provide information about the recent sales prices of comparable properties.
- familiarize you with the community you are considering (quality of schools, safety, traffic, and amenities).

- help you find a property to buy.
- help you obtain financing.
- provide suggestions to help you prepare your house for sale.
- use a multiple listing service (MLS) to advertise your home or find homes for sale.
- find and qualify buyers for property you want to sell.
- market your home, e.g., host open houses.
- negotiate contracts or agreements for you.
- prepare the contract and other pertinent paperwork.

Real estate brokers that help buyers usually represent the seller. (That's who is paying the commission.) Ask your broker if he or she represents the buyer, seller, or both. Ask how he or she would handle the conflict of interest that might arise if you (the buyer being represented) were interested in a property that his or her agency had listed (representing the seller).

When you plan to sell your house, ask at least three brokers to supply a market analysis on your home and their recommendation of a sale price. Be wary of a broker who suggests asking a price that is out of line with the suggestions of other brokers. Too high a price is likely to hurt the chances of a sale; too low a price will lose you money. Go with a broker who can place your home on the MLS, a broker information network that publicizes homes for sale.

Eight Steps to Hiring a Financial Professional—A Review

1. Determine your financial needs and objectives.
2. Check your conclusions with someone familiar with your financial status.
3. Learn as much as you can about various investment options.
4. Learn as much as you can about the various types of financial professionals and services.
5. Attend unbiased public seminars.
6. Get recommendations from others.
7. Get names from professional associations.
8. Interview at least three financial professionals for each advisor position you wish to fill.

> ### Questions to Ask a Real Estate Broker
>
> 1. Are you a licensed broker, an agent, or a sales associate?
> 2. How long have been licensed?
> 3. Are you a member of the National Association of Realtors?
> 4. Do you work full-time as a real estate professional?
> 5. How long have you been involved in this town/neighborhood/county?
> 6. Can you provide three references of recent clients?
> 7. What houses have you sold in the past 60 days?
> 8. What is your marketing plan to sell my home?
> 9. What services does your company offer?

How to Check Your Broker's or Planner's Background or Make a Complaint

To check a planner's or broker's background, start with your state securities administrator. That office will send you background materials on the advisor and can tell you about any pending or prior disciplinary actions against both the advisor and the firm.

Then move on to the FINRA public disclosure phone center at 800-289-9999 or use the SEC's Investment Adviser Public Disclosure database at www.finra.org. to find out if the agency has any complaints or cases pending against member broker-dealers.

References

A Money Management Workbook (1999). Washington, D.C.: American Association of Retired Persons (Women's Financial Information Program).

Bach, D. (1999). *Smart Woman Finish Rich*. New York: Broadway Books.

Chatzky, J. (2001). *Talking Money*. New York: Warner Books, Inc.

Dahl, B. (1996). *A Working Woman's Guide to Financial Security*. Urbana, Ill.: University of Illinois Cooperative Extension.

Ernst & Young (1999). *Financial Planning for Women*. New York: John Wiley & Sons, Inc.

Financial Insights (2000). Minneapolis, Minn.: American Express Financial Corporation.

Action Steps

SESSION IV: **Investing for Retirement**

- [ ] Determine your desired investment asset allocation model.

- [ ] Determine the minimum interest rate you need to break even with taxes and inflation.

- [ ] Use *Your Investment Portfolio* (Exercise IV-2, page 108) to list asset allocation and specific securities.

- [ ] Estimate the annual return for each of your investments or for your total portfolio.

- [ ] Answer the questions in *How Much Money Will You Need For Retirement?* (Exercise IV-5, page 114).

- [ ] Use Table IV-6 (page 117) to determine your full retirement age for Social Security.

- [ ] Use the *Estimated Cost of Living* worksheet (Exercise IV-7, page 118) to estimate retirement expenses.

- [ ] Use the *Estimating Your Retirement Income* worksheet (Exercise IV-8, page 121) to identify sources of retirement funds.

- [ ] Calculate your retirement savings need using the *Ballpark Estimate* worksheet (Exercise IV-9, page 123).

- [ ] Use a file folder for each investment to store account purchase and sale records.

- [ ] Interview at least three financial services professionals before hiring an advisor.

- [ ] Use the *Comparison of Financial Professionals* worksheet (Exercise IV-12, page 134) to compare advisors.

Garman, E.T., and Forgue, R.E. (2008). *Personal Finance*. Boston, Mass.: Houghton Mifflin Company.

Guide to Financial Planning and Selecting a Planner (1995). National Association of Personal Financial Advisors and Cooperative Extension System.

Investing for Your Future (2002). Publication E227. New Brunswick, N.J.: Rutgers Cooperative Extension.

O'Neill, B. (1999). *Investing on a Shoestring*. Chicago, Ill.: Dearborn Financial Publishing.

Personal Savings Rate (2008, April 30). Washington, DC: Bureau of Economic Analysis. Available online at: http://www.bea.gov/briefrm/saving.htm.

Planning Your Retirement—An Investment for Your Future (1997). Madison, WI: University of Wisconsin-Extension, Family Living Programs.

Quick Stats 2007 (2008). Washington, DC: Women's Bureau, U.S. Department of Labor. Available online at: http://www.dol.gov/wb/stats/main.htm.

Quinn, J.B. (2006). *Smart and Simple Financial Strategies for Busy People*. New York: Simon and Schuster.

Retirement Trends in the United States Over the Past Quarter-Century (2007, June). Washington, DC: Employee Benefit Research Institute. Available online at: http://www.ebri.org/pdf/publications/facts/0607fact.pdf.

Schwab, C. (2001). *You're Fifty—Now What?* New York: Crown Business.

Social Security Fact Sheet: 2008 Social Security Changes (2008). Washington, DC: Social Security Administration. Available online at: http://www.ssa.gov/pressoffice/factsheets/colafacts2008.pdf.

Study: Men Continue to Earn Higher Salaries (2003, March 28). Available online at: http://media.www.dailytexanonline.com/media/storage/paper410/news/2003/03/28/News/Study.Men.Continue.To.Earn.Higher.Salaries-495291.shtml.

Taylor, J. (1993). *Building Wealth with Mutual Funds*. Brightwaters, N.Y.: Windsor Books.

Women and Social Security: Benefit Types and Eligibility (2005, June). Washington, DC: Institute For Women's Policy Research. Available online at: www.iwpr.org/pdf/D463.pdf.

Women Closing Some Gender Gaps: Census (2003, March 30). Available online at: http://usgovinfo.about.com/cs/censusstatistic/a/aamenwomen.htm.

Planning for Future Life Events

Mary has a spouse and kids
And a very special niece
That's why she has a will and plans
To make sure they get a piece.

What will be covered in Session V

Estate Planning Lessons

1. Estate Planning Fundamentals
2. The Bare Essentials of Estate Planning
3. The Matter of Trusts
4. Estate Taxes

Money and Relationships Lessons

5. Widowhood
6. Divorce
7. Marriage and Remarriage
8. Cohabitation

Terms to Learn *(bolded in the text)*

Alimony	Estate planning	Pour-over will
Basis	Fair market value	Power of attorney (health care)
Child support	Generation-skipping trust	Probate
COBRA law	Gift tax	Replacement value
Codicil	Intestate/intestacy	Revocable
Cohabitation agreement	Irrevocable	Stepped-up basis
Durable power of attorney	Living trust	Testamentary trust
(financial)	Living will	Uniform Transfers to Minors Act

Exercises

1. Estate Planning Checklist
2. My Estate Inventory
3. My Will Planning/Updating Checklist
4. Letter of Instruction Checklist
5. Postdivorce Housing Analysis

Estate Planning Fundamentals

Susan is thoroughly confused about estate planning issues. Her eyes seem to glaze over whenever the topic comes up, but she knows she can't be in denial about the subject any longer. She and her husband Ben are both 48 years old. Recently, her best friend's spouse died suddenly and didn't leave a will. This is causing her friend and her friend's children big problems. It's difficult for Susan to think of her house and meager investments as an "estate." She knows that she and Ben had better get wills and maybe do more. But what?

These are her questions:

- What is estate planning?
- Don't you have to be rich to do estate planning?
- Why should I (we) plan our estate?
- What is the first step to take?
- What are the basic estate planning documents?
- What do I (we) need to take into consideration?
- How do I ensure that my wishes are carried out if I become terminally ill?
- Should I (we) appoint guardians for our children in case I (we) die prematurely? How can we do this?
- Are there any trusts that are appropriate for my (our) estate planning goals?

Estate planning is a critical part of the financial planning process. A goal of this session is to help you

> **Estate planning.** The process of organizing your financial and personal assets for use during your lifetime and distribution after death in accordance with prevailing laws. It ensures that your wishes are carried out with a minimum of inconvenience and expense to your family. It is an ongoing lifetime process that includes planning for the care of your dependents. Estate planning also includes gifting during one's lifetime.

understand the process and its importance in reaching your goals. In the estate planning process, you want to be assured that your assets, no matter how large or small, go where you want them to go when you pass on. You also want to minimize estate taxation and provide for minor children, survivors (e.g., your spouse), and dependents. Perhaps you anticipate an inheritance yourself that will affect your retirement assets and your future standard of living.

It is extremely common for people to procrastinate in planning their estate. One reason is that it is often viewed as a chore to do when one gets older and children are grown. It also can be time-consuming, and the process can also be overwhelming if the decisions that need to be made and the appropriate tools are not understood.

It is very uncomfortable for most of us to think about death and talk to our families about sensitive topics such as money and our own mortality. Another obstacle for many young families is not knowing whom to name as a guardian for their children, so they avoid the issue altogether by procrastinating.

Following (Exercise V-1) is an estate planning checklist to complete that will help you get started.

What Are Your Estate Planning Objectives?

Objectives of estate planning are personal. They should come from you (and your spouse/partner) and not be dictated by the attorney or other financial professionals you work with. They may include:

- financial security for your spouse/partner and/or self.
- giving your spouse/partner as much responsibility and flexibility in managing the estate as he desires or is capable of, while saving on potential taxes.
- minimizing the headaches and costs of probate.

Estate Planning Checklist

	Yes	No
1. I know what will happen to my children/dependents and my property should my spouse and I both die.	☐	☐
2. My spouse and I each have valid, updated wills. The signed originals are stored (indicate location) _____.	☐	☐
3. I have checked all of my property titles to make sure that they don't conflict with my will.	☐	☐
4. I have a clear understanding of the principal financial resources and liabilities of my estate.	☐	☐
5. I have checked the beneficiary designations on all individual retirement accounts (IRAs) and other retirement accounts to make sure they are correct.	☐	☐
6. I expect to receive substantial assets/property as a gift or inheritance in the next few years.	☐	☐
7. I know what papers and records will be important in the event of my death.	☐	☐
8. I have a separate record of the important papers I keep in my safe deposit box or lock box. The box, the key, and this record are located (indicate location) _____.	☐	☐
9. I know and understand what types of insurance policies I own. I last checked the beneficiary designations on _____.	☐	☐
10. I am aware that life insurance proceeds are subject to federal estate taxes and perhaps even probate (settlement of a deceased person's estate in a court of law).	☐	☐
11. I have put in writing my wishes regarding funeral and burial arrangements. This document can be found (indicate location) _____.	☐	☐
12. I have communicated my estate plans to family members and/or friends. Name: _____ Date: _____	☐	☐
13. I have determined what assets in my estate will require probate.	☐	☐
14.I have an estimate of the costs to my estate of possible estate taxes, funeral expenses, probate fees, legal fees, and unpaid property and income taxes.	☐	☐
15. I have heard about living trusts and will check/have checked to see if this is appropriate for my family.	☐	☐
16. I have completed separate forms for power of attorney for health care and durable power of attorney for financial matters.	☐	☐
17. An attorney has reviewed my will in the last 4 years, and it says what I want it to say.	☐	☐
18. I have prepared a living will.	☐	☐

> **Probate.** Proceedings involving a court of law to validate a will, pay debts of the deceased, and distribute the deceased's property to named beneficiaries.

- providing for minor children via guardianship if you were to predecease them.
- ensuring that children are not left too many assets at an inappropriate age.
- providing for enough liquidity so that assets do not have to be sold hurriedly to pay debts or estate taxes (e.g., having a life insurance trust to pay expenses).
- minimizing taxes at time of death and estate taxes after death.
- avoiding potential family conflicts and providing equitable treatment of children.
- organizing important papers and records affecting your estate plan in a place known to family members, including your executor/executrix, and letting them know of your overall estate plan.

> Important point: You can't avoid probate by not having a will. Should you die without a will, a.k.a., die "intestate," one will be written for you. Your assets will be distributed according to state intestacy laws.

Remember that even if you have prepared an estate plan in the past, either your estate holdings or your attitude toward it may have changed since you first developed your plan.

Periodically Review Your Estate Plan

- Have any new children or grandchildren been born since you last reviewed your will?
- Have any of your potential heirs died, married, divorced, or become disabled since your will was prepared?
- Are there any other life-changing events that have occurred that would prompt a revision of your will?
- Have federal or state estate tax laws changed?

To get started, you'll need to collect all the papers that show what you have to leave to heirs. Eventually, you will add a copy of your will, any trust documents, life insurance contracts, and powers of attorney to the estate file. Then you will have to find a safe place to store your estate planning documents. This can either be a fireproof lock box kept in your home or a safe deposit box held at the bank. Keep original documents in one location and copies in the other.

What Is Your Estate?

What it isn't is an expensive home that has a fence around it. Your estate is everything you own in your own name, and your share of anything you own with others (e.g., your spouse, children, business partners). This includes the fair market value of real property (e.g., land and buildings) and personal property. It also means investments, retirement benefits, and life insurance policies.

You will need to tally up "today's" net worth, but the actual value of your estate is computed only after you pass on. Knowing now what it adds up to will help determine whether any estate taxes will be due, whether there will be money to pay taxes or final expenses, and whether there should be anything left for heirs.

Here is a more comprehensive checklist of what you should count in an estate inventory:

- ☐ Real estate
- ☐ Securities (stocks, bonds, and mutual funds)
- ☐ Interest and dividends you're owed that haven't been paid
- ☐ Bank accounts
- ☐ All tangible personal property (e.g., car)
- ☐ Life insurance policies you own
- ☐ No-fault insurance payments due to you
- ☐ Annuities paid by contract or agreement
- ☐ Value of any qualified retirement plan, including IRAs and 401(k)s
- ☐ Unpaid judgments from lawsuits
- ☐ Income tax refunds
- ☐ Forgiven debts
- ☐ Closely held businesses

Complete Exercise V-2 (page 150), *My Estate Inventory.* You may find it helpful to refer back to the

Net Worth Statement that you prepared in Session I, page 24, to jog your memory about what you actually have.

This is what the columns in Exercise V-2 mean:

"What I own" refers to everything discussed on the previous page.

"How I own it" refers to how you hold title to the property (next topic to be discussed.)

"Percentage owned" refers to the part of an asset you own. You may own half your house, all of Aunt Gertrude's silver broach, and one-quarter of a flower business.

"Net value" is the value of an asset owned minus what is still owed on it. Example: Your home is worth $300,000 and you have a $100,000 mortgage on it.

$300,000 − $100,000 = $200,000 net value

Note to married women: More than likely, your net worth is not the same as your husband's. Your net worth and estate inventory statement will indicate:

- how much money you have to bequeath to your heirs, and
- what your financial situation would be in the event of widowhood or divorce.

It's All In a Name—
The Name on the Piece of Paper . . .

Depending on the state you live in, there are three basic ways to hold property. The property can be your primary residence, your beach cottage, your flower business, or anything else of value that you have bought alone or with another person.

Types of Ownership

Sole ownership. This is property owned solely by an individual. It is also known as outright ownership. When the owner dies, the property passes to heirs according to his or her will. However, solely owned property with a designated beneficiary(s), such as IRAs and life insurance, passes automatically to the beneficiary.

Tenancy in common (TC). Two or more persons own the property in distinct and separate shares. The shares need not be equal, and each "tenant" can will his or her shares to whomever he or she likes. The share does not pass automatically to a spouse or other tenant(s). An owner can sell his or her share without the consent of the other owner(s).

Joint tenants with rights of survivorship (JTWROS). The property is owned by two or more tenants together, and each agrees that if one of them dies, his or her shares automatically pass to the other(s). As with TC, a tenant can sell his or her share without the consent of the other.

Two other forms of ownership—"community property" and "tenancy by the entirety"—are available in some states. A third form of ownership, used often in elder law, is "life estate/remainder."

Community property (CP). The property and debts acquired by a married person in the CP states: California, Louisiana, Arizona, Nevada, Texas, Washington, Wisconsin, Idaho, New Mexico, and Puerto Rico. CP is owned 50/50, regardless of which spouse's name appears on the title. If one spouse dies, his or her half of the CP and all separate property are distributed according to the will or the state's intestacy law. It does not automatically pass to the surviving spouse.

Tenancy by the entirety. A type of ownership available to married couples in some states. Property is owned the same as in a joint ownership. However, it cannot be sold without the consent of both spouses. Upon the death of one spouse, it passes automatically to the surviving spouse.

Life estate/remainder. The life tenant has the right to the use and income on the property for so long as the life tenant lives and the remainderperson is entitled to the entire property upon the death of the life tenant. This is commonly used in Medicaid planning. (A remainderperson is an individual who has the right to possession or ownership of the property after the estate holder dies or surrenders the life estate.)

My Estate Inventory

What I own	How I own it	Percentage owned	Net value
Example: Home 4 Penndale Lane Morristown, NJ	JTWROS* with Ben	50%	Property value: $325,000 Mortgage owing: $75,000 Net Value: $250,000

*Joint tenants with rights of survivorship (see page 149).

What Is Probate?

In some states probate is a relatively simple court-supervised procedure for validating a will, paying the bills of the decedent, and distributing his or her property. In other states, this may not be the case. Procedures and costs vary from state to state.

The probate procedure does not apply to property that goes directly to heirs through beneficiary designations (such as life insurance and pension benefits), property titles (such as joint ownership with right of survivorship), or trust agreements. However, many people do have financial assets and personal property items that have to be transferred to beneficiaries by probate. The heirs for these items are designated by a will or, if there is no will, by the intestacy laws of the state.

How Does Probate Work?

After you pass on, your executor—sometimes working in tandem with a lawyer—will:

1. File your will in the probate court of the county where you reside. (Depending on where you live, the court that handles probate is called the "probate" or "surrogate" court.)
2. Inventory your assets and your debts.
3. Send a formal notice to each of your heirs saying that your will has been filed for probate. (If anyone wants to contest the will, he or she would do so at this point.)
4. If no one contests the provisions of your will, the judge will approve the will.
5. Your executor then pays any debts owed by your estate (including estate taxes) and distributes the remaining property to your heirs.

Estate Distribution Methods

There are six common ways to distribute your assets from your estate, and none of them are perfect:

Do nothing. Dying without a will is called dying **intestate**. When you die intestate, the probate court distributes your estate according to the intestacy laws of your state. The result may be contrary to your wishes and the needs of your family and heirs.

Create a will. A will is a widely used document to distribute assets. Remember, however, a will does not avoid probate. During the probate process, your family and heirs may not have access to your assets. In addition, your estate matters may become public record.

Create a living trust. This is also known as a revocable (changeable or cancelable at any time) inter vivos trust that permits you to place assets into trust while you live (see page 159).

Establish joint ownership. Joint ownership of assets, such as a home, car, or investments, is a common way to transfer property. Upon your death, your ownership is immediately transferred to your surviving co-owner. Although these assets avoid probate, there can be other problems such as loss of the stepped-up cost basis of securities and real estate when they are sold, disinheriting your children from a previous marriage, having your assets exposed to your co-owner's debts or obligations, and forfeiting an opportunity to fully use each co-owner's estate tax exemption. Property owned jointly with someone other than your spouse does not escape estate taxes.

> **Stepped-up basis.** When you inherit assets that have risen in value over the years, your tax basis typically is the value as of the date at your benefactor's death, rather than what your benefactor paid. An asset's value generally is "stepped-up" to the value as of the date of death.

Give your assets away. Gifting can be beneficial, but if you need the money later, it's gone. You can give up to $13,000 (in 2009) to as many individuals as you want in a year, $26,000 if you are a couple. This amount is indexed periodically for inflation.

Designate beneficiaries. Assets such as insurance policies, retirement plans, and some bank accounts let you name a beneficiary. When you die, these assets are paid directly to the person you named as a beneficiary without probate unless the beneficiary is your estate.

The Bare Essentials of Estate Planning

A basic estate plan can help save money, not only legal fees, but expensive probate delays, and ensure that your assets are distributed the way you wanted. A minimum estate plan should consist of the following four documents:

1. A Valid and Up-to-date Will

It's common knowledge to most adults that preparing a will is important. But surprisingly, many of us do not have wills. Do you? A will specifies exactly how your estate is to be divided, who your beneficiaries will be, and who is to be your executor/executrix (personal representative) to settle your estate and distribute your worldly goods.

To be valid, a will must conform to your state's rules. This is important to know if you are planning to relocate to another state after retirement. Your local bar association or area agency on aging can give you guidance here.

You can create a will in three ways:

- Ask your lawyer to draft a will for you.
- Use a step-by-step legal guide or computer program to draft your own will.
- Use a standard fill-in-the-blank will form.

What should you do?

Most experts agree that using a lawyer who specializes in wills and estates is smart and probably essential if your estate is at all complicated, involves real estate, or includes any bequests that might be challenged in court. One disadvantage may be cost, since a complicated will can be expensive. However, simple wills are generally reasonably priced.

If you use a guidebook or computer program such as those published by Nolo Press (www.nolo.com) to write your own will, you can spend less for a perfectly legal document. However, it is recommended that you have a lawyer review your work so that your estate doesn't end up paying in court fees or avoidable estate taxes everything you saved by doing it yourself—and more.

The pros of a fill-in-the-blanks will are easy access (you can purchase them in stationery stores) and economy. The major con is that they're inflexible and cover only the most generic situations, such as leaving everything to your spouse. Is a fill-in-the-blanks will better than no will at all? Maybe. But there's no substitute for sound legal advice.

Basic Information in Your Will

- Your full name, date of birth, and place of birth.
- The address of your principal residence.
- A statement that "this will revokes and supersedes all prior wills and codicils."
- The name(s) of the executor/executrix whom you appoint to settle your estate and contingent appointees in case your first choice designee is unable to serve.
- Your instructions for distributing your property. (State each person's legal name and relationship to you and describe the property he or she is to receive.)
- Directions for who is to receive any property not described above.
- Your directions for what is to happen to your property in the event none of your named beneficiaries survive you.
- The names of the persons whose consent you have obtained to serve as guardians of your minor children and/or dependents.

> *Codicil.* An instrument that revokes, changes, or adds to the terms of a will.

Making it official

The steps to making your will official are clearly spelled out in state law (again, check with your local bar association or area agency on aging).

Exercise V-3 (page 154) is a more detailed checklist that covers important things to consider as you prepare or revise an existing will.

2. Durable Power of Attorney (for Finances)

Do you have someone you would want to handle your financial affairs or make important decisions for you if you were not able to care for yourself? This can happen only if you appoint that person to act for you by signing a durable power of attorney.

A power of attorney is a legal document that authorizes your agent to act for you in matters as simple as writing or endorsing checks or as complex as selling real estate. A power of attorney can be given to anyone you choose and should be drawn up by a lawyer.

> *Durable power of attorney (financial).* Legal document that appoints someone to handle your financial affairs if you are unable to. The durable power of attorney, which terminates upon your death, can take effect immediately upon signing or can be designed to go into effect upon your incapacity.

Be very careful whom you select for your durable power of attorney. You must have complete faith and trust in this person. Be sure the person you have chosen is willing to serve. Also choose a back-up person (attorney-in-fact) and be sure that they, too, agree to serve.

A springing power of attorney takes effect only at the point that you are unable to act for yourself. In this case, the criteria for incapacity would be predeter-

mined, e.g., two doctors say you are no longer capable. Your attorney could hold this power of attorney document at his or her office until it is needed.

What can happen if you don't create a durable power of attorney? A court-appointed conservator (perhaps not one you would have chosen) would oversee the management of your affairs. It can result in a long and expensive process.

3. Power of Attorney (for Health Care)

A power of attorney for health care is sometimes known as a medical power of attorney or health care proxy. It authorizes the person you choose to make medical decisions for you when you are incapable of making them yourself. You specify the conditions when that person would exercise this power.

> *Power of attorney for health care.* A legal document that authorizes an agent you name to make medical decisions for you when you are not able to do so yourself.

You should discuss all your medical decisions, including those for life-sustaining treatment, organ donation, or experimental procedures, with your physician, close family members, and your agent. Make clear exactly what kind of care you would want to receive. If these people understand what measures you want taken, they will be better able to carry out your wishes. Just be sure they are not so emotionally close to you that they couldn't act as you want them to.

You have the right to end or change your durable power of attorney for health care at any time. Review it at least every year or two and whenever there are a major changes in your life, such as a death, a serious illness, or a move to another state. Be sure to give copies to your doctors, your immediate family, your lawyer, and the person you appoint as your agent. You should also keep a copy with your important papers.

It is a good idea to include in your health care document a living will. A living will formally spells out your wishes regarding the use (or exclusion) of medical treatments you specify when you have been

My Will Planning/Updating Checklist

Where I stand today   Date:_____

	Yes	No	N/A
Is my existing will representative of current times, including births or deaths of any of my intended beneficiaries?	☐	☐	☐
Does it reflect changes in tax laws and not contain obsolete sections, including a former state or residence?	☐	☐	☐
Will I make any specific bequests to anyone?	☐	☐	☐
Have I planned for the disposition of my personal property—furniture, jewelry, and automobiles? (This should not be a part of a will, but on a separate list referred to in the will.)	☐	☐	☐
Have I made provisions for the disposition of real estate or business interests?	☐	☐	☐
Does my will give directions for asset distribution if an heir predeceases me?	☐	☐	☐
Are trusts appropriate for certain beneficiaries, or should they receive assets outright?	☐	☐	☐
Is it necessary that particular beneficiaries be provided with periodic income?	☐	☐	☐
Does my will take advantage of the unlimited marital deduction (see page 160)?	☐	☐	☐
Have I provided for guardianship of my children?	☐	☐	☐
Should I give consideration to appointing a "financial" guardian for the children in addition to a personal guardian?	☐	☐	☐
Does my will specify that any minor children's share of my estate be held in trust until they reach maturity?	☐	☐	☐
Does my will provide for a special needs trust to protect my disabled or incompetent heirs?	☐	☐	☐
Have I named an appropriate and capable person or institution to serve as executor or trustee?	☐	☐	☐
Have I selected and named in my will an alternate executor, trustee, and/or guardian?	☐	☐	☐
Does my will grant specific powers to the executor, as necessary, such as to retain or sell property, to invest trust and estate assets, or to settle claims?	☐	☐	☐
Does the ownership of my assets match the provisions of my will?	☐	☐	☐
Have I set aside an easy access account to pay my funeral expenses?	☐	☐	☐
Does my will name who will receive property if the beneficiary disclaims it?	☐	☐	☐
Have I identified where the money to pay debts and estate administrative costs will come from?	☐	☐	☐
Will my survivors have enough cash to pay ordinary family living expenses while my estate is in probate?	☐	☐	☐

diagnosed as terminally ill, irreversibly unconscious, or in a chronic vegetative state. This document will be used if you are unable to provide instructions yourself at the time medical decisions need to be made.

> *Living will.* A written statement that expresses your wishes regarding prolonging your life by artificial, extraordinary, or heroic measures.

A living will is not a substitute for a power of attorney for health care and is often prepared as a combined directive. The living will provides guidance to health care personnel and family members as to your wishes regarding life-sustaining treatment. The health care proxy names the person who is responsible for making health care decisions on your behalf.

Each state that has legally authorized the living will has its own form. Whether you are moving to another state after retirement or staying put, you can get a free copy of your state's living will form from:

> Caring Connections
> 800-658-8898
> www.caringinfo.org
>
> They provide state-specific living will forms at www.caringinfo.org/stateaddownload.

County surrogate offices and area agencies on aging/senior services often have living will forms too. A living will generally must be witnessed by two people.

Under most state laws, there are two events that must occur before a living will can have legal effect:

1. You must be unable to make health care decisions for yourself.
2. For end of life decision-making purposes, you must be diagnosed to be terminal or in a persistent vegetative state or irreversible coma as decided by two doctors, one of whom is your physician.

4. Letter of Instructions

A letter of instructions is not as crucial as the other three essential estate planning documents, but your heirs will be thankful if you provide one. A letter of instructions is an informal document (you don't need an attorney to prepare it) that gives your executor information concerning important financial and personal matters. Although it does not carry the legal weight of a will, the letter of instructions is very helpful because it clarifies any further requests (e.g., your personal wishes as far as funeral preparations are concerned) to be carried out upon death, thus relieving the surviving family members of needless worry and guesswork. Be sure to tell loved ones that this document exists and where it is located.

Exercise V-4 will help you with what to include in your letter of instructions.

Letter of Instructions Checklist

Expected benefits

Employer: _____ Contact name: _____

Telephone number: _____

	Yes	No	Amount	Beneficiary
Life insurance	☐	☐	_____	_____
IRAs	☐	☐	_____	_____
Pension	☐	☐	_____	_____
Profit sharing	☐	☐	_____	_____
401(k), 403(b), 457 plans	☐	☐	_____	_____
Other insurance	☐	☐	_____	_____
Social Security	☐	☐	_____	_____
Veteran's benefits	☐	☐	_____	_____
Other	☐	☐	_____	_____

Contacts

Phone number

Employer: _____ _____

Funeral home: _____ _____

Lawyer: _____ _____

Social Security office: _____ _____

Bank: _____ _____

Insurance companies: _____ _____

_____ _____

Accountant: _____ _____

Financial planner: _____ _____

Your funeral wishes

Details of arrangements: _____

_____

_____

Cemetery location: _____

Plot deed location: _____

Special wishes (anything you want heirs to know)

_____

_____

_____

_____

Personal papers

Location of important documents, e.g., will, birth certificate, diplomas, military records, marriage certificate:

_____

_____

_____

_____

_____

Investments

List of accounts and location of statements and names of institutions where they are held:

_____

_____

_____

_____

_____

Bank records

List of accounts and location of statements/passbooks:

_____

_____

_____

_____

Credit cards

Company, name on card, number, and location:

_____

_____

_____

_____

Letter of Instructions Checklist
(continued)

Automobiles

Location of documents (e.g., titles, insurance): _____

House records

Title or deed, location of ownership documents, mortgages, property taxes, insurance, improvements:

_____

_____

_____

_____

Outstanding loans

Name on loan, account number, monthly payment:

_____

_____

_____

Debts owed the estate

Name on loan, account number, monthly payment owed:

_____

_____

_____

Untitled property (e.g., jewelry, furniture, clothing)

Location of list of who is to receive particular personal items (should be attached to will):

_____

_____

_____

_____

Signature_____   Date _____

The Matter of Trusts

In general, a trust can speed the estate administrative process, protect you (or your beneficiaries) from lawsuits and creditors (if it is an irrevocable trust), and allow for fair distribution of assets following death. Specific trusts can be designed to meet all of your estate planning goals.

> **Revocable.** The creator can change the terms or cancel the trust at any time.
>
> **Irrevocable.** The creator can never change the trust's terms or cancel it.

Example: A trust can specify exact conditions about the distribution of any inheritance (e.g., what age a child can receive it). You can also create a trust that will enable the trustee to distribute trust income to heirs in accordance with their needs. This could be particularly useful if you have a disabled child or if you have children of greatly differing financial means.

A simple will gives your assets to the beneficiaries outright. A trust, living or testamentary, can provide greater likelihood than a will that your exact wishes are carried out.

Depending on the type, a trust may be created to provide you with competent business and investment management, provide for the possibility of your incapacity, and save on estate administration expenses such as probate.

Trusts can be defined as either living trusts or testamentary trusts. A **living trust** is established during the creator's lifetime, usually funded during life, and may continue after the creator's death. A living trust may be revocable or irrevocable. **Testamentary trusts** are created by the will and come into being at the death of the creator. All testamentary trusts are irrevocable.

> **Testamentary trust.** A trust set up to manage property for one or more beneficiaries following the death of the creator.

Living Trusts

A revocable living trust enables you to stay in control of your assets. Therefore, you continue to pay taxes on the trust income. Often called an inter vivos trust, this tool can serve a variety of purposes, including:

- avoidance of probate, but not of estate taxes.
- management of assets in the event you become incapacitated.
- protection of your separate assets in case of divorce.
- protection of your separate assets from a spouse's creditors.
- ability to pass your home to your children after your death, while giving your spouse rights to live in it.
- ease of passing property to your heirs.
- avoidance of multiple probates if you own real property in more than one state.
- protection of privacy in your financial matters.

> **Inter vivos or living trust.** A vehicle for managing your property while you are alive and for transferring your property to heirs at death without being subject to probate. A "trustee" manages the property of others by distributing income and principal to the trust beneficiaries according to your instructions.

Table V-1 shows how a living trust is created and functions.

TABLE V-I

Living Trust

Grantor (you)   transfers assets to trust
Trust   (created by legal document)   owns assets
Trustee   (you or someone you designate)   buys, sells, and manages assets in trust
Beneficiaries   ultimately receive trust assets

Note: Be wary of "free" living trust seminars and high-pressure salespeople. Usually, these events are nothing more than come-ons for paying a lawyer (or a nonlawyer service) $1,000 or more to write up a living trust. Sponsors often try to push the idea that much of your estate is likely to be gobbled up by estate tax and probate costs unless you set up trusts now to avoid some of the estate tax. They encourage you to buy life insurance to pay the rest of the estate taxes owed. In truth, most people don't have estates large enough to owe estate tax. Be sure you need these benefits before paying a substantial amount for them.

To make maximum use of a trust, it is important that property titles be changed to the name of the trust. For example, the title would say "Susan Jones Trust," not just "Susan Jones." This process may include preparing a new deed for real estate, changing the title on bank accounts, or changing titles on brokerage accounts. A "pour-over" will should accompany the trust agreement to cover property not placed in the trust during your lifetime, so that it will go into the trust at death via a simple probate process.

Pour-over will. A will that directs that the property subject to it (e.g., IRAs, investments) be "poured-over" into a trust upon the maker's death.

Irrevocable trusts are less common and are generally used for very specific purposes such as management of assets going to family members the trust creator (you) believes are too young to manage the property themselves. For persons with estates larger than $3.5 million (in 2009), a major advantage of an irrevocable living trust is that the assets in the trust are removed from the maker's estate, assuming that the owner is not the trustee.

An irrevocable trust may be set up during your lifetime or provided for in your will. Either way, you give up all control of your funds in order to receive tax advantages. The trustee passes the funds on to your heir(s) as directed by the trust document. Variations include:

- support trusts that provide income for your dependents.
- bypass trusts that provide income to your spouse while holding the assets for children.
- qualified terminable interest property (QTIP) trusts that maximize the marital deduction (see "Spousal Transfers" below) while designating heirs to succeed your spouse. (Often used in a second marriage situation where one or both spouses have children from a former union.)
- insurance trusts that keep insurance proceeds out of your estate.
- charitable trusts that transfer assets to charities and enable you to claim an immediate tax deduction.

Spousal Transfers

The unlimited marital deduction allows one spouse to pass his or her entire estate, no matter what the size, to the other completely free of federal estate taxes. However, giving all of your estate to your spouse outright may not always be the best method of transferring property.

If your estate was valued at more than $3.5 million in 2009, consult a financial advisor for guidance about a bypass or "B" trust.

Uniform Transfers to Minors Act

A convenient way to make a moderate-sized gift to a person under age 18 or 21 (depending upon the state of residence) is to use the Uniform Transfers to Minors Act (UTMA). This allows a person to give property to a minor by transferring it to a custodian who holds and administers the property for the minor until he or she reaches age 18 or 21. The gift may be securities, life insurance policies, annuity contracts, money, or real property. A major advantage of a UTMA, rather than a trust, is the ease of creation and its limited expense. The custodian has broad discretion in managing the property and may expend the property for the minor's benefit. You may name yourself "custodian." You should also name a "successor custodian" in case you or your first choice can't do the job. However, if you name yourself custodian and die before the child comes of age, the money will be included in your taxable estate—as though you hadn't given it away.

> *Uniform Transfers to Minors Act.* Allows transfer of ANY type of property, real or personal, tangible or intangible, to a minor, to be managed by a custodian for the benefit of a minor.

Gifting Cautions: Titling Property with Others

Some families believe that adding names of family members to the titles of property is a wise move to avoid probate and formalities. Frequently, they have not estimated the associated costs based on the kind of ownership they already have—much of it may not even go through probate. If you or your parents are tempted to add names to titles, do consider the following cautions:

- You can lose control of the asset. Property can be "attached" if the recipient divorces, is sued, or needs cash for his or her needs (accident, illness).
- All owners must sign (agree) if they want to mortgage, remortgage, or sell in the future.
- If one owner dies, that share is in his or her estate, so the surviving co-owner must deal with heirs of the deceased co-owner.
- Homestead credit eligibility (a property tax break) can be lost if the co-owner is not living in the residence more than 6 months a year.
- Giving assets of more than $13,000 (in 2009) in any one year to any one person may create a taxable gift and require a gift tax return to be filed.

Estate Taxes

There is no secret about estate taxes. The government wants a share of your estate. Estate tax is the federal tax imposed on transfers of assets from one person to another at death based on the value of the decedent's estate assets.

But, before you dive too deeply into this subject, you should know that most people don't have to worry about it, especially now. Thanks to a tax law that became effective June 7, 2001, most estates are too small to be taxed. Generally, no federal estate tax is assessed if the net value of your taxable estate at death is less than $3.5 million (in 2009). Estate tax rates are determined by the size of a person's taxable estate. The more you own, the higher the rate.

A prosperous married couple, with a little bit of planning—starting by making sure that at least $3.5 million in assets is in each spouse's name (2009 figure)—can pass along $7 million tax-free (in 2009) under current estate tax legislation (see Table V-2).

Some states, in addition to federal estate tax, impose a state inheritance or death tax on the property of a deceased person who lived or owned real estate in that state (depending on whom your beneficiaries are). You can specify in your will that your estate should pay whatever inheritance taxes are due to save your beneficiaries from having to sell property they inherit so they can pay the tax.

Summary of Federal Estate, Gift, and Generation-Skipping Tax Changes

The Economic Growth and Tax Relief Reconciliation Act of 2001 made significant changes in the estate, gift, and generation-skipping tax (GST) regulations. Although the estate tax has been "repealed" effective January 1, 2010, the so-called **sunset provisions** restore the pre-2001 tax law regulations effective January 1, 2011. Thus, the estate tax has been repealed only for people who will die in the year 2010 (Table V-2).

- The estate tax exemption is $3.5 million for 2009. There will be no estate tax in 2010. The estate tax will be restored beginning in 2011, with a $1 million exemption, if no further legislation is passed (Table V-2).
- The lifetime gift tax exemption is $1 million. As the estate tax exemption increased from 2004 through 2009, the gift tax exemption did not.
- The GST exemption is $3.5 million for 2009.
- The top estate, gift, and GST tax rate is 45% for 2009. The estate and GST taxes will be zero in 2010 and, absent a new tax law, will be restored to 55% in 2011.
- The estate and GST taxes have been repealed as of 2010, but for 1 year only. What will really happen in 2010 and thereafter, we'll have to wait and see. New tax laws could be passed.
- Although the new law provides that there will not be any estate or GST tax in 2010, there will still be a gift tax. The top gift tax rate will be the top individual income tax rate (currently 35%).

> *Gift tax.* A tax imposed by the federal government on the giver of substantial gifts made during his or her lifetime. No tax is usually owed at the time that a tax return is filed unless you have used up your unified credit (the estate tax credit that exempts a certain amount of assets from taxation).

> *Generation-skipping trust (GST).* A trust set up for the benefit of grandchildren. Frequently, it is drafted such that the trust pays only income to the middle generation (the grandchildren's parents). When the middle generation passes on, the trust principal is divided among the grandchildren—the final beneficiaries.

- In 2010, when the estate and GST taxes are "repealed," inherited property will no longer receive a stepped-up basis (see page 151).

> **Basis.** The value assigned to an asset from which taxable gain or loss is determined. It is generally the original deposit plus additional deposits and reinvested distributions.

People who inherit assets do not have to pay income or capital gains tax on the value of those assets at the time of inheritance. However, once a person inherits assets, any income subsequently received from the assets is treated as regular income or capital gains and subject to federal and state income tax. One exception to this rule is inheriting someone's traditional IRA. Income tax payments are owed because when the deceased first invested the money, the contributions were tax deductible, as was any money the IRA earned. When the money is withdrawn, Uncle Sam wants his due, regardless of the death of the person who opened the account. However, a surviving spouse usually is able to roll over her husband's IRA to her own account and not pay tax on it until she makes withdrawals. Other beneficiaries may be eligible for similar treatment.

Calculating your required distribution from an IRA, beginning at age 70½, no longer requires a degree in math or accounting. Thanks to a 2002 change in government regulations, now all you have to do is add up the total amount in all of your IRA accounts on December 31 of the previous year and divide the amount in your IRAs by the appropriate figure in the Uniform Distribution Table. The table is available at many financial institutions that serve as IRA custodians (e.g., brokerage firms) and online at the Rutgers Cooperative Extension Web site at www.rce.rutgers. edu/money/ira-table.asp. You can also use an online calculator such as that at http://njaes.rutgers.edu/money/ira-table.asp.

> Note: The gift giver pays the gift tax, not the recipient.

TABLE V-2

Estate Tax Exemptions

Year	Estate tax exemption ($)	Top estate tax rate (%)
2008	2,000,000	45
2009	3,500,000	45
2010	Estate tax repealed	0
2011	1,000,000	55

> Important point: No income tax is owed on inherited property at the time of the inheritance.

> This advice bears repeating: Even people who do not have enough assets to be liable for estate taxes should have a will so that their property is disposed of as they intend. People with estate plans or wills should ask a lawyer to review them to make sure they take best advantage of current tax laws.

Gift Tax

Congress imposes a tax on substantial gifts made during a gift-giver's lifetime. The law came into being because the government figured out that if only property left at death were taxed, then everyone would give away as much as they could while they were alive—thus, cheating the government of its due. So, to nix tax incentives for making large gifts, gift tax rates are the same as estate tax rates, except starting in 2010 when the estate tax is due to phase out completely for that year alone. No such luck with gift taxes—you'll pay gift tax at the top individual bracket.

If you make a taxable gift, you will not have to pay the tax at that time. Instead, the total amount of the taxable gift must be deducted from your estate tax exemption.

Good news! Gift tax rules contain four exceptions:

Limited annual tax-free giving. Federal tax law allows individuals to give annual tax-free gifts up to $13,000 per year (in 2009) to as many persons as they choose. Married couples may give up to $26,000 per year tax-free to as many persons as they choose.

Example: Sharon gives $13,000 to each of her four children ($52,000 total) in 2009. All of these gifts are tax-exempt.

The marital exemption. All gifts between a husband and wife in which the recipient is a U.S. citizen are exempt from gift tax, regardless of the value of the gift.

Example: Susan leaves $2 million to her husband Ben. No estate or gift tax is owed.

Note: The gift tax exemption is indexed yearly to the cost of living. As the cost of living rises, the gift tax exemption will also rise, but only in increments of $1,000 rounded down to the lower thousand. So in this case, cost of living increases beyond 2009 must cumulatively add up to more than $1,000 before the annual exclusion is raised to $14,000 per year.

The marital deduction can be disadvantageous if a couple has assets worth more than the estate tax exclusion and each leaves everything to the other. The result is that the surviving spouse's estate could grow so large that there is an estate tax bill due at death, when there could be none had they taken advantage of each spouse's exemption. The result is a higher estate tax than necessary.

Gifts for medical bills. You can make unlimited gifts in a single year if you make the gifts in direct payment of medical bills for someone else. The requirement is that you must pay the money directly to the provider of the medical service.

Gift for school tuition. You can make a gift of school tuition (for any grade or type of school) by making a direct payment to the institution for tuition bills for as many students as you like. This exemption applies to tuition only, not dorm rental fees, college meal plans, or the purchase of books. You cannot reimburse someone who has already paid the tuition bill and receive the tax exemption.

Your Minimum "Need to Knows" about Estate Planning

- Two principal estate planning goals exist: to pass on as much of your assets with the least amount of taxation and to make sure that your property is distributed the way you want.

- A bare bones estate plan consists of three documents—a will, a durable power of attorney for your financial affairs, and a power of attorney for health care. It's also helpful to include a final letter of instructions.

- Plan to have enough liquid assets so that there is ready cash to pay for funeral costs and other expenses that follow death.

- Whenever there is a federal or state tax law change, have your attorney or accountant review your estate plan to see if any of the changes affect you.

- Put together an estate plan that is appropriate for today. If your circumstances change, e.g., divorce or widowhood, your estate plan can easily be updated to reflect these changes. Review your estate plan at least every 5 years.

- The consequences of not minimizing taxes on your estate (if it is substantial) are huge.

- Make sure that your assets are titled properly to ensure smooth distribution to your heirs. This is especially important if you have a trust.

- Beneficiary and contingent beneficiary designations on IRA and retirement benefits need to be reviewed periodically, perhaps every year or two.

- The Economic Growth and Tax Relief Reconciliation Act of 2001 increased the estate tax exemption in stages and decreased the top estate tax rate.

- A will is the only document through which you can legally name a guardian for your minor children.

- Four legal exemptions to gift tax rules exist: 1) the annual $13,000 exemption (in 2009) to as many people as you want; 2) the marital exemption that allows any amount to be transferred to a spouse; 3) unlimited gifts for medical bills; 4) unlimited gifts for school tuition.

- The biggest estate planning mistake people make is not having a will. This can create a nightmare for your loved ones. No matter how large or small your estate is, don't let this happen to you.

Money and Relationships

One of the certainties of life is change. Among the things that can change, sometimes abruptly, in a women's life are:

- job/career and employment status (e.g., full-time and part-time work)
- health (oneself and family members)
- amount of household income (increase or decrease)
- amount of assets and debts (i.e., household net worth)
- relationships (e.g., widowhood, divorce)

The next four lessons discuss the impacts of relationship changes on a woman's financial well-being. Four common life transitions are described below:

- widowhood
- divorce
- marriage and remarriage
- cohabitation with a nonspouse.

Financial planning strategies for each life stage are described. The objective of this unit is to help readers prepare adequately for the financial consequences of changed relationships. A change in marital status, for example, need not cause a financial crisis.

Widowhood

Few events can turn a woman's life upside down as can the death of a spouse. In addition to the shock and grief associated with death and the loss of a husband's emotional support and companionship, there is often less household income than before. Meanwhile, household bills stay the same or even increase if there are high medical or funeral bills to repay.

In addition, there are many decisions that need to be made (e.g., how to invest the proceeds of a life insurance policy), forms that need to be completed (e.g., pensions, Social Security), and suggestions from "helpful" family members and/or financial product salespeople. For some widows, the pressure to do something—anything—becomes unbearable. Decisions are thus made quickly, much like a "hot potato" that must quickly be tossed away.

The financial aftermath of widowhood is especially traumatic for women who have little understanding of their household finances. Suddenly there is this necessary "learning curve" that comes at the worst possible time. Financial knowledge and experience and marketable job skills, on the other hand, are resources for more effective coping.

Below are some suggestions to cope with financial issues related to widowhood.

- Take your time. Do not make any major financial decisions immediately. If you receive an insurance settlement or other payment, place it in a bank certificate of deposit or money market mutual fund until you have time to explore longer-term investment alternatives and/or educate yourself about personal finance.

- Make sure you're covered by health insurance. Assuming you have no health insurance of your own, call your spouse's employer to find out if you're still covered under the company plan. If not, you may be able to apply for continuation of coverage for up to 36 months under the federal **COBRA law** if you apply within 60 days of your spouse's death and pay the premiums. If you've always had employer-provided benefits, the premiums for COBRA coverage can be a shock. However, they will probably be lower than what you could qualify for as an individual. COBRA coverage is available to employees of companies with 20 or more workers.

- Get organized. Among the documents that you'll need to collect are original death certificates (you'll probably need about a dozen); insurance policies; your marriage certificate; birth certificates for dependent children; the deceased's will; retirement plan (e.g., pension) records; and a certificate of discharge from the military, if any.

- Retitle a spouse's or jointly held (with right of survivorship) assets, such as bank accounts, credit cards, auto titles, and the deed to your house, into your name. Expect minor hassles, such as the need to obtain a signature guarantee for some

---

Resources that Can Ease a Widow's Financial Distress

- adequate life insurance
- a joint and survivor pension that provides continued retirement benefits
- a stable source of income (e.g., employment or a small business)
- continued health insurance coverage
- savings/investments for financial goals (e.g., children's college)
- low or no household debt
- availability of Social Security survivor's benefits
- benefit counselors in a deceased spouse's human resources department

---

documents. Also review your will, retirement savings accounts (e.g., 401(k) or 403(b) plan and IRA), and insurance policies. You may need to change beneficiaries. Consider adding contingent beneficiaries as well.

- Identify and secure financial resources. Some examples include life insurance policy proceeds (both individual and employer-provided coverage); employee benefits (e.g., deceased spouse's 401(k) or 403(b) plan), and Veteran's benefits (e.g., burial in a national cemetery).

- If your deceased husband was employed, contact his employer regarding benefits due survivors. For example, your husband's estate may be due a final paycheck or payment for unused vacation and sick leave. If the death was work-related, there may be worker's compensation benefits. If he was retired and receiving a pension, check with the employer about continued spousal payments.

- Apply for widow's Social Security benefits. A widow must be at least age 60 or have children under age 16 living at home to collect these payments. If a widow collects a benefit on or after turning 60, when she turns 62, she can switch to a payment based on her own earnings record if it will increase her benefit. For additional information, visit the Social Security Administration Web site at www.ssa.gov.

- Review your income tax status and withholding amounts for pension payments and household income. Complete a new W-4 form to make changes. Widows can file federal and state taxes for their spouse for the year of death. They can file jointly for the year of death and for the next 2 years as a qualifying widow. For further information, check Internal Revenue Service (IRS) publication 559, *Survivors, Executors, and Administrators.*

- Adjust to the situation economically, however painful. This may require selling your home and moving to a smaller place if you cannot afford the payments. Whether you were a full-time homemaker or part of a two-income couple, you are bound to feel the effects of the loss of your husband's income. Develop a spending plan (budget) based on your changed financial status.

- Read and learn about financial planning. Subscribe to a financial publication and/or attend seminars to increase your knowledge. The Cooperative Extension basic investing course *Investing for Your Future* is available free online at www. investing.rutgers.edu.

- Evaluate your marketability as an employee, particularly if you were a full-time homemaker prior to your husband's death. Marketable skills and increased education are two of the best options available for gaining greater economic security and a higher standard of living. Community colleges and women's centers are good sources of information.

- Spend money and use credit wisely and try not to allow monthly consumer debt payments to exceed 15–20% of take-home pay. It is not uncommon for widows to act out their bitterness about being "abandoned," or to simply try to maintain their previous lifestyle, with credit cards. Another common error is dissipation of insurance proceeds within a few months of a husband's death.

- If you don't have credit in your own name, apply for a secured credit card that is backed by the deposit of a specific amount of money (e.g., $1,000) with the credit card issuer.

- Seek professional advice, where needed, such as an attorney to help with estate tax returns or a Certified Financial Planner (CFP®) for investment decisions. Ask questions about anything that you don't understand or feel comfortable with. There are no "dumb" questions when your future financial security is at stake. If a professional advisor does not answer your questions with patience and empathy, look elsewhere. For the names of local CFPs, call 800-282-7526 or check the Web site www.fpanet.org.

- Don't pay any large debts that your late spouse may have incurred until you check with a lawyer. Debts owed by the deceased are the responsibility of the estate and should be forwarded to the executor. Creditors will simply need to wait until the estate is settled. If you pay bills with out-of-pocket funds or personal savings, you could leave yourself short of necessary cash, both for living expenses and a financial emergency (e.g., car repairs).

- Review whether or not you need the same amount of life insurance as before and make changes accordingly. You might also want to sell assets, such as your spouse's car, if they are no longer necessary and/or require unwanted payments. Resist the urge to sell or give away your husband's "collectible" possessions (e.g., gun or coin collection) without first checking their value.

Divorce

Like widowhood, divorce can have a profound long-term effect on the financial well-being of a woman and her children. This is especially true for women who lack marketable job skills and/or those who earn no, or a low, percentage of household income. Unlike widows, there are no insurance settlements to receive when a spouse is gone. In addition, household assets and debts must be divided and the cost of retaining legal counsel and/or a mediator is an added expense. A number of well-publicized studies have found that divorce reduces the economic status of women by varying percentages. Many women must cope not only with the effects of divorce but with the financial challenges of single parenthood as well.

The goal of divorce, in many states, is to arrive at a settlement that is "fair and equitable" based on the facts and circumstances of an individual couple's case. For example, the earning ability of each spouse, their respective ages, the amount of their assets and debts, and the length of the marriage are key decision-making factors. In some cases, decisions made at divorce are carried out immediately. For example, if the only property to be divided is a bank account, it can be closed out and divided. Other divorces involve the promise of things that will take place in the future, such as spousal pension benefits, selling a house after the youngest child reaches age 18, or college expenses for children.

The period of time before and after a divorce is stressful for many women. They are expected to make rational and far-reaching decisions at a time of emotional turmoil. This may also be many women's first experience with the court system and hiring an attorney. Expenses often increase when a spouse moves out and sets up a separate household. It is important, however, to keep a clear head and not let emotions (e.g., revenge) result in missed payments, lapsed insurance, or other negative consequences.

Below are some suggestions to cope with financial issues related to divorce.

- Do not sign a property settlement agreement, or any other divorce-related document, that you do not understand or one that you feel contains unfair terms. Consult your own attorney—not your spouse's attorney—before signing anything.

- Estimate the dollar value of your household property using **fair market value**, which is the price at which a willing buyer will buy an item and a willing seller will sell it. **Replacement value**, on the other hand, is the cost of replacing an item (e.g., refrigerator) at current prices. As you and your spouse discuss how you'll divide property, whichever one of you plans to keep the property may think in terms of fair market value, while the other (who will be replacing a piece of property) may think in terms of replacement value.

- In addition to dividing your property, you must determine who will pay which part of debts incurred during your marriage. List all of your and your spouse's debts, including your home mortgage, car payments, and credit card accounts. Usually, one spouse or the other will assume an obligation and agree to "hold harmless" the other party. However, it is important to note that if either party doesn't pay a jointly held debt, creditors may collect from either spouse. Creditors are not bound by any agreement between spouses.

- Parents who are employable must support their children. The court will determine each parent's obligation by applying state **child support** (payments by one spouse to another to meet the needs of the couple's child(ren) after legal separation or divorce) guidelines based on combined gross monthly income and number of children. Courts generally do not require child support past age 18 unless the parents agree in their divorce settlement that support will continue while a child is receiving post-high-school training or a college education.

- A divorced person is eligible for Social Security benefits based on a former spouse's earnings, even if the former spouse is not yet retired. To qualify for benefits, the marriage must have lasted at least 10 years and both you and your ex-husband must be at least 62 years old. The amount paid to a qualified ex-spouse is a percentage of the benefit due the primary beneficiary. If the primary beneficiary has not applied for benefits, but can qualify and is age 62 or older, the spouse must have been divorced for at least two years. If the ex-husband was already receiving benefits before the divorce, there is no two-year waiting period. If you remarry, you lose the right to benefits based on a former spouse's earnings unless the subsequent marriage(s) also end in divorce. If more than one marriage lasts 10 years or longer, you can elect benefits based on the higher ex-spouse's earnings.

- Like widows, divorced persons may be entitled to continued group health insurance for up to 36 months under the federal COBRA law if they lose their status as a dependent spouse. The cost of coverage cannot exceed 102% of the premium (group rate) paid by your ex-spouse's employer. You must apply for this coverage within 60 days after a divorce is granted.

- A postdivorce spending plan (budget) is essential for making realistic support and property distribution decisions. Some women retain possession of the family home when they are actually unable to afford the mortgage, taxes, and maintenance on their salary alone. They subsequently get behind on payments and may have to sell the house at a loss. Difficult as it might be to accept, a much better alternative is often moving to a smaller home or renting and either selling the house and dividing the proceeds or having a higher-earning spouse "buy you out." Make a list of anticipated income and expenses and adjust the numbers until expenses are no more than what you earn after divorce. Use Exercise V-5, *Postdivorce Housing Analysis,* to compare the costs of staying in the family home and renting. If you are temporarily living with family members, be sure to make plans based on actual living costs.

- Know the tax consequences of divorce-related decisions. Marital status on December 31 determines your tax-filing status for the year; if you divorce before this date, you must file as either a single taxpayer or head of household. Usually, the custodial parent claims a couple's children as dependents. However, a custodial parent can waive the right to claim dependents as part of a divorce settlement, thus allowing the other parent to do so. A signed waiver statement (IRS form #8332) from the custodial parent must be attached to the noncustodial parent's tax return.

- Child support is neither deductible by the spouse who pays it nor is it included in the income of the recipient. **Alimony** (according to Webster's dictionary, payment made to one spouse by another pending or after legal separation or divorce), on the other hand, is taxable to the recipient and deductible as an adjustment to the payer's gross income. Alimony generally ceases upon remarriage while child support continues until children are grown.

- Protect your child support and/or alimony income stream with life and disability insurance on your ex-spouse. Otherwise, if he dies or becomes disabled, future support payments may cease. If necessary, take ownership of a life insurance policy and/or request third-party notification of nonpayment if there's reason to believe that your ex-spouse would let it lapse or change the beneficiary.

- Consider hiring a professional mediator to resolve issues related to divorce. Mediators are trained not to take sides but rather to work out a settlement that is fair and equitable for both spouses. This includes both financial issues and other

Postdivorce Housing Analysis

Part 1: Estimated proceeds from sale of home

Estimated sales price   (a) $ _____

Selling expenses

    Amount required to pay off loan(s) in full $ _____

    Fix-up costs connected with sale (paint, minor repairs, etc.) $ _____

    Realtor's commission (often 6% of sales price) $ _____

    Seller's portion of closing costs (often 1% of sales price) $ _____

    Other sales costs $ _____

    Total selling expenses   (b) $ _____

Estimated proceeds from sale (a minus b) $ _____

Part 2: Estimated cost of staying in the family home

    Monthly mortgage payment $ _____

    Monthly insurance payment* $ _____

    Monthly property tax payment* $ _____

    Electricity, gas, heating oil $ _____

    Water and sewer charges $ _____

    Garbage pickup $ _____

    Yard work $ _____

    Homeowner fee, association fee $ _____

    Upkeep and repairs $ _____

    Other $ _____

    Total monthly cost $ _____

* These may be included in the mortgage payment; if not, divide the yearly expense by 12 to arrive at the monthly cost.

EXERCISE V-5

Postdivorce Housing Analysis
(continued)

Part 3: Estimated cost of renting

Monthly costs

    Rent $_____

    Electricity, gas, heating oil $_____

    Water and sewer charges $_____

    Garbage pickup $_____

    Yard work, if it is the renter's responsibility $_____

    Renter's insurance $_____

    Other $_____

    Total monthly costs $_____

One-time costs

    Moving $_____

    Deposits (security, cleaning, pet, key) $_____

    Utility hookups and deposits $_____

    Other $_____

    Total one-time costs $_____

Adapted from: Ford, R., *Financial Concerns at Divorce* (1990). Rutgers Cooperative Extension Curriculum.

considerations such as child custody. Once these issues are resolved, each spouse's attorney can assist with a final agreement. This is usually a far less expensive and time-consuming process than letting lawyers negotiate a settlement.

- Recognize that 50/50 splits of assets are not necessarily equal. For example, if one spouse takes sole possession of the family home, he or she also shoulders the burden of future property taxes and repairs. The other spouse who, for example, receives the same dollar value in the form of a pension has an asset that will continue to grow tax-deferred. Clearly, this property distribution is not equal even though the dollar value may be the same at the time of divorce.

Marriage and Remarriage

Getting married or remarried means blending the financial management practices and beliefs, not to mention the income, assets, and debts, of two different people. Sometimes, this is not easy. For example, "spenders" married to "savers" are bound to experience some conflicts. For people who remarry, there are additional challenges, such as relationships with stepchildren and handling child support payments to or from a former spouse.

One of the dilemmas that all couples face is developing a successful way of handling their money and paying bills. Some couples choose to pool their money in one account, while others keep their income and/or assets separate. Another issue is how much each spouse contributes toward household expenses and how much each keeps for personal expenses.

There are also "technical" details, such as who keeps the checkbook register, pays the bills, and makes investment decisions. Although one spouse often assumes these tasks, the other should also be familiar with the couple's cash flow and net worth. If both spouses receive employer benefits, they need to be coordinated. In addition, spending decisions, such as the choice of furniture or a vacation destination, must be made and often involve compromises.

Below are some suggestions related to financial decisions upon marriage or remarriage.

- In two-paycheck households, prorate the amount that each spouse contributes toward joint household expenses. The fairest way to do this is to base each spouse's deposit upon his or her respective income. For example, if a husband and wife earn 65% and 35% of household income, respectively, the husband should pay about two-thirds of family bills and the wife the other third. After all bills are paid, each spouse should have some spending money that is theirs to do with as they please without consulting their partner.

In one-earner households, a system should be established for providing spending money for the nonearning spouse.

- Take advantage of each spouse's access to retirement savings such as 401(k) and 403(b) plans. Contributions can be written off against a couple's joint income, and both spouses benefit. If cash is limited for retirement plan contributions, fund the plan with the higher employer match. Two other important considerations are the investment options offered by each spouse's employer and the time required for benefits to become vested.

- If the lower-earning spouse is the only one with access to an employer-sponsored retirement plan, he or she should contribute as much as possible. In return, the higher-earning spouse can provide the lower-earning spouse with some additional spending money to offset the reduction in salary or pay for a higher percentage of household expenses.

- Review and revise the beneficiary designations on life insurance policies and pension and retirement plans (e.g., 401(k)s) and name your spouse as primary beneficiary, where appropriate. When you remarry, you'll probably want to provide for your children from your former marriage as well as your new spouse. One way to do this is with a bypass trust or a QTIP trust (see page 160). Income from these trusts goes to the surviving spouse but, upon his or her death, assets are distributed to children or whomever the trust maker designates. In addition, it is important to have a will drafted or revised to reflect your changed marital status.

- Communicate openly and honestly about financial matters with your new spouse. One effective way to do this is with "I messages." Instead of blaming or accusing each other (e.g., "You're spending too much money and we're going to end up in the poorhouse"), start the message with the word "I" and explain how you feel. An example of an "I message" is "I get worried when we charge more than $300 per month because I'm afraid we won't be able to pay it back."

- Set common financial goals, such as the purchase of furniture, or retirement in 2017. Agree to provide support to each other for shared goals and develop an action plan to make each goal a reality. In addition, discuss your childhood financial influences, assets and debts, and money management habits (e.g., use of direct deposit or online banking and debt repayment practices). Money values should also be discussed because they underlie financial decisions.

- Maintain at least one separate credit card in each spouse's name in case something happens to the other person (e.g., illness or accident) or in the event of a divorce.

- Adjust tax withholding on form W-4 to account for the fact that as a couple your combined in-come may place you in a higher tax bracket than if you filed as two single taxpayers.

- If health benefits require employee contributions, select the plan that provides the most comprehensive coverage at a reasonable cost. If both plans are of high quality and provide spousal coverage, ask if extra pay is available (from either employer) for waiving coverage.

- Think of each spouse's individual investments as part of one larger portfolio and diversify accordingly. This is especially true for retirement plans, for which there is a tendency to view investments as "his" and "hers" because they are connected with different employers.

- Weigh the pros and cons of a one- vs. two-pay-check lifestyle. Sometimes, especially when the second income is a lot smaller than the first, it hardly makes any difference at all financially to have both spouses working. Work-related expenses, such as income taxes, child care, and transportation, may consume most of the second income. Of course, there are also other factors to consider such as the self-fulfillment and socialization that work provides.

Cohabitation

Unmarried couples head well over 6.5 million U.S. households. People choose to live together but not marry for a number of reasons. Some are financial, such as a desire to retain Social Security and pension benefits (common among older unmarried couples) and/or to reduce income taxes (the so-called "marriage tax" requires many couples to pay more taxes than they would if they filed as two single taxpayers).

Other reasons frequently cited for not marrying include concerns about leaving an inheritance for children from a prior marriage, fear of becoming legally responsible for a partner's debts or medical bills, and a personal bias against, or previous bad experience with, marriage or remarriage. For same-sex couples, most states' laws prohibit legally sanctioned marriages.

Nonmarriage relationships lack many of the legal protections afforded to married couples. Thus, special planning must be done to ensure the long-term financial security of each partner. This is especially critical with estate planning. If you haven't clearly stated your property distribution desires in a will, it is almost certain that the surviving partner will lose out. This is because state intestacy laws (which cover people who die without a will) require possessions to be distributed to your closest living relative. In addition, most employer benefits (e.g., health insurance and pensions) cover only employees and a spouse. Unmarried couples often must pay more for health insurance and save more for retirement as a result.

Below are some suggestions for unmarried couples.

- Inquire about joint property insurance instead of paying more for two separate policies. Some major property insurance carriers allow unmarried partners to share a renter's or homeowner's policy. Each party must own part of the property that is covered, however.

- Consider signing a **cohabitation agreement**. This is a legal document, similar to a prenuptial agreement, that is drafted by a lawyer and describes each partner's responsibility for household expenses and who will get what in the event of a breakup.

- Draw up a durable power of attorney and health care power of attorney if you want your partner to make financial and medical decisions for you in the event of your incapacitation. Otherwise, the courts will probably appoint a blood relative to manage your affairs.

- Consider maintaining separate financial accounts to avoid liability for each other's debts and to protect each partner's assets. This means individual bank and brokerage accounts and credit cards. Otherwise, if assets and debts get commingled, one partner's creditors can seize jointly owned assets to repay a debt for which the other partner would otherwise not be responsible. With joint bank accounts, either partner could withdraw all the funds at any time.

- Consider owning some property, such as a house, jointly with a right of survivorship. This allows jointly held assets to pass directly to your partner upon your death, thereby avoiding probate. This is especially important when your unmarried partner does not get along with your family. The surviving partner automatically becomes the sole owner of the property when the other partner dies.

- Understand that if both partners sign a lease, mortgage, or other financial contract, each is responsible for making full payments regardless of what happens to the relationship (e.g., if the relationship ends and one partner moves to another state). Consider whether you can handle joint obligations on your income alone, if necessary.

Your Minimum "Need to Knows" about Money and Relationships

- One of the certainties of life is change. Changed relationships (e.g., divorce, marriage) have financial consequences for women and their children.

- When confronting a financial crisis, such as widowhood or divorce, take your time with major financial decisions, such as investing a large sum of money.

- If possible, continue health insurance provided through a former spouse's employer. Check to see if you are eligible for COBRA coverage, which can extend benefits for up to 36 months at group rates.

- Widows should identify and secure resources, such as Social Security benefits, life insurance proceeds, and a deceased spouse's pension and retirement savings.

- A change from married to single status may necessitate painful adjustments such as moving to a smaller home.

- Consult your own attorney before signing a divorce property settlement agreement.

- A divorced person is eligible for Social Security benefits on an ex-spouse's record if the marriage lasted at least 10 years.

- Many divorce property settlement decisions have income consequences.

- 50/50 splits (by value) of marital assets are not necessarily equal.

- Two-earner households could prorate each spouse's contribution toward joint household expenses based upon their respective incomes.

- "I" messages are effective ways to communicate with family members about financial matters.

- Each spouse in a married couple should have at least one credit card in his or her name.

- A two-earner couple should coordinate employee health benefits and retirement plan investments.

- Nonmarriage relationships lack many of the legal protections afforded to married couples and, thus, require special financial planning strategies.

Action Steps

SESSION V: **Planning for Future Life Events**

☐ Complete the *Estate Planning Checklist* (Exercise V-I, page 147) to identify estate planning strengths and gaps.

☐ Use the *My Estate Inventory* worksheet (Exercise V-2, page 150) to total the value of property in your estate and to provide information about your financial affairs to your heirs.

☐ Check that ownership titles on property do not conflict with terms of your will.

☐ Contact an attorney to draft a first-time will or review and revise an existing will.

☐ Review the *My Will Planning/Updating Checklist* worksheet (Exercise V-3, page 154) to identify planning gaps.

☐ Contact an attorney to draft durable powers of attorney for finances and health care.

☐ Prepare a living will to express your wishes about prolonging life by artificial means.

☐ Prepare a letter of instructions to list requests to be carried out upon your death.

☐ Consider using the annual gift tax exclusion to assist others and reduce your taxable estate.

References

A Money Management Workbook (1999). Washington, D.C.: American Association of Retired Persons (Women's Financial Information Program).

Brandt, E., Kirk Fox, L., and Hardcastle, K. (1997). *Making Financial Decisions When Divorce Occurs: An Idaho Guide*. Bulletin 733. Moscow, Idaho: University of Idaho Cooperative Extension.

Chatzky, J.S. (1995). Splitsville. *Smart Money* 9: 98–109.

Clark, J.B. (2007, July). Leave Your Legal Affairs in Order. *Kiplinger's Personal Finance*, 81-82.

Clifford, D. (1999). *Estate Planning Basics*. Berkeley, Calif: Nolo Press.

Connors, P., and Nelson, S.B. (1995). Divvying up your retirement money. *Kiplinger's Personal Finance Magazine* 8: 95–97.

Coordinating benefits as a couple (1999). *Loose Change* 3/4: 3.

Dahl, B. (1996). *A Working Woman's Guide to Financial Security*. Urbana, Ill.: University of Illinois Cooperative Extension.

Dale, A. (2007, April 5). Estate Taxes Flummox Planners. *The Wall Street Journal*, D2.

Estate Planning News (2001). Kleinberg, Kaplan, Wolff, and Cohen, PC.

Financial Insights (2000). Minneapolis, Minn.: American Express Financial Corporation.

Ford, R. (1990). *Financial Concerns at Divorce*. New Brunswick, N.J.: Rutgers Cooperative Extension Curriculum.

How divorce affects women's Social Security (1994). *Kiplinger's Personal Finance Magazine* 10: 132.

Keown, A.J. (2001). *Personal Finance: Turning Money into Wealth*. Upper Saddle River (NJ): Prentice-Hall.

Levonson, D.H. (2006, July). 8 Steps That Will Make Life Easier for Your Heirs. *AAII Journal*, 20-220

Matlin, E.G. (2004). *The Procrastinator's Guide to Wills and Estate Planning*. New York: New American Library.

Nowak, R.E. (n.d.) *Divorce and Social Security Benefits*. Available online at: www.divorcesource.com/NY/ARTICLES/nowak7.html.

Planning Your Retirement—An Investment for Your Future (1997). Madison, Wisc.: University of Wisconsin-Extension, Family Living Programs.

Pond, J. (1993). *ABCs of Managing Your Money*. Denver, Colo.: NEFE Press.

Quinn, J.B. (1997). *Making the Most of Your Money*. New York: Simon & Schuster.

Rosenberg, L. (2000). Newlyweds must set financial goals. *Ticker* 10: 92–94.

Sander, J., Boutin, A., and Brown, J. (1999). *The Complete Idiot's Guide to Investing for Women*. New York: Alpha Book.

Schwab, C. (1998). *Charles Schwab's Guide to Financial Independence*. New York: Three Rivers Press.

Schwab, C. (2001). *You're Fifty—Now What?* New York: Crown Business.

Separation and Divorce: A Guide For Decision-Making (2003). Bulletin 175. New Brunswick, N.J.: Rutgers Cooperative Extension.

Siskos, C. (1998). Build a future for richer, not poorer. *Kiplinger's Personal Finance Magazine* 6: 45–48.

Spinale, L. (1999). *Smart Guide to Estate Planning*. New York: John Wiley & Sons.

Willis, C. (2006, February). Could You Please Die Sometime in 2010? *Money*, 44A-44B.

Appendix: Action Steps

Money Talk: A Financial Guide For Women

Action Steps

Every idea on this list of action steps will not apply to every reader. You may have already taken some steps, and others may not apply to your situation. It is easy to get overwhelmed when looking at such a long list. Don't!

Simply mark those steps that apply to you, check off the ones you've already done, and take action on the others at your own speed. Every action taken is a step toward securing your financial future.

☐ Complete the *Money Coat of Arms* worksheet (Exercise I-1, page 4) and use it to identify your values.

☐ List short-, intermediate-, and long-term financial goals with a date and cost for each.

☐ Start or increase emergency savings to equal 3 months' expenses.

☐ Take the *Financial Fitness Quiz* (Exercise I-5, page 11) to identify financial strengths and weaknesses.

☐ Track household income and expenses for a typical month to identify spending patterns.

☐ Identify specific ways to increase income and/or reduce expenses.

☐ Use the *Spending Plan Worksheet* (Exercise I-9, page 19) and expense tracking data to prepare a budget.

☐ Calculate your net worth (assets minus debts) annually to analyze financial progress.

☐ Contact existing creditors and request concessions, such as a lower interest rate.

☐ Request a copy of your credit file and correct any errors. Check your credit score.

☐ Complete the *Credit Card Safety Record* (Exercise I-14, page 30) to summarize credit card account data.

☐ Calculate your debt-to-income ratio (monthly consumer debt payments/net earnings).

☐ Set up a simple, user-friendly financial record-keeping system.

☐ Review existing insurance policies and identify weaknesses, such as low liability limits.

☐ Identify "big ticket" insurance gaps (e.g., lack of disability and long-term care coverage).

☐ Complete the *Life Insurance Needs* worksheet (Exercise II-1, page 52) or ask an agent to determine policy needs.

☐ Read the coverage limits and exclusions of your health insurance policy.

Action Steps
(continued)

☐ Determine if you receive any disability insurance (DI) through your employer.

☐ If not, contact an insurance agent for three price quotes for an individual DI policy.

☐ If you have a DI policy, read the coverage limits and exclusions.

☐ Read the coverage limits of your auto and homeowner's policies.

☐ Ask your property/casualty agent for ideas to reduce premiums and improve coverage.

☐ Get a price quote for umbrella liability coverage from your auto or homeowner's agent.

☐ Get three price quotes for long-term care coverage and consider buying a policy.

☐ Identify your risk tolerance with the *What Kind of Investor Are You?* worksheet (Exercise III-2, page 76).

☐ Review the list of Rung 1 investments (page 78) and select those appropriate for your goals.

☐ Review the list of Rung 2 investments (page 80) and select those appropriate for your goals.

☐ Review the list of Rung 3 investments (page 81) and select those appropriate for your goals.

☐ Review the list of Rung 4 investments (page 82) and select those appropriate for your goals.

☐ Automate your investments with payroll deductions and/or automated deposits.

☐ Use the *Comparing Stock Investments* worksheet (Exercise III-4, page 86) to compare equity investments.

☐ Use the *Comparing Fixed-Income Investments* worksheet (Exercise III-5, page 90) to compare fixed-income securities.

☐ Determine the type(s) of mutual funds that best match your investment objectives.

☐ Use the *Comparing Mutual Fund Investments* worksheet (Exercise III-11, page 97) to compare mutual funds.

☐ Determine your desired investment asset allocation model.

☐ Use *Your Investment Portfolio* (Exercise IV-2, page 108) to list asset allocation and specific securities that will help you reach your financial objectives.

☐ Determine the minimum interest rate you need to break even with taxes and inflation.

☐ Estimate the annual return for each of your investments or for your total portfolio.

☐ Answer the questions on *How Much Money Will You Need for Retirement?* (Exercise IV-5, page 114).

☐ Use Table IV-7 (page 117) to determine your full retirement age for Social Security.

☐ Use the *Estimated Cost of Living* worksheet (Exercise IV-7, page 118) to estimate retirement expenses.

☐ Use the *Estimating Your Retirement Income* worksheet (Exercise IV-8, page 121) to identify sources of retirement funds.

☐ Calculate your retirement savings need using the *Ballpark Estimate* worksheet (Exercise IV-9, page 123).

☐ Use a file folder for each investment to store account purchase and sales records.

☐ Interview at least three financial services professionals before hiring an advisor.

☐ Use the *Comparison of Financial Professionals* worksheet (Exercise IV-12, page 134) to compare advisors.

☐ Complete the *Estate Planning Checklist* (Exercise V-1, page 147) to identify estate planning strengths and gaps.

☐ Use the *My Estate Inventory* worksheet (Exercise V-2, page 150) to total the value of property in your estate.

☐ Verify that ownership titles on property do not conflict with terms of your will.

☐ Contact an attorney to draft a first-time will or review and revise an existing will.

☐ Review the *My Will Planning/Updating Checklist* worksheet (Exercise V-3, page 154) to identify planning gaps.

☐ Contact an attorney to draft durable powers of attorney for finances and health care.

☐ Prepare a living will to express your wishes about prolonging life by artificial means.

☐ Prepare a letter of instructions to list requests to be carried out upon your death.

☐ Consider using the annual gift tax exclusion to assist others and reduce your taxable estate.

Abbreviations

AFC – Accredited Financial Counselor

AIP – automatic investment plan

APR – annual percentage rate

CD – certificate of deposit

CFCS – Certified in Family and Consumer Sciences

CFP – Certified Financial Planner®

CHC – Certified Housing Counselor

ChFC – Chartered Financial Consultant

CRPC – Chartered Retirement Planning Counselor

DI – disability insurance

DRIP – dividend reinvestment plan

FDIC – Federal Deposit Insurance Corporation

FINRA – Financial Industry Regulatory Authority

GNMA – Government National Mortgage Association

HMO – health maintenance organization

IRA – individual retirement account

IRS – Internal Revenue Service

JTWROS – joint tenant with rights of survivorship

LTC – long-term care (insurance)

MLS – multiple listing service

NASDAQ – National Association of Securities Dealers Automated Quotation System

NAV – net asset value

NYSE – New York Stock Exchange

OTC – over-the-counter stock

PE – price/earnings ratio

PFS – personal financial specialist

RR – rate of return

S&L – savings and loan

SEP – simplified employee pension plan

SHIP – State Health Insurance Assistance Program

TC – Tenancy in common

Glossary of Investment Terms

401(k) plan – Employer-sponsored retirement plan offered through for-profit companies. Allows an employee to make tax-deferred contributions by reducing his or her salary. The employer often matches at least part of the employee contribution.

403(b) plan – Employer-sponsored retirement plan offered through nonprofit organizations, schools, and colleges. Allows the employee to make tax-deferred contributions by reducing his or her salary. In some cases the employer may match at least part of the employee contribution.

alimony – Payment made to one spouse by another pending or after legal separation or divorce.

American Stock Exchange (AMEX) – Stock exchange located in New York City that has less rigorous standards than the NYSE and lists smaller companies.

annual percentage rate (APR) – The total annual cost for a loan or other type of credit.

annuity – A contract by which an insurance company agrees to make regular payments to an individual or couple for life or for a fixed period in exchange for a lump sum or periodic deposits.

any-occupation disability insurance – Insurance that pays benefits when the insured is unable to engage in any type of employment.

appreciation – An increase in the value of an asset.

asset allocation – The placement of a certain percentage of investment capital within different types of assets (e.g., 50% in stocks, 30% in bonds, and 20% in cash).

assets – Things of value that you own.

automatic investment plan (AIP) – An arrangement in which you agree to have money automatically withdrawn from your bank account on a regular basis (e.g., once a month or every quarter) and used to purchase individual stock or mutual fund shares.

basis – The value assigned to an asset from which taxable gain or loss is determined. Generally, it is the original deposit plus additional deposits and reinvested distributions.

benefit coordination – Clause in an insurance contract designed to prevent people from collecting from two insurance policies for the same expense. The total claim cannot exceed 100% of the cost.

bond – A debt instrument or IOU issued by a corporation or government entity.

business risk – Risk caused by events that affect only a specific company or industry, thereby influencing the value of an investment.

buy and hold – Investment strategy that involves long-term ownership of high quality securities.

call risk – The risk that the issuer of a bond may buy it back, or call it, from an investor prior to maturity.

capital gain – An investment's increase in value.

capitalization – The total market value of all shares of a company's stock; calculated by multiplying the share price by the number of outstanding shares.

cash flow – The relationship between household income and expenses.

certificate of deposit (CD) – Time deposit accounts available at banks, savings and loan associations, credit unions, and brokerage firms. CDs pay a fixed return for a specified period of time.

child support – Payments by one spouse to another to meet the needs of the couple's child(ren) after legal separation or divorce.

COBRA law – Requires employers with 20 or more workers to offer continued group health care coverage to departing workers for up to 18 months and to eligible dependents for up to 36 months. Employees or dependents are responsible for paying the full cost of coverage, plus a 2% administrative fee.

codicil – An instrument that revokes, changes, or adds to the terms of a will.

cohabitation agreement – A legal document for unmarried couples, similar to a prenuptial agreement, that is drafted by a lawyer and describes each partner's responsibility for household expenses and who will get what in the event of a breakup.

coinsurance – The amount (usually stated as a percentage) of a claim that an insured person is expected to pay out-of-pocket.

commodities – Bulk goods, such as food, coffee, grain, livestock, and metals, that are traded on a commodities exchange.

compound interest – Interest credited daily, monthly, quarterly, semiannually, or annually on both principal and previously credited interest.

contingent beneficiary – A person who is second in line to receive a distribution.

copayment – The amount (usually stated as a dollar amount) that an insured person must pay out-of-pocket for a medical service or prescription drug.

core – The foundation of a portfolio (e.g., a stock index fund) to which an investor might add additional securities.

cost basis – An investment's original cost. This number, which is used for tax purposes, includes transaction costs plus reinvested dividends and capital gains.

credit risk – Relates to the financial strength of the company that is issuing a bond and is based on the ability of the company to repay principal and interest on time.

custodian – A person who holds and administers property for a minor until the minor reaches age 18 or 21.

debt-to-income ratio – The total monthly payment for household consumer debts divided by net household income.

deductible – The dollar figure, usually a flat dollar amount, that an insured person must pay out-of-pocket before an insurance policy reimburses him or her for the remainder of a loss.

defined benefit plan – A type of pension that guarantees a specified monthly payment in retirement based on income and/or years of service. The amount is often not adjusted for inflation.

defined contribution plan – A type of retirement savings plan that grows tax-deferred but does not guarantee a specific retirement benefit.

depreciation – A decrease in the value of an asset.

diversification – The policy of spreading assets among different investments to reduce risk of a decline in the overall portfolio as well as a decline in any one investment.

dividend reinvestment plan (DRIP) – A stock or mutual fund purchase option that allows investors to automatically reinvest any dividends their stock or mutual fund pays in additional shares, as well as to invest optional lump sum cash payments.

dividends – The share of profits or earnings that a company passes on to its shareholders.

dollar-cost-averaging – Investing equal amounts of money (e.g., $50) at a regular time interval (e.g., quarterly) regardless of whether securities markets are moving up or down. This reduces the average share costs to investors, who acquire more shares in periods of lower securities prices and fewer shares in periods of higher prices.

durable power of attorney (financial) – Legal document that appoints someone to handle your financial affairs if you are unable to.

elimination period – The number of days, starting from the date of an insurable event, before benefits are paid on certain kinds of insurance policies.

emergency fund – Savings set aside specifically to meet emergencies or unanticipated bills or to cover monthly living expenses if your paycheck stops.

equity investing – Becoming an owner or partial owner of a company or a piece of property through the purchase of investments such as stock, growth mutual funds, and real estate.

estate planning – The process of organizing your financial and personal assets for use during your lifetime and distribution after death in accordance with prevailing laws.

exclusions – A description of risks that are not covered by an insurance policy.

executor – A personal representative of an estate holder, named in a will, who sees to the financial affairs and the distribution of property after the estate holder's death.

expense ratio – The percentage of fund assets deducted for management and operating expenses.

fair market value – The value for which you could reasonably expect to sell an item.

fee-only planner – Financial planners who are compensated only from client fees.

fixed expenses – Costs such as housing, car loan payments, and insurance premiums that don't vary over time.

fixed-income investments – Investments such as long-term corporate bonds, Treasury notes and bills, CDs, and money market mutual funds.

flexible expenses – Household expenses such as food, transportation, and gifts that vary from month to month.

generation-skipping trust (GST) – A trust set up for the benefit of grandchildren, through which the grandchildren's parents often earn income. At their death, the trust principal is divided among the grandchildren.

gift tax – A tax imposed by the federal government on the giver of substantial gifts made during his or her lifetime.

Ginnie Mae (GNMA) fund – Mortgage-backed security issued by the Government National Mortgage Association.

guaranteed renewable – An insurance policy that will continue for life or until a certain specified age, assuming no lapse in premium payments. Premiums will not increase unless they are raised for everyone with the same type of policy.

index fund – A type of mutual fund that aims to match a particular stock or bond index by investing in the securities found in the index.

individual retirement account (IRA) – A retirement savings plan that allows individuals to save for retirement on a tax-deferred basis. The amount of savings that is tax deductible varies according to an individual's access to employer pension coverage, income tax filing status, household income, age, and the type of IRA that is selected.

inflation – Increase in the cost of goods and services.

inflation risk – Refers to a loss of buying power that can occur if the rate of inflation is higher than the rate of return on an investment.

insurance – A guarantee against risk of loss or harm in consideration of a payment proportioned to the risk involved (premium).

inter vivos trust – See "living trust."

interest rate risk – The risk that the value of fixed income securities will decline when interest rates rise.

intestate – Dying without a will.

irrevocable trust – A trust whose terms the creator can never change or cancel.

Keogh plan – A qualified retirement plan for self-employed individuals and their employees to which tax-deductible contributions up to a specified yearly limit can be made if the plan meets certain requirements of the Internal Revenue Code.

laddering – Creating a bond or CD portfolio with a combination of assets with different maturity dates. As each bond or CD matures, the proceeds are reinvested at the longest time interval to maintain the ladder.

large-loss principle – The idea that the amount of a potential loss—rather than its probability—should be the determining factor in purchasing insurance.

liquidity – The quality of an asset that permits it to be converted quickly to cash without a loss of value.

living trust – A vehicle for managing your property while you are alive and for transferring your property to your heirs at death without being subject to probate.

living will – A written statement that expresses your wishes regarding prolonging your life by artificial, extraordinary, or heroic measures.

load fund – A mutual fund that carries a sales commission of up to 8.5% of the amount invested.

long-term care insurance – Insurance policy that pays for a wide range of services for the elderly or disabled, such as home health care and nursing home costs.

managed care health insurance – Coverage provided by a health maintenance organization (HMO) or preferred provider organization (PPO) that emphasizes wellness and preventive care, controls the care that is given, and limits the selection of medical providers.

marginal tax rate – The rate you pay on the last (highest) dollar of personal or household (if married) earnings.

market risk – The risk that prices of individual investments will be affected by the volatility of financial markets in general.

maturity – The date on which the principal amount of a bond or loan must be paid.

money baggage – Harmful thoughts and beliefs about money that can hold people back from achieving personal and/or financial success.

money market deposit account – Insured bank and credit union accounts that may provide a slightly higher rate of return than savings accounts. May limit access to funds (e.g., limited number of checks and withdrawals per month).

money market mutual fund – A type of mutual fund, available in taxable and tax-free versions, that invests in the lowest risk, shortest term (less than 90 days), most highly rated debt securities. It is not federally insured but is extremely safe and liquid.

mutual fund – A portfolio of stocks, bonds, or other securities that is collectively owned by thousands of investors and managed by a professional investment company. The shareholders of a particular fund have similar investment goals.

NASDAQ – A stock exchange made up of brokers networked together around the country who trade stocks back and forth using computers. Many high-tech companies trade here. Volatility is generally the highest of the various stock exchanges.

net worth – Assets minus debts or liabilities.

New York Stock Exchange (NYSE) – The largest and oldest of the U.S. stock exchanges. Located in New York City. Trades the shares of many large and well-established companies.

no-load fund – A mutual fund that requires no up-front fees to purchase shares and has no marketing fees.

noncancelable – An insurance policy that will continue for life or until a certain specified age, assuming no lapse in premium payments.

own-occupation disability insurance – A policy that defines disability as the inability to work in the particular field or trade for which you were trained.

pension – A type of savings plan that pays benefits to workers at retirement.

periodic expenses – Costs that occur only once or a few times per year (e.g., quarterly property taxes).

permanent life insurance – A policy that combines protection for the life of an insured person with a savings component known as cash value. Specific types of policies include whole life, variable life, and universal life.

policy limit – The highest dollar amount that an insurance policy will pay.

portfolio – The combined holding of stocks, bonds, cash equivalents, or other assets by an individual or household, investment club, or institutional investor (e.g., mutual fund).

portfolio rebalancing – Periodically adjusting the holdings in your investment portfolio to maintain a certain asset allocation.

pour-over will – A will that directs that the property subject to it be "poured-over" into a trust upon the maker's death.

power of attorney (health care) – A legal document that authorizes the person you choose to make medical decisions for you when you are incapable of making them yourself.

principal – The original amount of money invested or borrowed, excluding any interest or dividends.

probate – Proceedings involving a court of law to validate a will, pay debts of the deceased, and distribute the deceased's property to named beneficiaries.

profit sharing – Employer-sponsored retirement savings plan in which contributions depend on a company's profits. Employer contributions can vary from year to year.

reinvestment risk – The risk of having to reinvest existing funds at a lower return than previously earned, resulting in a decline in income.

remainderperson – An individual who has the right to possession or ownership of property after the estate holder dies or surrenders the life estate.

return – Investment gain or loss.

revocable trust – A trust whose terms the creator can change or cancel at any time.

riders – Additional clauses to an insurance contract that add coverage in exchange for a higher premium.

risk – Exposure to loss, harm, or danger.

risk acceptance – Intentionally accepting small financial losses that you can afford to pay for out-of-pocket, if needed.

risk avoidance – Eliminating the possibility of a loss by avoiding activities that expose you to a risk.

risk reduction – Taking measures to reduce a loss, should one occur, instead of avoiding a risky activity altogether.

risk tolerance – A person's capacity to emotionally and financially handle the risks associated with investing.

risk transfer – Transferring the risk of loss to a third party (insurance company) in exchange for a specified payment (premium).

S&P 500 Index – A stock market index consisting of the stocks of the 500 largest U.S. companies.

SEP (simplified employee pension) plan – A tax-deferred retirement plan for owners of small businesses and their employees, if any.

spending plan – A budget; a written plan for spending and saving money.

stepped-up basis – An inherited asset is valued as of the date of the donor's death.

stock – Security that represents a unit of ownership in a corporation.

stockbroker – Someone who is employed by a registered broker-dealer firm and who is authorized to buy and sell stocks, bonds, mutual funds, or certain other securities for investors.

stop-loss limit – A limit on the amount you must copay per year on an insurance policy.

sunset provisions – When a federal law, such as tax legislation, expires.

taxable distribution – Payment to investors of profits realized upon the sale of securities within a mutual fund.

term life insurance – Provides life insurance protection only for a specific period. Has no cash value at the end of that period.

testamentary trust – A trust set up to manage property for one or more beneficiaries.

time risk – The greater volatility of bond prices as their length of maturity increases.

total return – The combination of income and capital gains or losses on an investment.

Treasury bill – A short-term federal debt security that matures within a few days to 52 weeks (1 year). Interest is exempt from state and local income tax.

Treasury bond – A long-term federal debt security with a term of 30 years. Interest is subject to federal taxes but is free from state or local taxes.

Treasury note – An intermediate-term federal debt security with terms of 2, 3, 5, and 10 years. Interest is subject to federal taxes but is free from state or local taxes.

trustee – A person or financial institution who manages the property of others. He or she distributes income and principal to the trust beneficiaries according to the estate holder's instructions.

umbrella liability coverage – Excess liability insurance that supplements the liability limits of a homeowner's or renter's policy and automobile insurance policy.

Uniform Transfers to Minors Act (UTMA) – Allows transfer of any type of property, real or personal, tangible or intangible, to a minor, to be managed by a custodian until the minor comes of age.

values – Beliefs about what is important in a person's life.

vesting – Refers to the date when you are entitled to the money that your employer has contributed to your retirement account.

volatility – The degree of price fluctuation associated with a given investment, interest rate, or market index. The more price fluctuation that is experienced, the greater the volatility.

zero-coupon bond – A corporate, municipal, or Treasury bond that sells at a deep discount and whose value increases every year.

About NRAES

NRAES, the Natural Resource, Agriculture, and Engineering Service, is a not-for-profit program dedicated to assisting land grant university faculty and others in increasing the public availability of research- and experience-based knowledge. NRAES is sponsored by eleven land grant universities in the eastern United States. Administrative support is provided by Cornell University, the host university.

NRAES publishes practical books of interest to fruit and vegetable growers, landscapers, dairy and livestock producers, natural resource managers, SWCD (soil and water conservation district) staff, consumers, landowners, and professionals interested in agricultural waste management and composting. NRAES books are used in cooperative extension programs, in college courses, as management guides, and for self-directed learning.

NRAES member universities are:

University of Connecticut
University of Delaware
University of the District of Columbia
University of Maine
University of Maryland
University of New Hampshire

Rutgers University
Cornell University
University of Vermont
Virginia Polytechnic Institute & State
    University
West Virginia University

Contact NRAES for more information about membership.
NRAES
PO Box 4557
Ithaca, New York 14852-4557

Phone: (607) 255-7654
Fax: (607) 254-8770
E-mail: NRAES@CORNELL.EDU
Web site: WWW.NRAES.ORG